SOCIAL WORK IN CONTEXT

SOCIAL WORK IN CONTEXT

A comparative study of
three social services
teams

Jim Black

Ric Bowl

Douglas Burns

Chas Critcher

Gordon Grant

Dick Stockford

Tavistock Publications
LONDON and NEW YORK

To
John, Zoë, and Anisa

First published in 1983 by
Tavistock Publications Ltd
11 New Fetter Lane, London EC4P 4EE

Published in the USA by
Tavistock Publications
in association with Methuen, Inc.
733 Third Avenue, New York, NY 10017

© 1983 J. Black, R. Bowl, D. Burns,
C. Critcher, G. Grant, R. Stockford

Printed in Great Britain by
J.W. Arrowsmith Ltd, Bristol

British Library Cataloguing in Publication Data

Social work in context.
1. Public welfare – Great Britain – Cast studies
2. Great Britain – Social policy – Case studies
I. Black, Jim
361'.0941   HV248

ISBN 0-422-78270-X

Library of Congress Cataloging in Publication Data
Social work in context.

Bibliography: P.
Includes index.
1. Public welfare – Great Britain – Case studies.
2. Welfare State.   1. Black, Jim.
HV245.S6235   1983   361.3'0941   83-9171
ISBN 0 422 78270 X

Contents

Preface

This book is concerned with the practice of social work within local authority social services departments in Britain. The three case studies that comprise its core were a product of research conceived in 1977 and completed in 1981 by researchers based at the UCNW, the University of Birmingham, and the University of East Anglia. As we explain in the opening chapter, the themes that provided the original impetus for the study were subject to a number of changes in direction. These changes were a product not only of the reflexive nature of the research process; they were also influenced by a more general debate about the role of social workers within the framework of the welfare state. In this respect, we were aware that while this book was in preparation, the Barclay Report was yet to be published. For both the authors and the social workers we interviewed, it was a report that was anticipated but about which direct comment was impossible. Field-work and analysis were concluded in 1981 and it was not feasible to integrate the working party's conclusions as this would have placed a retrospective gloss on the study. However, we are mindful that our findings and conclusions will be compared with those of Barclay. Thus we have added a postscript that provides our own commentary on the working party's recommendations and that helps the reader to draw some comparisons.

The title of this book, *Social Work in Context*, reflects our own view that social work practice and area team functioning cannot be divorced or examined in isolation from the wider context. If social work is to be concerned with serving rather than servicing, with becoming both responsive and responsible to its users and local people, arguments that rely solely on administrative reform (post-Seebohm reorganization) or on changes in attitude of workers and managers (Barclay's prescription) are not sufficient.

We believe that the ability of teams to recognize and respond to the problems of the locality they serve is crucial. These problems, the resources available to social workers, their practice skills, and the way in which the organization is managed, all form part of the context within which people are helped by social workers. Nevertheless, it would still be naive to present the difficulties that beset social work and the welfare state today solely in these terms, for overarching all this are legal and administrative structures operated by the central and local state. Hence, in drawing some conclusions to our research we have tried to link the empirical world we observed to what we consider to be a much more fundamental debate concerning the relationship between the state, social work, and the users of personal social services.

There are many people to whom acknowledgement must be made. The work at Birmingham and Norfolk was financed by the Joseph Rowntree Memorial Trust and in Wales by the Department of Health and Social Security and the Welsh Office. It was only made possible, however, by the agreement of three social services departments and, more especially, three area teams who bravely allowed us to subject them to close scrutiny. To each we offer our grateful thanks, mindful of their patience and forbearance.

The most important individuals in this venture are too numerous to name: the workers and clients of the three departments. We only hope that we have done justice to the views they have expressed.

The suitably anonymous names of 'Aber' and 'Glyn' have been used for the Welsh study and its employing agency. We trust that these fictionalized replacements will not unduly affect the reader's ability to identify with the area. Otherwise we have been able to use the real names for the teams and their employers: Selly Oak and Birmingham Social Services Department; and Dereham and Norfolk Social Services Department. The three case studies describe the organization and activities of the teams at the time the research was undertaken. We are aware that some significant changes have taken place since then. Thus, inevitably, these descriptions are historical. Some of the problems identified have been resolved, while no doubt other issues have emerged since the research ended.

Six names appear as authors of the book: Ric Bowl, Gordon Grant, and Dick Stockford, who jointly initiated the idea of the study; Jim Black, Doug Burns, and Chas Critcher who were subseqently employed as contracted researchers to conduct much of the field-work. We have, since that point, worked together and would emphasize the collective nature of the enterprise.

Many individuals from the sponsoring and host bodies have pored over early drafts of this manuscript and provided invaluable feedback and advice. To them all, we express our gratitude. However, this book is the product of the joint authors, and does not represent the views of the departments in which the research was undertaken. If our joint efforts still contain flaws then the responsibility is entirely ours.

In bringing this collaborative exercise to fruition we acknowledge the direct help received from other quarters: from Jon Bloomfield, who worked for a short time on the Birmingham research; from the small groups of committed souls who helped us to interview the elderly at home; from Dai Davies, Barbara Morris, Angie Rowlands, and Jayne Coombe, who provided secretarial support during the course of the project; and most particularly from Angie Martin, who undertook the awesome task of typing the many drafts of this book, often from indecipherable copy. We hope they will feel that the final product justifies their hard work.

Finally, we wish to pay tribute to John Turner, who started this journey with us, but whose untimely death robbed him of the chance to witness its fruits and, more importantly, left us bereft of a close friend and colleague. This book is dedicated as a small token to his memory and to his wife, Zoë, and daughter, Anisa.

Jim Black
Ric Bowl
Doug Burns
Chas Critcher
Gordon Grant
Dick Stockford

PART ONE

STARTING POINTS

1

Theoretical and Methodological Approach

INTRODUCING THE INTRODUCTION

This book is the end result of a comparative study of social work teams in the districts of 'Aber', Selly Oak, and Dereham. This introduction explains where the research started, how it developed, and its progress to book form. Two considerations have led us to inflict upon the reader a more than usually detailed account of the research process. One is to make explicit the logic underlying the structure of this book, which was not inherent in the research design but had to be worked for. The other is the general case for a more honest and reflexive acknowledgement that research has a dynamic: it experiences uncertainties, undergoes transformations, and reflects conflicts and compromises of interests (Bell and Newby 1977; Payne *et al.* 1981).

In the first part of this introduction, we explain the issues that provoked the original research proposal and its theoretical and methodological intentions. In the second part we evaluate the status of our evidence, so that it will be clear how conscious we are of its strengths and limitations. In the final part we address the ambiguities of a comparative approach, in principle and practice. If nothing else, we may be able to alert future researchers to a range of difficulties, primarily but not exclusively methodological, which comparative study of this kind entails.

ISSUES FOR RESEARCH

The original concerns of the project stemmed from two debates emergent in the last decade about the nature of social work in its post-Seebohm form. One debate was about how social work could best be organized and administered; the other was about how social work practice could meet the increasing demands and needs of the elderly as a client group. These are the essential contexts for our approach to 'social work in context' and require some elaboration.

The first debate, about the organization of social work, received particular impetus from those who questioned how far new organizational models took account of the special circumstances in rural areas. Although research in Britain had paid considerable attention to the activities of area-based teams (e.g. Goldberg and Warburton 1979; Stevenson and Parsloe 1978), this first debate had received little attention. In contrast it had been most widely articulated in the United States, where growing disaffection with conventional social work training and centralized modes of service delivery had given rise to a social work caucus (Ginsberg 1976; Green and Webster 1976) that subsequently became something of a movement (Martinez-Brawley 1982).

To underpin their concern, some attempt was made to develop a theory of 'rurality' as a fundamental way of differentiating between communities in receipt of public services. If there were problems in giving theoretical status to what were often no more than empirically observable variations in population density, the identification of the apparently unique problems of rural areas found favour with many of those evaluating the provision of services in such regions. In Britain, by the late 1970s, the thesis of rural deprivation had become well established (Association of County Councils 1978; Child Poverty Action Group 1978; Shaw 1979).

One strand of this thesis was the need to defend what earlier studies focused on kinship and friendship ties (Davies and Rees 1960; Emmet 1964; Frankenberg 1966; Williams 1963) had identified as a high degree of interdependence and mutual exchange in rural social relationships, in contrast to the more impersonal social relations assumed to exist in urban areas. The discovery of working-class urban villages in British cities (Jackson 1968; Young and Wilmott 1962) only partly qualified the interest in studies emanating from the USA which sought to compare and contrast rural and urban areas in terms of the degree of social care and community involvement (Bultena 1969; Johnson and Knop 1970; Michaux Pruim, Foster, and Chelst 1973; Rojek, Clemente, and Summers 1975; Sauer, Shehan, and Boymel 1976).

It has subsequently become evident however that living in a rural area does not in itself determine or explain levels of social and communal involvement. Rather what has emerged is a set of problems in maintaining or servicing the social infrastructure of rural areas. These have particular implications for the health and social services in Britain. The assumption behind post-war welfare policy has been that uniform models of administration will produce equitable access to services. There has thus been an inherent resistance to any great decentralization or diversity in administering state benefits and services (Hadley and Hatch 1981; Nissel, Maynard, Young, and Ibsen 1980).

The inception of this study thus reflected the uneven state of this debate and the variety of positions tenable in relation to it. The evidence for some of the basic propositions of the rurality thesis – the distinctive nature of rural deprivation, higher levels of informal care in rural areas, the inappropriateness of urban-based models of welfare organization – was at best suggestive. Nor was it clear what status a theory of rurality had; whether or how, for example, it modified class-based analyses. There was thus some scepticism amongst the originators of this research as to the validity of the rural–urban dichotomy. But it seemed to merit systematic empirical examination and it had raised a number of key issues for social services organization which could not lightly be dismissed.

The second debate informing our interest in comparative study came from a separate but related source. It concerned the nature of social work intervention with the elderly. In particular it focused on the ideal of community care as a potential solution to the increasing pressure from an expanding elderly population on the limited resources of the health and personal social services. Some enterprising secondary analysis of comparable surveys of the elderly undertaken in the 1960s and 1970s (Bebbington 1979) had verified concerns that despite considerable expansion of various domiciliary services care from families was still under pressure. Other surveys have continued to demonstrate, however, that the family remains the single most important and immediate source of care for the elderly (Abrams 1978; Hunt 1978). Less evident from such studies were qualitative aspects of family care – obligations, stresses, or rewards involved in caring for dependent elderly relatives – which are now coming to light (Wenger 1982).

With more elderly people needing health and social service support, the policy problem was how to ensure that services were appropriate, efficient, and channelled to those most in need. Whilst surveys of social work clients had indicated the elderly to be satisfied with the mainly practical services they were receiving

(Glampson and Goldberg 1976), there was countervailing evidence showing that certain groups, such as those living alone, were often pushed to the front of the queue for services, much to the disadvantage of families caring for the elderly at home (Isaacs, Livingstone, and Neville 1972). Further problems were that the services provided were not always those most appropriate to elderly clients' needs (Plank 1977) and that social workers accorded low status to work with this group (Rowlings 1981). Additionally there were gaps in the supply of such essential services as day care and meals on wheels, while liaison between health and social services was often improvised rather than systematic.

Thus the extent of informal support to the elderly, the appropriateness, efficiency, and distribution of services supplied, gaps in service provision, social workers' perceptions of the elderly as a client group, and clients' evaluation of social services support, formed a cluster of questions for a second level of comparative study. We were also able to compare the apparent effects of generic and specialist forms of team organization on the range and depth of work with elderly clients and how these related to underlying philosophies.

CHANGES IN DIRECTION

Our concern with the elderly as a focus of comparative study was relatively unproblematic in principle. While it clearly encroached upon the rural dimension, especially on the area of the nature of informal care, it had an autonomous trajectory of its own. We were able to place special but by no means exclusive emphasis on the elderly as a client group within the profiles of the context and practice of social service delivery which we began to obtain in one urban and two rural areas.

The urban–rural comparison proved more difficult. Some of the work revealing considerable gaps in the basic theoretical model only became available after the research had commenced. We therefore had to come to terms with some conceptual deficiencies which the original research proposal only partly acknowledged. But equally if not more important was the failure of much of our early empirical data to validate the rural–urban paradigm. As the study progressed, very few of the differences we found between the areas in their demographies, patterns of expressed demand, or structures of service delivery in response, could be accounted for by any one-dimensional rural–urban dichotomy or continuum. Thus on the indices thought to differentiate rural from urban social services – population profile, common social problems, levels of expressed need, available resources, the organization of social work teams – the differences were not as we had been led to expect them. The differences existed within the same range of problems; they were not differences in the nature of problems. This is a generalization which needs to be set against the detailed comparison of Chapter 6, where some consistent differences are recounted. But their significance, as we interpret them, did not validate a rural–urban contrast, in however weak or modified a form, as the crucial explanatory paradigm.

To a certain extent this finding was the outcome of the specific social work teams we studied. The urban 'control', for example, turned out to have a larger proportion of elderly clients than neighbouring (and indeed most other) teams in the city. As a consequence its client profile was less heavily weighted towards child care than had been anticipated to be typical of urban areas. But if such a social work team could be found in the heart of a major city we had to throw into question the whole problem of what constituted uniquely rural characteristics for the purpose of social services delivery. Other indices amplified this uncertainty. A declining local economy was found in all three areas – different in form and extent, but similar in its impact upon inhabitants. Housing problems, though again different in degree, appeared consistently across all three areas. The provision of social service resources in the three areas was uneven but the variations were not consistent and in some instances the rural areas appeared to be, on paper at least, better resourced. The division of labour of the social work teams and their relationship to the locality appeared to throw up similar patterns and problems almost regardless of rural or urban definitions. Finally, in this brief review of potential indices of a rural–urban dichotomy, the factor of space did superficially appear to divide urban from rural areas. Groupwork, for example, was virtually impossible to organize in rural areas outside the main townships. Yet as a counterweight we found that problems of access, of potential clients to social work services and case-workers to their current clients, were no less prevalent in the urban than in the rural context – especially for the elderly.

Thus by the time we came to the protracted stage of writing up our research we found that we had gathered data around a number of problems yet at least one of the frameworks which might have held them together had been found wanting. The crucial questions for us, as for the 'rurality' debate generally, no longer centred simply on whether social work organization and practice took account of distinctively rural characteristics. It was now the more valid, if more complex, problem of how far social work had been adapted to the particular circumstances of the locality, whether these were defined in demographic, spatial, or cultural terms. The move away from a rural–urban contrast towards this question of adaptability was one of our crucial changes of direction. But as the subsequent discussion shows, this entailed strategies in writing up the research which were rather different from those originally envisaged.

MORE ANSWERS THAN QUESTIONS

At an early stage in the research, when the rural–urban paradigm was still strong, we identified four clusters of questions. These remained central to comparative study.

1 What are the identifiable characteristics of rural and urban clients? What factors account for variability in levels of expressed need both within and between different territories?
2 What activities are involved in meeting the needs of clients? What influence is exerted on adopted intervention strategies by (a) geographic/territorial factors *per se*, (b) organizational factors, (c) client need?
3 How do members of area teams evaluate present approaches to practice? What factors do they perceive as influencing their own approaches to service delivery?
4 How do different groups of elderly social services clients view and assess the support they have received from social services departments within the context of care provided by family, friends, neighbours, and significant others? What outstanding or unmet needs remain to be tackled? Are these idiosyncratic, related to situational factors in each area, or reflective of common needs?

Clearly such questions involved more than simple fact-finding. We wanted to know not only who received which social services and how, but which factors appeared to affect the whole process of service delivery. To identify such factors and incorporate the important question of whether or not a sense of satisfaction was experienced, we needed the evidence of the perceptions of those involved. A degree of evaluation is always present in any research, but this was not primarily an evaluative exercise in which the success of a system is judged by its ability to meet certain prescribed objectives. (Evaluation in that sense would have required at least some analysis of face-to-face contact between worker and client.) Our main focus was explanatory, involving both straightforward descriptions of service delivery systems and the identification of those factors which affected their functioning.

Three areas of data collection relevant to the above questions were identified. The first was the agency's official records of the process of service delivery to clients as represented by case files; the second the social workers' perception of their role in the process of service delivery as revealed in semi-structured interviews; the third the clients' reactions to the intervention of social services as elicited by an interviewer using a structured questionnaire. Each of these involved the selection of a sample, the choice of a research instrument, the gathering and processing of data, its interpretation, and, not least, selection of the most meaningful data for publication. These are the canons of social scientific enquiry and were applicable across all areas of data collection, though the nature of the data was different in each case.

Such a procedure was given considerable strength by having different kinds of data to draw on. We were and are appreciative of the advantages of a triangulated methodology (Denzin 1970; Smith 1975) and its all too rare application to social work (Goldberg and Connelly 1981). However, the complexity involved in multiple methods of data collection was increased by the need in a comparative study to maintain consistency across three research sites. Reliability as well as validity had to be maintained in data collection. How we endeavoured to achieve this at the level of explicit comparative analysis will be discussed after an explanation of the methods used to analyze agency cases, social workers' perceptions, and clients' responses.

The cases

Initially we had to draw a sample of cases which was both manageable and representative. Eventually two main samples were taken. One was of 'new' work consisting of all referrals dealt with by the social work teams in a six-month period. We excluded enquiries redirected without social work assessment and only counted once those cases with multiple episodes within the six-month study period (July–December 1978 in Aber and January–June 1979 in Selly Oak and Dereham). Given the recently reviewed problems of such procedures (Crousaz 1981) we were reasonably confident that we included all referrals resulting in the opening or re-opening of a case. The second sample was of 'long-term' work defined as cases that had been open at least six months. We therefore identified all those cases open at the end of the relevant study period but referred before it.

We also took more selective samples of equivalent referrals and cases of home help and meals on wheels services, even where they were administered by a separate arm of the social services department. Such data were of only indirect concern and were sparingly used in the final analysis. They are excluded from *Table 1(1)* which refers to social work cases only.

Table 1(1)

	referrals	long-term cases	totals
Aber	269	514[1]	783
Dereham	481	255	736
Selly Oak[2]	418	269	687

[1] A variably stratified random sample was taken of this group, 182 in number.
[2] Some case files were never accessed. The actual numbers used were 384 and 246 totalling 630.

Because of differences and deficiencies in agency recording systems, it was sometimes a substantial task to identify these cases and the social workers responsible for them, especially where we were reconstructing case-loads which had existed some months previously. Once identified, a specific set of information was compiled on each case by means of the case review form (Appendix A). This elicited three kinds of information about each case:

1 the client's biographical circumstances;
2 the agency's processing of the case;
3 the social work activities and resources involved.

The instrument was modelled on the system devised by Goldberg and Fruin (1976), the development of which was subsequently reported (Goldberg and Warburton 1979).

As its name implies, the case review form was originally designed as a means of managing and monitoring social workers' activity. Thus not only did we make some alterations in the information required to suit our needs, we also changed its very purpose: it became an instrument of research rather than reflection. Further, since we were dealing with episodes in the past, often in cases subsequently closed, we used the form retrospectively rather than prospectively. Overall, therefore, we altered the precise format, original purpose, and intended time-scale of the form. Hence, the problems in using the form we describe may be as attributable to our modifications of it as to its design in principle.

Firstly there were some problems of a technical nature, where the design of the form resulted in unnecessary ambiguity. One example was the categorization of a case as one of, or a combination of, physically handicapped, elderly, mentally ill, mentally handicapped, family problem, child care, or other. These categories have different bases: age, disability, agency definition. Some are vague, like 'family problem'. Some duplications were produced when a case was classified as, for example, elderly and physically handicapped, or child care and family problem.

The second set of problems revolved around who was actually filling out the form. Because of local circumstances, our research included a number of different situations, from that where the social worker filled out the form according to the set of written instructions, with no cross-checking by the researcher, to that where a researcher filled out the form from a case file in the absence of the past or current social worker involved. This caused problems of reliability: social workers' individual interpretations were, despite careful briefing, beyond the control of the researcher. This is apart from the temptation facing harassed social workers confronted with such a task, to guess about information not immediately to hand and to describe what they would like to have done rather than what they actually did. Occasionally we achieved the most valid if not the most reliable method, for the researcher and social worker to fill out the form together, but this was very time-consuming and open to interpretation by the social worker as a kind of interrogation.

The third set of problems in our use of the form was more fundamental. Much of the data was straightforwardly factual. Age and family circumstances, date and source of referral, specific services provided and other agencies' involvement could be taken as a clear and reasonably accurate picture of the main elements in the processing of a case. From this, significant factors in the agency's response to a request for help could be identified. Each case study has taken this information as its empirical base. We have also used data which we know to be more subjective. In part this is inevitable since these were the areas of social workers' own judgements; in part it reflected some inadequacies in the form which did not recognize the very different kinds of information it was eliciting.

The description of social work activity is a prime example. In asking the social worker to list 'problems tackled', there was no way of identifying clients' problems that the social worker acknowledged but would not or could not do anything about. Thus, the form came close to endorsing as accurate information the agency's redefinition of the client's problems in terms of what services could be delivered. Similarly, the characterization of work with the client (by choosing from a list of possible descriptions) was as likely to reflect the social workers' own ideals as to provide accurate information about what had actually transpired between agency, client, and social worker. Perhaps such difficulties are inherent in the process of reducing the intangibles of case-work to the tangibles of activity classification. Yet the status of such information remains unclear. More than just problems of validity and reliability is evident: it is not clear whether we are dealing with reasonably objective descriptions, professional judgements, or self-validating accounts. The three are not synonymous and consequently there were real and enduring problems in interpreting the meaning and significance of such data.

For these and other reasons, notably that the agencies had not always recorded the kinds of information we wanted (for example, housing tenure), we did not use all the information on the form. Though used less selectively than either social work or client interviews, some case review form data was rejected on the grounds of unreliability or inadequacy, including all forecasts about future work, statutory registration, and case transfers. Such necessary omissions reinforced the usefulness of a triangulated methodology, especially the social work interviews as alternative sources of information.

The social workers' perceptions

Originally we had hoped to interview senior management as well as field-workers but were unable to spare the time from other kinds of data collection. Hence the accounts of social services departments we received from the inside were partial. Views emanating from field-workers could not be balanced against those which might have come from other points in the hierarchy.

Thus our interviews were limited to every member of the three teams studied plus relevant area-based specialists who were asked about their perception of the context and process of service delivery and their own role within it. Context questions covered perceptions of the local community (unmet needs, major problems, caring networks) and other agencies present (especially potential referral sources). Process questions included agency response (intake and allocation, adequacy of services, priorities, and objectives) and agency organization (from division of labour on the team to the role of centralized management). Role questions included objectives and principles (for individual cases and social work as a whole), and felt limitations (of skills, resources, or responsibilities).

The interviewing was undertaken mainly by the three full-time researchers using a check-list of topics rather than pre-set questions (Appendix B). Hence the interviews were semi-structured and open-ended. In practice they lasted an average of ninety minutes. Altogether forty-five such interviews were conducted. The well-known and apparently intractable problems of interviewing as a methodology were not absent, if mitigated by the availability of other sources of information. How far the situation and especially the tape-recorder affected social workers' willingness to talk openly and honestly about the department and their role within it seemed to us to vary within and between teams. Some appeared to enjoy it, others not; some were reserved, others loquacious; some defensive, others offensive.

As a partial check on the possible contamination of interview material, some limited observation was undertaken in the teams' offices. This involved attendance at team meetings as well as the noting, by no means always systematically, of the kinds of things habitually happening or being said around the office – where the researcher would often have good reason to be. Such observations served to explicate and occasionally to modify interpretation of interview material. The strategic importance of such interview and observational material changed as the study progressed. Originally intended as material illustrative of agency processes, it came to have a significance in its own right. Social workers' perceptions of their roles were themselves an integral part of the agency's functioning, not something existing outside it. Nor could assessments of the adequacy of services provided be divorced from social workers' perceptions of the relationship between the local community's needs and the remit of the social services department.

In supervising the completion of case review forms, carrying out interviews, and conducting informal observation, the three field-workers maintained relationships with the social work teams for periods of eighteen months or more. There was some depth to our understanding of social workers' perceptions which has not always survived the necessarily ruthless editing of our case studies. A similar sacrifice had to be made over client perceptions.

The 'client' view

The client view remained for us, as for social work research generally, a difficult yet essential area. We even found the terminology awkward, specifically rejecting the label of 'consumer', since it connotes an element of commercial choice inappropriate for monopolistic public service provision. 'Users' seemed nondescript; our own preference for 'citizens', since we are all potentially elderly and vulnerable, seemed too idiosyncratic for a readership used to other terms. We have therefore used the word 'client' despite its ambiguity, implying as it does a reciprocal or at least contractual agreement absent in most social work transactions. This is not a mere semantic quibble: the uncertain status of those for whom social services are provided is mirrored in the language used to describe them. Further, the status of the client response was from the first defined differently from that of other sources. The sheer numbers involved (826 in the original sample, of whom 338 were interviewed) precluded the flexible style of interviewing adopted with social workers. Instead a 91-itemed interview schedule was designed and piloted (Appendix D). This covered three kinds of information. The first, on biographical circumstances, covered a range of questions similar to those on the case review form, with the addition of data on family networks and geographical mobility. The second included various indices of dependency, from access to shops and potential sources of help to measures of physical mobility (Harris 1971) and psychological morale (Lawton 1975). A third set of questions referred to their experience of social services: how they felt about being referred to the department, their knowledge of, and willingness to contact social services, and their satisfaction with services.

Despite careful pilot work, we were unexpectedly presented with difficulties in contacting elderly clients in the sample for whom we had case review form data. Because one team felt unable to release names and addresses directly to the researchers, the clients were originally contacted by letters, one from the department, one from the university (Appendix C), asking if they would co-operate in the survey. Not surprisingly, given the difficulty of understanding what was involved by reading a letter, a good proportion refused. Since we had to maintain comparability, this method was used in the other areas, with similar effects on the proportion of the original sample eventually interviewed.

All these factors resulted in just over one-third of our original sample being interviewed. The remainder were unable or unwilling to participate. Those unable to participate included some who had gone into permanent residential care and others in hospital for indefinite periods. The mortality rate was also rather higher than we had anticipated. Such cases were by definition those involving multiple crises; the possibly more intensive social work intervention likely in such circumstances was thus underrepresented in the group ultimately interviewed.

Those unwilling to participate introduced another set of imponderables. Some gave explanations, directly or by proxy, often referring to physical or mental ill-health. But without having comprehensive information about refusers, we cannot judge whether as a group they might have had particular circumstances or attitudes different from the group who did participate.

It was partly such doubts about the representativeness of our respondents which led us to be highly selective in our use of the client interview material. This data could have been expanded in several ways: into some of the more technical aspects of mobility and morale measurements; into some areas peripheral to this study but central to many of the interviews, especially the whole question of income; into the often extraordinary qualitative richness of elderly clients' perceptions of their lives. It is intended that at least some of these aspects will be written up separately. But here the view of the client has mainly been used to illustrate points highlighted by other sources. The partial loss of its unique value was the price to be paid for a gain in comparability.

The major initial task for comparative analysis was how to achieve consistency of data collection across all three case studies to enable systematic comparison to be made. To an extent this was helped by the fact that one area was at any one time between three and six months ahead of the others. All they had to do was follow suit even if this meant adopting research strategies inappropriate to different organizational settings. Few *ad hoc* decisions could be made since research procedure had to be more formal and systematic than is often the case on individual projects. To achieve the necessary mutual collaboration and control, the three field researchers and their three supporters would all meet as a group for day-long meetings at roughly two-month intervals. Decisions made would be binding, so that minutes of such meetings became a kind of research manual for those involved, supplemented by frequent (occasionally frantic) telephone calls.

This care in co-ordinating our research activities gave us, as we came to compare our empirical findings, considerable confidence that we had achieved a systematically comparative study of a unique kind. While there had been difficulties in constructing samples and utilizing research instruments, these did not invalidate the objectives or results of the analysis. We could compensate for doing scant justice to the interview material by the greater breadth afforded by a triangulated methodology. If we already suspected that the studies of individual teams might lose something to the stress on standardization, we could see how they might gain from being set in the context of the other teams, enabling us to compare their capacity to adapt to local circumstance. Given our initial objectives, it did not seem to us that we had done at all badly.

However, our difficulties were not all past. We had achieved comparative data collection; we had now to achieve comparative interpretation. Some ambiguity was evident about the nature of comparative analysis. In one sense all research is inherently comparative, since it compares reality with some implicit or explicit ideal. Our emphasis on explanation rather than evaluation only partly resolved this question, since explanation can never be entirely disinterested.

How to achieve comparative interpretation also appeared in more specific forms. One example was the status of our concern with the elderly. This was specific but not exclusive. We wanted to place the elderly as a client subgroup within the context of other subgroups and thus social services clientele as a whole. This is a kind of comparative analysis – it compares the needs of, and service delivery response to, the elderly, with those of and to other client groups. Yet it was difficult to make such comparison explicit or, crucially, to build some indices of comparison into the research instruments. The case review form, for example, is designed to produce information on individual cases; it cannot, except in the form of aggregated tables, produce comparisons between groups. Neither did the interview and observation of social workers always yield information which explicitly compared client groups in terms of presenting problem, assessment, or service provision. The client interviews were similarly of limited use for the purposes of comparison between client groups, since the sample did not include any non-elderly clients, such as the younger physically handicapped, with whom explicit comparisons might have been made.

More complex still was the tendency for different data sources to provide ambiguous information, even when just the elderly were being considered. The strength of a triangulated methodology lies in its comprehensiveness. A set of defined problems can be approached from different angles. The problem is that complementary methods can also be contradictory if they supply incompatible evidence about the same problem. Unless one accepts the ethnomethodological view that all accounts are of equal validity since they are true for those who offer them, preference has to be given to one version of reality, often a composite of those available. For factual information, strategies to achieve this preferred version were straightforward: a client's account of their age was more likely to be accurate than the agency's, though the reverse was true for the date and source of referral. For attitudinal information, the aggregated responses of clients to questions about service satisfaction were taken as more accurate than social workers' individual or collective perception of the gratitude or otherwise of clients. For some kinds of data, however, inconsistencies were sharper and less easy to resolve. For instance, what social workers said in interview about the competence of referral sources was not always borne out by how team meetings reacted to referral letters for particular cases brought before them for allocation. Such disjunctions between attitudes and behaviour are commonplace in social science but frequency of occurrence does not guarantee ease of resolution. Here the comparative methodology was double-edged: it gave us otherwise buried indications of social workers' ambivalence towards referral agents, yet left us less confident in what we had to say about the nature of the relationship between the social work teams and those referring potential clients.

These ambiguities in the different levels and kinds of comparative analysis were evident more sharply than ever in our consideration of the form to be taken by the final write-up. Originally we had thought that a 'running' comparative analysis, in which data from the three teams was pulled together under a number of headings, would be a feasible and necessary way of writing up the comparison. It ceased to be either of these. It was no longer feasible as there was now no fixed framework to organize the comparative discussion. Such a framework could only evolve from consideration of each case study on its own and then in relation to the other two. It was no longer necessary because we were now as interested in similarities as in differences between the two teams. Since such similarities had taken shape as one of our key findings, the act of discovery should be demonstrated to the reader.

Hence we eventually decided to write up each case study separately, even in the knowledge that the result might well make turgid and repetitive reading. Each followed a constant set of subheadings and tables, as described in the introductory note to the case studies, though some flexibility was allowed in the weighting and introduction of factors unique to each situation. Even so, we were conscious that the logic of each case study was externally imposed in the interests of comparability. Left to its own internal dynamic, each case study might have produced a different organizing framework. It did feel at times as if what we wanted to say about individual teams, especially that which might have been of most direct interest to them, was being suppressed by the drive towards the necessary comparability.

The decision to write up each case study separately still left us with the need to bring our findings together in an explicitly comparative fashion, without too much repetition of detail from the case studies. Eventually, after much debate, we decided to have two kinds of explicit comparison. The first was to build directly out of the case study data into a discussion of the practice of social work and service delivery. The second, more abstracted, was to take an overarching view of the organizational forms of social work and service delivery. The distinction is analytical rather than empirical; the reality of social services departments is that practice and organization appear indivisible. Nevertheless, we felt it was a useful way of inflecting the discussion in rather different directions. It also helped us to address two types of audience, the practitioner and the policy-maker, who might see their specific interests highlighted within an overall view.

In a sense, these two forms of comparative analysis constitute our attempts to explain our empirical findings. But we also wanted to relate these to what we felt had emerged as the main influences on the interaction of practice and organization. Thus we have written a self-consciously polemical and speculative conclusion, focusing primarily upon teamwork: what in practice it appears to mean and what in principle it might be made to achieve.

These are some of the processes of research which led to the structure of this book. This opening chapter has been an account of the theoretical and methodological development of the project. Chapter 2 compares the characteristics and resources of the three study areas. Chapters 3, 4, and 5 are the case studies. Chapter 6 extracts some comparative issues of practice, Chapter 7 those of organization. Chapter 8 is the concluding argument. We have also added a Postscript on the Barclay Report, published by the National Institute for Social Work as this book reached draft form. This was clearly too significant to ignore yet we could hardly re-write the whole book so as to incorporate it. We therefore decided briefly to examine in a separate comment the convergences and divergences between the concerns of that report and those of this research.

2

Study Locations:
Contrasts and Similarities

THE AREA TEAM AS THE FOCUS OF STUDY

The focus for our study has been three social services area teams. As a method of organization within social services departments, the area team is long accepted and operates at the lowest level of the managerial/supervisory hierarchy. It also has the most immediate level of contact with the community. Whether it is the most effective or appropriate form of organization for its task has been raised elsewhere (Webb and Hobdell 1980) and is not a question to which we address ourselves directly. What we hope to do in this chapter is to provide a description of the context in which our three study teams operated.

In order to understand why certain resources are used and particular client groups are given priority, it is necessary to look both at the place of the teams within their organizations and to the policies and overall pattern of expenditure of those social services departments. The characteristics of the areas in which needs are to be met are also important. Here we highlight first the prevailing socioeconomic characteristics of the areas and second the organizational context in which the study teams operated.

While an attempt was considered in each case to find a team 'typical' of their respective urban and rural areas, the unique aspects of each particular team and its context bedevilled such an approach. Our teams were part of local authorities of different administrative status. Dereham is part of Norfolk, a non-Metropolitan County; Aber part of a Welsh non-Metropolitan County; and Selly Oak part of Birmingham Metropolitan District. At the time of our study Birmingham and Norfolk were controlled by the Conservatives, Glyn by Independents.

The study areas were prescribed by the boundaries set by each team for their catchment areas. Loosely based on local government areas they did not always coincide with those served by other related services. This presents challenges for liaison and co-operation between the services concerned and, for us, problems in comparing statistics of need and service provision.

TOPOGRAPHY AND POPULATION

The areas were very different topographically. The mountainous features of Aber and consequent low population density stood in

Figure 2(1) The study areas

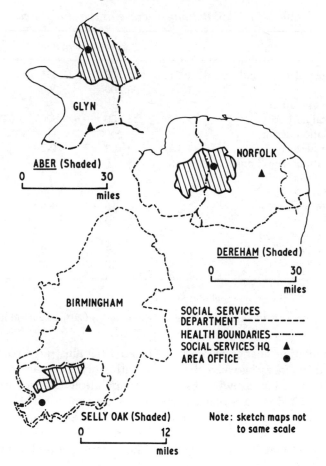

GLYN

ABER (Shaded)
0   30
         miles

NORFOLK

DEREHAM (Shaded)
0   30
         miles

BIRMINGHAM

SOCIAL SERVICES
DEPARTMENT ――――――――
HEALTH BOUNDARIES―・―・―
SOCIAL SERVICES HQ ▲
AREA OFFICE   ●

SELLY OAK (Shaded)   Note: sketch maps not
0   12   to same scale
         miles

marked contrast to the arable plain of Norfolk and the high population density of urban Selly Oak. As a result only in Aber were there major natural barriers to communication, though Dereham had the problem of poor public transport, common to Norfolk, and which particularly disadvantages the elderly, children, and housewives (Moseley *et al.* 1977).

The population structures in the areas showed a clear contrast with fewer old people and more children in the urban area (*Table 2(1)*). The area figures masked considerable internal differences and the Selly Oak ward for example, which formed two-thirds of the team's total catchment area, had over 16 per cent of its population aged over 65.

Table 2(1)   *Population structure in the study areas*

		Aber	*Dereham*	*Selly Oak*
total population (study area)	1971	31,505	37,355	39,607
	1979	30,700	46,200	37,825[1]
total population (local authority)	1979	226,400	679,800	1,041,000
population density (per hectare)	1979	0.2	0.7	38.6[1]
population projections 1971–1986 (% plus or minus)				
Total		−3	+30	−6[3]
0–14 yrs		−16	+5	−18[3]
65+		+10	+37	+18[3]
age group % 1979				
0–14 yrs		19	20	23[2]
65+		18	17	13[2]

[1]1976: [2]1971: [3]projection for all Birmingham.

Source: OPCS 1971 Census and Planning Depts of individual local authorities.

Population change between 1971 and 1979 illustrated considerable differences between the areas, with only Dereham showing any population growth. Estimated population change between 1971 and 1986 also revealed some interesting contrasts between the two rural areas. Whilst the population of the Dereham area was expected to increase by just under one-third, in Aber it was predicted to fall by over 3 per cent. The situation of decline in Aber was made more significant by the fact that the proportion of elderly was predicted to increase by nearly one-tenth in the same period. In Dereham the population under fourteen years was to grow by nearly 5 per cent and the elderly population by 36 per cent. Unfortunately, population projections for the Selly Oak study area were not available and the evidence of 1971–6 suggests that those for Birmingham as a whole underestimate the population decline there. Overall, Birmingham was predicted to lose just under 6 per cent of its population between 1971 and 1986 and, significantly, the under fourteen age group was anticipated to drop by 18.4 per cent, a figure slightly higher than for Aber. Birmingham expected to experience an 18.1 per cent growth in its population over sixty-five years (41 per cent in the more dependent over seventy-five age group) by 1986. Thus in each of the study areas, as in the country as a whole, there will be variable but still significant increases in the elderly population, with contingent consequences for health and social services agencies.

In each area, these variations were due not only to *natural* changes in birth and death rates, but also to the impact of migration. In the rural areas, retirement migration has had important implications for the provision of social services facilities. Matched against this there has been a continuous out-migration of younger people to the towns in search of jobs, further education, careers, and housing, which has had the effect of gradually increasing the proportion of elderly people remaining. Notably, Aber had the highest proportion of Welsh speakers anywhere in Wales. It was anticipated that the problems associated with the integration of ethnic minorities might thus, for different reasons, be present in both Aber and Selly Oak, which had a small black population.

EMPLOYMENT PATTERNS

A major problem for Selly Oak was found in the sharp increase in youth unemployment over the decade ending in July, 1979 (*Table 2(2)*). There has also been an increase, though less marked, in the Dereham study area where youth unemployment trebled in the decade. Similar figures were not available for Aber but a major increase in youth unemployment seems likely. As a result it might reasonably be expected that increased social problems associated with youth unemployment would be reflected in the work of the social services departments.

Table 2(2)　*Employment sectors and unemployment
in the study areas*

Employment	Aber	Dereham	Selly Oak
% by key sector			
1977: primary	10[1]	15	0
manufacturing	4[1]	26	56
service	80[1]	50	41
construction	6[1]	9	3
total unemployment %			
June 1969: summer	4	3	3
winter	8	3	4
June 1979: summer	6	7	8
winter	9	6	7
youth unemployment (numbers)			
July 1969	na	43[2]	55
July 1979	na	132	1774[3]

[1]1976; [2]May 1969; [3]July 1978. A change in catchment area renders the 1979 figure
inappropriate.

Source: Planning departments of the individual local authorities, based on returns
made available to them by the Department of Employment.

Unemployment in total had not experienced the rapid increase
associated with that of school leavers. Nonetheless in June 1969
unemployment in each of the study areas was under 5 per cent, but
in the decade to June 1979 the unemployment rate had more than
doubled in Selly Oak and nearly trebled in the Dereham study area.

All three areas had suffered the recent loss of major employers.
Comparison of winter and summer rates showed Aber to have wide
seasonal variations in employment opportunities which meant that
between June and December 1979 unemployment increased by 50
per cent. This is a feature of many rural areas where tourism creates
seasonal imbalances in employment opportunities, leading to
instabilities in the labour market and in many cases poor wage
levels and hence multiple job holding (Wenger 1980).

A more significant difference between the study areas concerned
employment opportunities. For both rural areas the highest proportion of the employed work force were to be found in the service
sector, with agriculture, forestry, and fishing (the primary sector)
absorbing only 10 per cent and 15 per cent of the work force in

Aber and Dereham respectively. Employment in Selly Oak was focused almost exclusively on the manufacturing and service sectors. The greatest difference between the study areas lay in the size of the manufacturing sector with the proportion in Selly Oak being fourteen times greater than that in Aber though only twice that in Dereham. The heavy reliance on the service sector for employment is a well-known feature of rural areas and indicates the importance of the public sector as an employer, and their dependence on public policy.

For Selly Oak this dependence took a different form. The severe contraction of the British motor vehicle industry in particular, and manufacturing in general, has created severe problems of structural unemployment. While it too has become increasingly dependent on the employment opportunities in the shrinking public sector, it particularly looks to government intervention to aid the necessary rejuvenation of local manufacturing industry.

STANDARDS OF ACCOMMODATION AND PENSIONER HOUSEHOLDS

Local authority intervention in the provision of accommodation varied quite markedly between the study areas. In 1971 (the latest date for which comparative data were available) only 17.1 per cent of accommodation in the Selly Oak area was rented from the council, a considerably lower proportion than in the rural areas. Whilst in each area one-half of households were in owner-occupation, a large proportion of Selly Oak households were rented from the Bournville Trust, a local housing association (*Table 2(3)*).

The rural areas suffered from the clearest signs of sub-standard housing. Aber had the highest proportion of overcrowding though it was low in all three areas. The differences in standards were reflected more sharply in the other basic amenities. The proportion of households sharing or without a bath or shower in Aber was over twice that of Selly Oak. Exclusive use of all three basic amenities (bath or shower, inside WC, and hot water supply) was lowest in Aber and highest in Selly Oak. Parallel differences have been found between rural and urban areas in Wales as a whole (Fisk 1980).

To an extent of course these measures are outmoded as indicators of housing stress. The best standard of housing within the Selly Oak study area was on a council estate dominated by 'high-rise'

Table 2(3)   *Housing characteristics in the study areas*

	Aber	Dereham	Selly Oak
tenure			
% households in 1971			
owner-occupied	57	51	53
council rented	21	28	17
rented privately (unfurnished)	22	19	25
overcrowding			
% households with more than			
1.5 persons per room	2	1	1
basic amenities 1971			
% households without or sharing			
bath/shower	19	15	8
inside WC	18	17	10
hot water	12	13	6
exclusive users of these amenities	78	81	89
pensioner households			
% households in 1971			
1 person pens.	16	12	12
2 person pens.	19	18	8

Source: OPCS 1971 Census.

blocks. As if to emphasize internal differences the worst were in the 'core' area of urban renewal where many low income families were concentrated. By coincidence it was also an area in which a high proportion of pensioner households were found. In Aber, with its large elderly population, the more vulnerable single pensioner households represented a sixth of all households and two pensioners together another fifth. In Dereham, too, two-pensioner households were more prevalent than in Selly Oak, a pattern reflecting migration flows as much as long-term patterns of residence.

THE SOCIAL SERVICES DEPARTMENTS

Examination of expenditure on personal social services per head of population showed Birmingham to be the highest spender of our three authorities (*Table 2(4)*). Each department had a net expendi-

Table 2(4) *Expenditure on personal social services:
net budget allocations 1978/79[1]*

	Glyn	Norfolk	Birmingham
	%	%	%
residential care			
children	7	12	27
elderly	26	27	16
younger physically handicapped	2	2	1
mentally handicapped (children and adults)	4	3	3
mentally ill	2	1	1
total	41	45	48
day care			
children	1	2	5
adults			
physically handicapped	1	1	0
mentally handicapped	4	5	3
mentally ill	0	0	0
elderly	3	1	0
multi-purpose	3	0	1
total	12	9	9
field-work	10	11	12
domiciliary and other services	20	21	21
administration	17	15	10
total net expenditure (£1000s)	5,873	13,277	31,049
net expenditure per head of population	£25.9	£19.5	£29.8
% on social services compared with other council services	10	11	14[2]

[1] Figures in this table are given to nearest whole number. Totals may not sum to 100%.
[2] Metropolitan districts do not have as wide a range of functions as non-metropolitan counties.

Source: CIPFA Personal Social Services Statistics 1978/9 (Actuals).

ture per head slightly higher than the average for their respective types of authority. Although all three authorities had a policy of encouraging non-institutional care, each to varying degrees (as a result of the higher unit costs of residential care) spent proportionately more on residential than any other form of care.

The higher proportion of elderly people in the rural counties was clearly reflected in the expenditure allocations, particularly those for the provision of residential care. Also Glyn devoted relatively large proportions of its budget to residential care of the 'Cinderella' client groups (physically and mentally handicapped and mentally ill). It also spent higher proportions of the budget supporting day care for the elderly and physically handicapped.

Comparison of the levels of revenue expenditure, broken down by client group, confirms this pattern (*Table 2(5)*).

Clearly the elderly were more prominent in Norfolk and Glyn. The dominance of child care expenditure in Birmingham contrasted with restricted proportions of expenditure on the other client groups, particularly the mentally ill. At the other extreme, the rela-

Table 2(5)   *Revenue expenditure and caseloads divided into client groups*

	Glyn	Norfolk	Birmingham
revenue expenditure in 1978/79 (gross)			
% spent on each client group			
elderly	63	62	39
children (and families)	12	20	48
mentally ill	4	2	1
mentally handicapped	11	10	8
younger physically handicapped	11	5	4
caseloads (March 1979)			
% receiving active social work support by client group			
elderly	29	28	18
children (and families)	22	38	48
mentally ill	11	9	3
mentally handicapped	10	8	3
physically handicapped	28	17	28
total	100	100	100
	(n = 4805)[1]	(n = 9321)	(n = 14,040)
cases per 1000 population	21	14	14

[1] June, 1979.

Source: Individual social services departments returns.

tive lack of pressure from child care expenditure led to comparatively high levels of financial allocation in Glyn to the younger
physically handicapped particularly.

The difficulties of collecting comparative information on case-
loads across the departments hamper taking a clear view of how
these expenditure priorities might affect the pattern of social work
support. Nonetheless children and families dominated social work
case-loads in Birmingham and the mentally handicapped and ill
formed a very small proportion of this work. In Glyn the elderly
were the primary client group (and the physically handicapped
second) while Norfolk demonstrates a pattern somewhere between
the two extremes.

THE STUDY TEAMS AS PART OF LARGER ORGANIZATIONS

The three agencies employed different organizational structures to
manage their departments, though each had a stated emphasis on
decentralization of control and four layers of management between
social workers and the Director of Social Services (*see Figure 2(2)*).

Norfolk had a structure based on geographic 'divisions', each in
turn divided into a number of social work 'areas', of which Dereham was one. The area officer was responsible for field-work and
home help services and also controlled the allocation of places in
elderly persons homes within the area. The divisional managers
took a broader resource allocation and co-ordinating role across
the areas, though specialists, such as the intermediate treatment
and occupational therapy workers, were accountable to headquarters personnel. Placements in children's homes were also allocated
from county hall.

Although the area officer at Aber had a similar range of control
to his counterpart in Dereham, higher level co-ordination and management in Glyn was based on client group specialisms and operated from county headquarters. With the exception of places in
elderly persons homes, day and residential resources were allocated
from headquarters.

Birmingham's structure incorporated assistant directors with
functional specialisms – field-work and care services (subdivided
into adult day care, residential services, and direct meals) – with
group leaders co-ordinating field-work services for four geographic
districts, which were in turn divided into social work 'areas'. Area
managers hence had responsibility for field-work services but many

resources were controlled at district level and some, such as placements in elderly persons homes, allocated by staff based at headquarters. The Selly Oak team was one of four 'ward' teams that
formed part of Birmingham's Area 12.

These structures produced similar feelings about the centre on
the part of many field-workers. For Dereham and Selly Oak headquarters seemed very remote, since decisions on resources were
largely taken centrally or at district/divisional level and only their

Figure 2(2) Line management responsibilities to social work teams

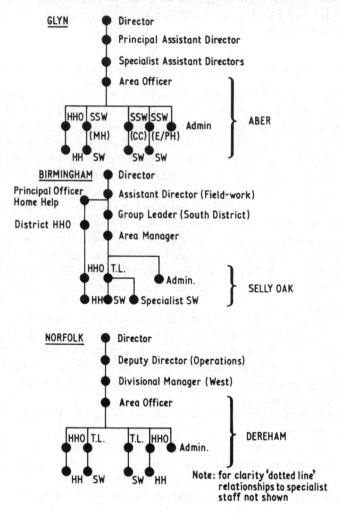

area officers were represented at district/divisional management teams. In Aber communication with county hall was more direct managerially because although formal communication went via the area officer, staff from across the county would sometimes meet at headquarters with the assistant director for their specialism. Nonetheless headquarters was remote geographically and direct contact with it seen as something of a 'special event'.

ORGANIZATION AND LOCATION OF THE TEAMS

Selly Oak's team was generic and served the Selly Oak ward itself and a small part of neighbouring Weoley, though its base was shared with other Area 12 teams some way from the ward. Dereham's two teams also operated generically and shared accommodation within one of the two areas served. Aber staff were located in the largest settlement in the area and formed three specialist teams but allocated work within the teams on a geographic basis. The geographic orientation of the areas did not, however, carry the connotations of multi-disciplinary methods of work and emphasis on prevention typical of the true 'patch' system (Hadley and McGrath 1981). None had developed sub-offices or similar contact points. But the generic teams had specialist workers available to them and had encouraged an interest in particular client groups amongst their workers – to some extent determined by client demand. Additional resources were involved in 'duty' arrangements. Each team offered a standard day-time system which meant Selly Oak's duty referrals might well be handled by members of other ward teams on the rota. Out of hours or stand-by duty was handled in Birmingham by a specialist centralized team, while Norfolk operated a centrally co-ordinated voluntary 'long-stop' arrangement, and in Glyn two alternating central co-ordinators used a team of retained 'runners' to undertake these emergency visits and investigations.

The offices of all three study teams were not ideally sited for many of the populations they served and this was compounded by the problem of physical access to the building in Dereham and Selly Oak. Nor was accommodation ideal for staff and the lack of suitable interviewing accommodation was an issue in all the areas.

The teams had a similar balance of qualified and unqualified staff, though their designations varied considerably (*Table 2(6)*). They were augmented by a range of specialist resources and it is those we now consider.

Table 2(6)   *Staffing in the study areas*

	Aber	Dereham	Selly Oak
management	1	1	0.25
admin. and clerical	4	6	2.75
fieldwork			
team leaders/seniors	3	2	4.0
qualified social workers	6	7	2.5
unqualified social workers	6	2	1.0
social work assistants	0	2	1.5
trainee social workers	0	0	1.0
community workers	1	0	–
family aide	0	0	1.0
part-time visitor	0	0	1.0
occupational therapist	0	1	0.33
care services			
home help organizer	1	2	1.25

Source: DHSS staffing return September 1979 and research observation June 1979.

RESOURCES IN ABER

The elderly and physically handicapped

The distribution of residential care for the elderly was concentrated on the main centres of population. This produced a pattern in which the five homes were scattered throughout the district. Aber had 152 places available with a waiting list of 25 at the time of the study. The team controlled the admission process and often was faced with having to place someone outside their local area. Social workers had to look outside the area for specialist residential services for the deaf, blind, and physically handicapped.

Some day care was offered at homes for the elderly and the team had also attempted to encourage a network of social clubs. A meals on wheels service was provided to a number of local communities, in conjunction with the Women's Royal Voluntary Service who were responsible for managing the individual schemes and recruiting helpers to deliver meals. Meals on wheels kitchens were based usually in school canteens or in county-run homes, though certain communities lacking a central kitchen or available volunteers were without this service. In Aber there were thirteen schemes providing two mid-day meals per week for recipients.

Although there was no occupational therapist available to the team, two social workers specialized in work with the deaf and blind respectively.

The mentally ill and mentally handicapped

Nearly all services to the mentally ill were provided from outside Aber. However, a weekly club run jointly by the social workers and a community psychiatric nurse in one of the towns provided a focal point for clients and families.

For the mentally handicapped, an adult training centre was available within the area, situated centrally and catering for up to fifty members a day. Most attenders lived in their own homes. However, the team looked outside Aber for short and long-term residential care for mentally handicapped adults and children. In addition the area supported Gateway Clubs for the mentally handicapped providing venues for meetings and financial support.

Children and families

A community home, a county resource, catering for fourteen children, was situated within the area. Activities for young people were organized in the community centre funded by the social services department with urban aid in Slatetown. These resources were complemented by twenty-five foster parents, pre-school play groups, and Ysgoliau Meithrin (the Welsh pre-school play group movement) which had been set up in a number of centres with the support of the social services department. Each area held a register of child minders but this latter service was little developed because of lack of demand. Social workers had to rely on resources outside the district for assessment placements, intermediate treatment for 'children in trouble', and also for community homes with education on the premises.

Health services

Centres for acute services lay outside the area boundary, but the local area health authority pursued a policy of maintaining cottage hospitals to provide both short and long-stay beds for elderly patients and limited acute, convalescent and maternity services. In addition, Estuarytown hospital provided day facilities for the elderly. A large psychiatric hospital over 50 miles away served as the in-patient facility for psychiatric patients from Aber but some effort had been made to provide regular out-patient clinics in Estuarytown on a twice-monthly basis. The region's major hospital for the mentally handicapped lay outside the area, also some 50 miles distant. Two long-stay hospitals were situated in Aber but neither provided either assessment or short-term care facilities.

There was no local child guidance centre though a county-wide service was available. The majority of general practitioners were based in group practices to which community nursing services were often attached, though some nursing services operated over wider areas. Community psychiatric nurses were also in the process of expanding their services to patients living at home.

Table 2(7)   *Social services department resources situated in the study areas*

	Aber no.	places	Dereham no.	places	Selly Oak no.	places
adult training centre	1	50	0	0	0	0
homes for elderly	5	152	2	76	3	100
children's homes	1	14	2	25	2	30
day nursery	0	0	0	0	1	40
homes for the mentally handicapped	0	0	0	0	1	25

Source: Individual Social Services Departments (June 1979).

RESOURCES IN DEREHAM

The elderly and physically handicapped

There were two residential homes for the elderly in the study area, located in Dereham and Swaffham, with thirty-six beds and forty beds respectively. These beds were allocated through the area officer who was able to call on a number of beds in another home just across the southern border of the area. Both homes took a limited number of short-stay and day care clients and both were in the process of being extended to provide more beds through the use of joint financing money. Day care was generally limited. A voluntary centre in Dereham provided twelve places two days per week but in Swaffham, although a centre was planned, no current provision existed.

Meals on wheels were provided in just over a quarter of the parishes in the area by the Women's Royal Voluntary Service and mainly supplied through school kitchens. Other than the occupational therapist and craft organizer, there were no specialist services available within the area for the blind, deaf, or physically handicapped. Voluntary organizations provided some facilities for the elderly and physically handicapped in the area. A 'Crossroads' care attendant scheme provided relief for relatives and care for handicapped people. In Dereham a Disabled People's Club met once a fortnight and in Swaffham a similar club organized meetings once a month. A club for the blind met in Dereham and Swaffham each month and also arranged holidays. Seven old people's clubs met in the rural areas.

Mentally ill and mentally handicapped

Little community provision existed for either of these client groups in the area; only a group home for the mentally handicapped in a village to the south of Dereham. Two Adult Training Centres outside the area had to be used to meet the area's needs, though another is planned. In spite of the paucity of statutory facilities voluntary organizations were quite active in the form of local branches of MIND and MENCAP. Both organizations had a local adviser and clubs in the area and MIND sponsored two group homes. The Carr Gomm society operated a hostel in Dereham which was complemented by the work of the MIND day centre which opened three days per week.

Children and families

There were two residential homes for children in the area with a total of twenty-six places. Both were situated in Dereham but one served a wider catchment area. It was the policy of the social services committee to encourage fostering and the team was able to use the services of a specialist fostering officer who was shared with another team. This resulted in the area being able to foster the majority of its children in care. Similarly, a play group and child minding officer attached to the division was available to provide a service in each area using village halls and youth clubs. Occasionally house groups (play groups held in private residences) had been developed in order to augment the shortage of public physical resources. The divisional intermediate treatment officer was, with some success, attempting to organize the provision of school-linked community-based schemes.

Health services

Links with the health service developed through work with clients. There were for example no GP attachments or specific linkage schemes, the only regular meetings taking place informally at monthly social worker lunches. There were small community hospitals at Dereham and Swaffham which provided largely geriatric and convalescent beds for the Norwich and King's Lynn health districts. Treatment facilities for the mentally ill, physically handicapped and mentally handicapped were located outside the area as were child guidance and other major clinics.

RESOURCES IN SELLY OAK

It is more difficult to outline clearly the resources available to the Selly Oak area team because many resources within both the statutory and voluntary sector, whilst they may well be located in the Selly Oak area, were available for allocation or use to people living in larger administrative areas – often the social work area as a whole or the social work district. To give one specific example, places in day or residential care, even where the homes or centres may be located within Selly Oak, were managed on a divisional basis and allocated according to need, and within the constraints of geographical distance, by a placement officer working from the department's headquarters. Nevertheless, what follows gives some idea of the range and depth of resources available to the team.

Elderly and physically handicapped

There were three homes for the elderly, with a total of 100 beds, located in Selly Oak itself. Birmingham had a policy of homes taking a small number of day care clients but staff shortages meant that this was not always achieved. Hence day care in homes tended to be limited to those clients being considered for long-term placement.

Day care for the elderly was largely restricted to the voluntary sector, though the district did have a social welfare centre for the physically handicapped, with over 100 places. Effectively there were ten voluntary organizations concerned with the elderly of the ward itself, as well as others providing housing or nursing services over a wider catchment area. Provision was largely social activity, often for the ambulant elderly. Most provided their service on only one day a week, though a work centre for the elderly is open daily from Monday to Friday. There was little known voluntary activity in the small part of Weoley appended to the Selly Oak team's patch though one Leyhill Tenants' Association ran an active over sixties' club each week.

There is no doubt that this voluntary care was an important contribution to the care of elderly people in the Selly Oak area. However, whilst those we interviewed about these activities were enthusiastic and committed, they expressed reservations about their ability to meet the full range of needs of the elderly people in the ward. They felt many areas of need were not being covered, particularly among the less ambulant elderly and those living in the core area of Selly Oak. They also felt there was little likelihood of them being able to extend provision of the present services. Three particular problems were access to suitable buildings, finding further volunteers, and the dependence of many activities on local authority funding which was becoming increasingly difficult to secure.

The home help service was managed by an area home help organizer, responsible for three other wards in addition to Selly Oak, with four assistant organizers supervising 260 home helps. The social work team had available to them the services of one part-time occupational therapist, a specialist worker for the blind (both Area 12 resources), and a part-time visitor for the elderly (although this post was vacant for the duration of the study). There was also a night watch service administered city-wide.

Mentally ill and mentally handicapped

Facilities for these two client groups were at a low level both in the statutory and voluntary sectors. There was located within the study area one home for mentally handicapped adults providing twenty-five places and a voluntary home for mentally handicapped children. A day centre for the mentally ill and an adult training centre were available within the district. The specialist mental health worker attached to the Selly Oak team and the part-time handicraft instructress, both resources shared with the area as a whole, also made important contributions.

Children and families

There were two children's homes with a total of thirty places and one day nursery with forty places within Selly Oak. These, however, were resources managed on a district basis and were shared, as were the observation and assessment facilities, residential nurseries, working children's homes, and the community homes located within the other areas of the district. Two senior social workers in the team specialized in juvenile liaison, court work, and welfare rights respectively. They were available to the area as a whole in much the same way as the intermediate treatment officer and the fostering and adoption senior from another team were available to the Selly Oak team. Much of the work with juveniles was contracted out through the intermediate treatment centre at 870 House, a local voluntary organization, and as a result the intermediate treatment officer was not used to any great extent by the team. A further social services intermediate treatment centre was to be opened on the Ley Hill Estate and a social worker from the team was later to take up the management of this resource.

Voluntary services and facilities available to this client group were few and far between. There was a National Children's Home, ten flat units for single mothers within the area, and a number of play groups and youth clubs. There were, however, very few service-giving organizations outside the statutory sector and the lack of structured play facilities and nursery education was apparent.

One important statutory resource was the Family and Child Advisory Service Centre (formerly Child Guidance). There were six such centres in the Birmingham area and one covered the southwest part of the city. It provided a multi-disciplinary service with a psychologist, social workers, and a speech therapist, as well as a school refusal unit for children between eight and thirteen.

Health services

Links with the health services were largely informal and based on individual clients. During the course of the study the first formal GP attachment at a local health centre got under way, but other-

wise social work lunches at the local library – an important informal meeting – were the only regular form of liaison. A small
local hospital, with its own medical social work department, was
situated within Selly Oak itself. Other important health resources
were the huge Queen Elizabeth II hospital just outside the ward
boundary and psychiatric and geriatric day and in-patient services
available within the district in Rubery. There was no local specialist
provision.

CONCLUSION

Although our analysis has been a crude one, it does provide an
important background to the understanding of the case studies and
subsequent comparative analysis. This perfunctory comparison has
tended to concentrate on manifest differences rather than underlying similarities and in conclusion some attempt must be made to
rectify this.

For example, clearly there were differences in the growth and
decline of population in the study areas, both in total and age structures. Nonetheless the proportions of population in the younger
age group were broadly similar and all areas faced the problem of
growing proportions of elderly people. Differences in employment
structure and levels of unemployment were also balanced by shared
problems of decline in the dominant sectors of the economy.

There were also major differences in levels and proportions of
the authorities' budgets spent on the care of the elderly, children
and families, and the physically handicapped but similar small
amounts spent on the mentally ill and mentally handicapped. At
the study team level this was to some extent reflected in the
resources available, though the picture was clouded by the allocation of these over wider areas. Many of the resources available to
the elderly and physically handicapped in Glyn, for example, were
not always close to Aber and this created its own difficulties. Similarly, Birmingham had perhaps a wider range of specialist resources
than the other areas but their availability was limited by the dilu-
tion of the service across a larger population base rather than by
geography. Hence there were differences in organization and
budget that reflect, to an extent, the obvious differences in the
crude indices of need that we have examined. It remains to be seen
how this picture helped shape the work of each team when studied
in detail. It is to that detailed examination that we now turn
through the medium of the case studies.

PART TWO

CASE STUDIES OF THE THREE AREA SOCIAL SERVICES TEAMS

The Case Studies

The following three chapters report the results of our linked case studies. They are presented in a consistent format that makes use of the same basic subheadings and table numbers (in order that the readers might make their own comparisons). The common structure reflects first a description of work process and then wider influences on the nature of provision in the areas.

The subheadings are:

1 Referral to the social services department
2 Reception, intake, and allocation
3 Social work practice and service provision
4 Social workers' perspectives
5 The influence of management

Within each section we have not necessarily reported our data in precisely the same order or with the same emphasis. This would have been tiresome for the reader and cut across the logic of the individual case studies. Similarly we have held back direct cross-references between the case studies themselves or other research until the comparative chapters.

Further consistency is introduced by adopting a client group classification for the presentation of much of the information, including the sections on practice. There could be many alternative classifications of different levels of validity. Ours was chosen because it reflected the distinctions made by the workers we studied, is most often adopted by others writing about social work, and is therefore most likely to make sense to a wide variety of potential readers. The common tables reflect this classification and are headed:

1 Characteristics of Elderly People Referred to Social Workers and the Home Help Service

Within this structure we have allowed for differences in the situations we studied to be reflected by the inclusion of extra tables determined by the logic of a particular case study. Two other variations are made in the light of local circumstances to enhance comparability: in the home help referrals included for the enumeration of referral sources (*Table 3(2)*) and in the proportion of study referrals eligible for inclusion in the information on referral allocation (*Table 3(6)*). Finally because we drew separate samples from new and longer term work without counting workers' total case-loads, the figures on those case-loads (*Table 3(5)*) are drawn from separate departmental sources and, whilst they are approximately comparable across the study teams, they produce what might otherwise appear minor inconsistencies within the individual case studies.

It is our hope that despite the demands of enhanced comparability, each individual case study retains some of its value as detailed description and analysis of the operation of a particular social work team.

Further information about the three individual studies is available from:

Aber   –   Gordon Grant,
              Dept. Social Theory and Institutions,
              University College of North Wales,
              Bangor.

Dereham   –   Dick Stockford,
Social Services Dept.,
Norfolk County Council,
County Hall,
Martineau Lane,
Norwich.

Selly Oak   –   Ric Bowl,
Dept. Social Administration,
University of Birmingham,
PO Box 363,
Birmingham.

3

Aber

3.1 REFERRAL TO THE SOCIAL SERVICES DEPARTMENT

The nature of the area served by the Aber team was discussed in Chapter 2. We begin by considering the process of referral as it was affected by Aber's particular characteristics.

The field-workers were housed in an office in the main administrative centre. Though only a few steps from the main shopping centre, the office was hidden down a narrow alley and there were no directional signs apart from a nameplate by the door. A ramp was provided for wheel-chair users. There was genuine concern amongst the team about being concealed from the public and about the kind of image a closed hidden door conveyed to the occasional passer-by.

Workers operated in specialist sub-teams defined in terms of client group but as a concession to the sheer size of the district each team subdivided work according to varying sizes of geographical patch. Some liaison schemes with GPs were operated as a means of picking up referrals, the form of liaison varying from a literal 'popping in and out of the surgery' to regular attendance at health clinics. Territorially these schemes were less than comprehensive. Social workers saw this as due less to their own lack of commitment to this form of out-reach than to the prejudiced or uncompromising views held by their health care peers of the social services' role. Collaboration, as we shall see in subsequent chapters, was also affected by other factors.

The team had rather tenuous links with a detached community worker based in a town in the north of the district. Failure to respond to long-standing problems of economic decline, depopulation, unemployment, and poor housing had induced local hostility towards officialdom. The department had placed the community worker there but did not otherwise intervene. In collaboration with youth workers and local voluntary groups, the worker's main emphasis was to encourage self-help from within rather than on calling on assistance from without. However, few referrals to the social services team came from this source.

Thus little 'out-reach' work was evident. Referrals were expected to follow established routes to the team. Demand had to be expressed through such channels. This had particular implications for the distribution of referrals between client groups.

Excluding enquiries dealt with exclusively by the home help organizer, elderly persons accounted for almost 60 per cent of the incoming cases. Most of the elderly were women, over a half were widowed and nearly half were living alone. All but four of the thirty-one cases referred to the home help organizer involved elderly persons. In some biographical respects these were similar to cases referred for social work investigation, though more likely to be female, widowed, living alone, owner-occupiers, very old, or a combination of these. Contrary to our expectations the home help group manifested more signs of 'at riskness' than the social work group. Further confirmation of the vulnerability of individuals referred for home help is presented in *Table 3 (1)* which separates all home help referrals, including those processed by social workers, from all other elderly cases handled by the social work team.

Social workers were aware of the referral pressures emanating from old people but a subject of dispute was which groups of elderly were getting referred and for what reasons. One view

Table 3(1)   *Characteristics of elderly people referred to social workers and the home help service*

	social work referrals (n = 125)	home help referrals (n = 63)
	%	%
aged 75+	48	77
female	62	68
widowed	48	61
living alone	41	61
in council accommodation	26	25
in owner-occupation	48	61

maintained that articulate middle-class retirees from England were the dominant force behind referral demands. It was argued that they lacked adequate support networks and that distance from kin put them at risk. By definition they were deemed to be in greater need of support from the agency. A contrasting view maintained that depopulation, out-migration of the young and economically active, and consequent decline in chapel membership left local elderly people with weak social networks and thus equally vulnerable. Our data showed the ethnic characteristics of elderly clients to be almost identical to those of the elderly population at large so both arguments may well have some validity but with the effect of balancing each other out.

Within family and child cases nearly a half involved more than one principal client. Workers generally saw the problems of these families as linked to low pay, unemployment, and a poor economic infrastructure. Aber had some of the worst pockets of unemployment in the whole of Wales. Seasonal work produced by the short-term summer boom in tourism alleviated some of the worst effects of unemployment but child care workers pointed out that they all had clients who needed 'massive' support in the winter when unemployment peaked again. Wage levels in the area were also well below national norms. Hence it was common for financial problems and poor housing to be mentioned as going hand in hand in such cases. Typical of many comments was the following:

'Well, basically you see financial problems. It covers a lot of things ... homelessness, bad housing, lack of furniture, lack of heating, lack of employment ... You find men not working but for no fault of their own or you can get that way because of the level of wages around here. This is the reason behind a lot of child care. We talk of things like inadequate parents but I often wonder if they are that inadequate or whether the situation is inadequate and they just respond accordingly.'

The observation that some needs were rooted in the structural problems of society was illuminating since it underlined the misplaced notion of a rural idyll which protected families from the worst effects of contemporary living. However, workers often saw many clients as a conservative, retiring, or insular group holding on to values of self-help and independence still considered to be prevalent in small farming communities. Coupled with the small scale of community these features were seen by workers as exerting a controlling influence over more deviant forms of behaviour.

Indeed vandalism and crime were perceived as emanating almost exclusively from tourists letting rip during the summer months. As if in reflection of this, fewer Welsh families ended up on child care and family problem case-loads than would be anticipated from extrapolation of population data.

Amongst the younger physically handicapped roughly equal proportions were male and female but most were older persons of working age. Few were living alone so the worst effects of immobility were often mitigated by the presence of others in the household. Again, fewer than anticipated were Welsh speaking. Only a handful of mental handicap cases were referred but this was because the Aber team only occasionally shut these cases down. They remained part of long-term work.

The mentally ill also only formed a small proportion of social work referrals. This group presented a wide range of problems, from alcoholism, to anxiety neuroses, to psychotic conditions and situations involving complex family relationships. Contrary to expectations, more males than females presented themselves in this small group. Six cases involved confused or dementing old people, which accounts largely for the third who were living alone. Community psychiatric nurses received most of the referrals coming from the main regional psychiatric facility so new work with mental illness cases was becoming something of a rarity.

Since the sampled long-term cases formed an important part of social workers' cases a brief mention will be made here of their obvious biographical differences from referrals. Work with families involved proportionately more children, many of whom were in the care of the local authority. All the mental handicap cases were single, aged less than sixty-five and the vast majority were living at home with relatives. Of the small number of mental illness cases sampled the majority were females of older working age. The age distribution of the younger physically handicapped indicated the existence of more children in the long-term group, many of whom were multiply handicapped and destined to be on case-loads for some years to come. The elderly displayed similar personal characteristics to the referral group.

Sources of referral

Referrals came from many sources, details of which are summarized in *Table 3(2)*. Several pertinent features are worthy of mention. In all groups except the mentally ill, roughly one-half of the referrals emanated from informal channels, that is directly from clients, their families, neighbours, or other members of the public. Elderly clients were more likely to be referred by family and relatives than other client groups and less likely to refer themselves.

As regards formal sources, most referrals came from health personnel but these were not limited to the more obvious client groups like the elderly. Social workers acknowledged the gatekeeping role played by primary health teams but attitudes towards the smoothness of this function appeared to vary greatly: '... health visitors ... they have got a good idea of what the department is all about. I think they're very good. They come on the phone and discuss the case before they actually make a referral.'

Table 3(2) *Social work and home help referrals: sources of referral*

	elderly (n = 161)	younger physic. h'capped (n = 39)	mentally ill (n = 18)	mentally h'capped (n = 6)	children and families (n = 45)	home help only (n = 27)
	%	%	%	%	%	%
informal sources						
self	11	33	13	★	25	27
family relatives	26	19	6	★	10	8
neighbours/ friends	4	3	0	★	5	4
other members of the public	4	3	0	★	3	12
total all informal sources	(45)	(58)	(19)	★	(43)	(51)
formal sources[1]						
primary health	18	22	25	★	23	35
other health	11	11	25	★	5	8
other SSD worker	13	6	25	★	10	8
juvenile liaison officer	0	0	0	★	10	0

[1] Only categories accounting for at least 5 per cent are listed; hence column percentages do not sum to 100.

★ Referrals for the six mental handicap cases came via SSD personnel (2), psychiatrist (2), education department (1), and a neighbour (1).

One worker felt that GPs saw referral to social services as a last resort, coming often far too late in the day:

'GPs don't let us know about people until it actually is an extreme situation but they might have been seeing [a patient] for a long time. We don't know about them because the GPs also don't know how to use the SSD. I think that is a great pity because they are in touch with so many people . . . I think there is a lot of work to be done with GPs, but they are an institution, in a way, as we are.'

Mutually ambiguous definitions of responsibility occasionally led to conflict such as a 'demand' from a GP for a home help or the anger of another at a decision to defer provision of domiciliary services. Such incidents tempered enthusiasm for greater collaboration.

The only other agency responsible for a substantial proportion of referrals was the juvenile liaison office whose referrals were less the result of individual initiative than the outcome of legal processes. Long-term cases were more likely to have been referred through an agency, possibly because the intensity of their problems made the need for social services intervention self-evident.

Generally there were many potential referral agents who scarcely appeared at all. Less than 2 per cent of newly referred cases, and scarcely any more of long-term cases, were referred by each of MPs, councillors, DHSS, education department, housing department, Department of Employment, probation department, fuel agencies, voluntary organizations, and the church. If the health service recognized the relationship between its work and that of social services this seemed less true of other agencies, even those thought to be an integral part of the welfare state.

For nearly all client groups informal sources were at least as important as formal ones. For the elderly especially such informal sources were their own families. Despite the evidence about the existence of enhanced levels of neighbouring amongst the elderly in rural communities, the indications were that family and relatives made the critical, and perhaps more personal, decisions about care and support for dependants as evidenced by their role as referral agents.

Whoever makes the decision to refer, contact still has to be made with the social services office. Across all the client groups there were common features about modes of referral. As can be seen from *Table 3(3)*, telephone and written communication together accounted for virtually all cases. Visits made to the office by enquirers were most uncommon. In fact, only twenty-one persons were referred by an actual call at the office over the six-month study period. Predictably, the proportion of office callers was significantly higher from parishes lying closest to the area team base. Virtually no one living more than 10 miles away ever visited the office for referral purposes. With this exception rurality measures had little apparent impact on the incidence of referrals. Factors such as parish population sparsity and population size did not help to explain the prevailing distribution of either referrals or long-term cases. However, it must be remembered that the whole area was characteristically 'rural', the largest town having a population of only 5,000.

Table 3(3)   *Social work referrals: method of referral*

	elderly (n = 161)	younger physically handicapped (n = 39)	mentally ill (n = 18)	mentally handicapped* (n = 6)	children and families (n = 45)
	%	%	%	%	%
telephone	66	56	75	★	75
letter	17	14	0	★	13
office visit	5	17	13	★	8
other	11	14	13	★	5

★ Methods of referral of the six mental handicap cases were telephone (2), letter (2), and other (2).

Social workers were conscious of the difficulties involved in calling at the office, especially for those living far afield. However one non-indigenous worker felt these reasons were not sufficient explanation for the apparent under use of social services:

'I wonder whether people know how to use the social services department in this area. I'm amazed at the lack of use. This could be due to geography, transport, access. It is physically difficult to see what the social worker is about. ... I think we are terribly underused. People just don't know about us ... There could be other reasons; people might have difficulty getting hold of us. It

could also be our reputation ... but I also think there is a lot of
ignorance.'

There was little evidence of strategies which might have
improved the situation by providing more direct points of access
for the public or more systematic liaison with formal agencies.
The overriding picture of referral was therefore one in which
clients were left to contact the team. An active case-finding
approach was not in vogue. A low profile was adopted and almost
all social work activity took place in clients' homes, very little of it
happening or being sparked off from office calls. As we shall see
this had important repercussions for duty, intake, and allocation
work.

3.2   RECEPTION, INTAKE, AND ALLOCATION

For the vast majority of clients referral did not involve them in
visiting the social work office but for those who did visit reception
facilities were not ideal. One of the social workers in the team
described her own experience on coming to the office for her job
interview:

'I came into the front door and there was this massive corridor,
and doors and a staircase and a room that said "enquiries". I
went in and there was nobody there. Many clients are faced with
that since the duty officer isn't always sitting there because he has
to do other things.'

The formal reception process was relatively uncomplicated. The
duty social worker was expected to occupy the enquiry room and
act as the first point of contact with the agency for the person who
visited the office. Hence, there was no need for the caller to explain
their problem to administrative staff before meeting the social
worker on duty. However, the demands made on the duty officer
went beyond this role and involved the taking of telephone
messages for other social workers. It was this latter task that
presented problems for duty workers since telephone calls were
directed to individual workers' extensions from a central
switchboard which served other departments. In consequence, the
duty officer was often absent from the enquiry room. The ideal was
seen to be a receptionist in charge of an area switchboard who
could act as a filter for incoming telephone calls and be available

behind an enquiry desk for callers to the office. However, area management were in a weak position to argue for the necessary resources since the number of daily callers averaged no more than three or four.

For potential clients and other informal referrers who attempted to negotiate help via the telephone or by letter, skill in articulating problems and knowledge of the services available from the area office were important factors determining whether their needs would be met. However, the way in which the team processed enquiries came some way to dealing with these problems since it was tacitly accepted that taking a referral involved a home visit. Thus, having negotiated the problem of initial contact, the potential client was usually visited within the week following referral. It was typically at this point that an assessment of the problem was made. Administrative processing of referrals reflected this practice. Referrals were automatically opened as cases. Hence, apart from the few dealt with by the duty officer at first contact, all referrals were allocated to workers in the sub-teams.

Being on duty required both qualified and unqualified social workers from the three specialist teams to deal with problems outside their field. That all but two of the workers on the duty rota had worked generically before clearly minimized the potential problem. Furthermore, the senior social workers were readily available for consultation if the need arose. They actively encouraged the duty worker to use them so that enquiries inappropriate for team action could be dealt with and redirected.

The duty role occasionally bought with it the need for immediate action but crisis work was a rarity. For example, during the six months in which information on referrals was collected just three cases involving possible child abuse and only five compulsory admissions under the Mental Health Act were identified. Where an immediate response was required two options were open. Either the duty officer went out or, more usually, the case was given to a social worker who had planned a visit to that part of the district. When out on district, workers regularly telephoned in to meet this eventuality.

Thus the duty role in this rural area had certain defining characteristics. Apart from occasional personal callers whose demands were met in an office interview initial assessment for most cases extended beyond the role of the individual worker concerned. This was the norm for 'routine' referrals as well as 'crises' requiring immediate action. For the latter, it was accepted by the whole team that an individual's programmed visiting might have to be put on one side if an emergency had to be dealt with in the area they were visiting. One of the features of duty work in this rural area was that it was not equated with work pressure. Social workers saw their day in the office as a time to catch up with paper work on their own case-loads. Compared with duty in the urban team studied not only was the volume of personal callers lower, but the nature of the duty officer role and the response of the team qualitatively different.

Some mention should be made of the out-of-hours service operating in the county. At the time of the study an experimental emergency service was in operation which had been set up recently in response to a dispute over the organization of the service. It was organized on a county level with two qualified social workers employed as 'co-ordinatiors' to process all out-of-hours emergencies. At their disposal were a number of casually employed people who had been trained to deal with emergencies. Members of the Aber team were unable to assess the scheme's success but they were sceptical that it would be able to make the right decisions about emergencies, especially in those cases with which workers were already involved. Furthermore, standby duty had never been an onerous task, and it had been a rare event for the team member concerned to have to take emergency action. To overcome some of the problems faced by the scheme's co-ordinators, both the child care and the mental health senior had made it clear that they were available for consultation outside office hours if the need arose.

Allocation

Since it was unusual for referrals to be dealt with and closed at the point of contact, the overwhelming majority were passed to the three senior social workers in charge of sub-teams, or, if solely for home help, to the home help organizer. Thus, allocation of social work referrals was dominated by categorizing potential cases into 'child care', 'mental health', or 'elderly and physically handicapped' groups and then distributing them to workers via the appropriate senior social worker. Categorization, as such, was 'self-explanatory' for the majority of referrals. Where this was clouded by multiple problems a joint decision was arrived at by the senior social workers concerned.

Tables 3(4) and *3(5)* give figures for relative referral demands and

Social work in context

Table 3(4) Social work referrals in the study period

	all	elderly and physic. handicapped team		mental health team		child care team
		elderly	younger physic. h'capped	mentally ill	mentally h'capped	
	(n = 269)	(n = 161)	(n = 39)	(n = 18)	(n = 6)	(n = 45)
referrals per client group (%)	100	60	14	7	2	17
number of referrals per 1000 population	8.8	5.1	1.2	0.6	0.2	1.4
number of referrals per 1000 population pensionable age		23.1				
referrals to specialist sub-teams	267[1]	188[1]		24		45
number of referrals per week	11	8		1		2
number of referrals per individual worker per week	1	1.6		0.3		0.7

[1] Excluding cases referred to social worker for the deaf.

case-loads held by the three sub-teams. Over the six-months period that information was collected about social work referrals the Aber team dealt with 269 cases. This represents a referral rate of 11.3 cases per week, out of which 8.3 cases per week were allocated to the elderly and physically handicapped team. The different referral pressures placed on this team compared to the two other teams was commented upon by a number of workers, and seemed an inevitable result of the specialist team structure. This structure had been implemented county-wide, partly to prevent the high rate of referrals from the elderly detracting from the work with family and

Table 3(5) *Social work case-loads*

	all	elderly and physic. handi- capped team	mental health team	child care team
case-loads held by team at end of six months	783	485 (331)[1]	158	140
average case-load per worker	65	99 (82)[1]	52	47

[1] Figures in parenthesis represent case-loads of sub-team excluding those cases held by specialist worker for the blind.

mental health cases. Consequently workers in the latter two teams had more time for complex and intensive case-work. Since these teams and their seniors had clear interests in maintaining this division of labour, and in the absence of a high level of referral bombardment, it would appear that social work response to the elderly was disadvantaged.

Since referral demand was in no way unmanageable, it was to be expected that the team had found it unnecessary to develop priorities in dealing with cases. While the seniors were in a good position to monitor the expressed demands of clients within their own specialisms, neither they nor area management saw a need to re-evaluate staffing levels so that these would reflect the referral pressures coming to the team. The two seniors in charge of the child care and mental health teams inevitably strove to preserve their own team establishment, which had been determined by a county rather than by an area-based decision.

Two specialists who concentrated on work with the blind and the deaf worked relatively autonomously, receiving and processing their own referrals. While the former was accountable to the senior of the elderly and physically handicapped team and participated in duty work, the worker for the deaf had responsibility for cases in two districts and was accountable to line management at county headquarters, This worker held a nominal area case-load but there was no regular pattern of meeting between him and the sub-team.

Having identified the appropriate team to deal with the referral, the next step was for the three seniors to allocate referrals to individual workers. *Table 3(6)* presents the distribution of referrals

Table 3(6)   *The distribution of social work referrals at allocation*

	eldery (n = 161)	younger physically h'capped (n = 39)	mentally ill (n = 18)	mentally h'capped (n = 6)	children and families (n = 45)
	%	%	%	%	%
allocated to:					
qualified social worker	28	29	89	★	37
unqualified social worker	63	57	11	★	61
specialist worker for the blind[1]	9	14	0	★	0

[1] The specialist social worker for the blind received twenty referrals, out of which eleven were for blind clients.

★The six mental handicap referrals were allocated to qualified social workers.

to team members. Apart from the specialist for the blind and the social worker for the deaf, there was no formal division of labour on the basis of task or case complexity. Furthermore, it should be remembered that both qualified and unqualified workers were found in all the teams and each worker tended to concentrate his work within a smaller zone in the district. Indeed geographical source was a major factor governing case allocation. This enabled the teams to respond to referrals from Aber's scattered communities and minimized the time social workers spent travelling. The patch focus for an individual worker was flexible because of the different demands placed on the teams from different areas over time. However, in placing individuals on their 'patches' two seniors both had reasons for not placing workers in their home area: 'It's not my policy to have them working in the district they live in. ... I feel people are very sensitive to this; it makes no difference to the social worker, although it saves the problem of clients knocking on the door at night.' Workers saw the virtue of this but it was not identified as a ground rule by the senior in charge of the elderly sub-team. It seemed that the risks involved of being visible to clients were interpreted differently and were linked to the perceptions of practice held by workers across client groups.

While geographical source was a primary indicator for allocation other factors were sometimes taken into accout. Ethnicity, that is the ability of a worker to speak Welsh, was considered by all the senior social workers as and when seen to be necessary. Also, for the child care and mental health workers, social contact outside work and gender match between worker and client were mentioned. Seniors were also aware of more subtle factors affecting allocation decisions. In this respect, no relationship was found between case complexity and worker qualification. Reasons for worker choice nevertheless often demanded judgement reflecting the senior social worker's perceptions of team members' strengths and weaknesses in particular areas of work. However, some attempt was made to give less experienced workers a varied caseload. In fact from the evidence available from the case review data, no relationship existed between worker qualification and social work activity within any of the client groups. Whether this reflected similarity of social work practice or that the categories available failed to pick up more qualitative differences in method was more difficult to identify. Interviews with team members did not suggest that qualified workers employed different methods of work. Referrals were passed to individual workers on a day-to-day basis rather than through formal team allocation meetings. Given the factors governing allocation and the relatively low referral bombardment rate, this rather informal system could be readily understood.

3.3 SOCIAL WORK PRACTICE AND SERVICE PROVISION

The elderly

Details of work carried out with elderly persons by social workers are summarized in *Table 3(7)*. Problems dealt with were generally typified in health and self-care terms, reflecting the weight of referrals coming from the health service. Problems of a socio-emotional order, though not widely reported, were more evident in work with long-term clients. These active cases contained a good number of frail elderly, identified as being at risk, who were supported with the available array of services. Despite the size and topography of the team's catchment area, transport did not figure as a major problem at all and indeed in none of the long-term cases was this even reported.

Given that elderly social services consumers are usually older, more likely to be widowed, living alone, and in poorer health than the elderly at large in the community, the relative absence of loneliness and family problems reported by the team was interesting to note. However, our interviews with a sample of elderly clients living in the community revealed an altogether contrasting picture. Respondents' scores on the Philadelphia Geriatric Center Morale Scale (Lawton 1975) showed 27 per cent displaying low morale responses in eight of the seventeen items comprising the scale and independent probes built into the interview indicated similar quality of life deficits. Eight per cent admitted to not having someone in whom they could confide; 10 per cent said that there was no one from whom they could ask favours; and 22 per cent said that they wished they had more friends. If this can be taken as indicative of depression, loneliness, or difficulties with human relationships it is significant that social workers did not talk about social work with the elderly in these terms.

With this picture in mind what sorts of responses were evoked from the team? *Table 3(7)* shows that work with the elderly typically involved the provision of practical services, most often aids, home helps, adaptations, and meals on wheels. Predictably, long-term cases received more of everything. With the referral group, workers typically withdrew once domiciliary services had been mobilized and awaited re-referral. In this way case-loads were controlled, and the problems inherent in the otherwise large number of check-up visits necessary were minimized.

Social workers' perceptions of their methods of work with the elderly seemed qualitatively different from those with other clients. Problems dealt with and the activities and services provided were variously described by workers as 'routine' and requiring 'less in-depth work' or seen as being less complicated by interpersonal and emotional factors. Difficulties in dealing with cases were perceived more in terms of shortfalls of existing services. Investigation, advice-giving, and mobilization of resources emerged as the major social work activities but for long-term cases general support work was also widely reported.

However, social work visits were less frequent than with other client groups. Although home helps, meals on wheels, and day care services provided continuity of contact with clients, the responsibility of field-work and domiciliary workers for monitoring and review were less than clear. Social workers appeared to operate on the premise that if domiciliary workers were visiting clients then the latter would refer cases to them if needs and circumstances demanded. However, the criteria by which this should work and

	referrals (n = 161) %	long-term cases (n = 52) %
social work activities[1]		
investigating/assessing	69	78
giving information/advice	47	71
mobilizing resources	34	18
advocacy	1	6
educating/developing skills	1	4
problem-solving	10	18
supervising/reviewing	2	10
supporting/sustaining	20	51
providing group activity	0	8
visiting frequency		
monthly or more	45	31
monthly to quarterly	14	6
less than quarterly	41	63
service provided[1,2]		
aids	41	67
adaptations	5	21
home help	22	35
meals on wheels	10	17
clubs	3	19
day care	8	12
residential care	12	10
holidays	2	17
financial/material	3	17

	referrals (n = 161) %	long-term cases (n = 52) %
problems tackled[1,2]		
health/self-care	54	67
loneliness/isolation	5	15
family relationships	6	14
finance	9	19
housing	15	11
transport	5	0
other	22	4
none	13	21
major problem		
health/self-care	51	57
other agencies contacted[1,2]		
general practitioner	31	47
health visitor/district nurse	19	41
other health	8	8
housing department	14	14
DHSS	10	20
voluntary agencies	5	22
other[3]	5	2
none	38	20

[1] More than one category could be used so figures do not necessarily sum to 100.
[2] Categories which accounted for less than 5 per cent of cases in both the referral and long-term group have been excluded.
[3] For the most part 'other' in terms of agencies reflects contacts with fuel agencies.

the procedures to be adopted were not readily apparent.

Despite concerns in the team about poor housing in some communities, relationships with the housing department seemed to operate on the basis of a common understanding of the problem. Thus, the team saw their work of assisting clients with applications for adaptations or alternative accommodation as support work rather than advocacy. Difficulties over fuel debts were rare and work in the welfare benefit field only occasionally resulted in negotiation with the DHSS. More usually cases were simply referred across. *Table 3(7)* confirms that more long-term than newly referred cases required some form of contact with outside agencies. Here the data illustrate the key place of primary health teams although the housing department and DHSS also figure to some degree. As regards voluntary agencies it was usually the WRVS, in connection with delivery of meals, with whom the team were in touch. The home help organizer did not report any contacts with outside agencies so this activity was more generally perceived as a defining characteristic of social work.

In terms of services provided, household composition appeared to be a major factor that influenced team response. Clients living with families were far more likely to receive assistance with aids to daily living than those living alone. On the other hand, those living alone were more likely to be in receipt of both home helps and meals on wheels. The problems of self-care, loneliness, and isolation were identified by the team to be more prevalent amongst the elderly living alone. There seemed little doubt that this led workers to justify need for certain domiciliary services for this 'at risk' group. The elderly living alone certainly received the lion's share of these services. On the other hand, family problems were mentioned much more often where old people were living with family or others than when they were living alone. This may have been a first indicator of stress borne not only by clients but also by their carers.

A contrasting perspective was offered by the client interviews in relation to needs and service provision. First, it was apparent that the elderly living alone were not as vulnerable in self-care terms as many of their peers living with spouses, children, or other relatives. Those living alone were more able to perform all the personal care tasks without assistance on a dependency scale (based on Harris 1971), than the elderly living with others. Indeed six of the thirteen items comprising the scale discriminated the two groups at the p<0.01 level (chi square). Increasing dependency appeared to motivate elderly people to move in with their children. Second, when the items on the morale scale were correlated by household composition no significant associations were apparent so the elderly living alone were no more likely to be faced with problems of morale or a poor self-image than those living with family. Thus the stereotype of need held by the team would appear to be in need of some revision, since families living in the same household as their elderly dependents were supporting more highly incapacitated individuals whilst receiving fewer practical services. They also received no more frequent visits from social workers.

The views of elderly clients

There can be few doubts about the clients' feelings towards services received, however. Almost all said they derived at least some benefit from each service received and most said they either derived great benefit or could not do without them. Even when hesitant to commit themselves about the usefulness of particular aids or domiciliary support, clients were seemingly grateful for the security that being able to contact the department would bring. Overwhelmingly, elderly clients were relieved or glad rather than apprehensive, embarrassed, or ashamed at first being referred to the social services, and 83 per cent said they would have no hesitation in recommending the kind of support they had received to other persons. Although rather more than 60 per cent had no regular arrangement for seeing their social worker, these findings portray a picture of considerable and widespread consumer satisfaction. Clients' comments on the sort of difference contact with the team had made to their lives suggested that their expectations were generally fulfilled, although the actual impact of social work intervention, beyond the initial mobilizing of services, seemed rather marginal for them. Some typical comments:

'The social worker visit made no difference but I could not manage without my home help.'

'I'm very grateful for what's been done for me as the telephone is handy and they have adapted the house and the back drive for the wheel-chair.'

'The aids made my life easier. They were prompt, sympathetic, but I only received one visit to deliver the aids.'

While satisfaction with social work contact seemed to be evaluated in terms of practical services, the importance of a home help to a client was a different matter. In this respect the majority of respondents had nothing but praise for the helper involved and for many the service provided vital sources of support that enabled people to remain in their own homes.

'My home help is very good, I would not manage without her.'

'My circumstances are much better now I have a home help, it was a great relief.'

'It would be impossible for me to manage living alone without my existing help.'

'She has been so good to me. They helped me so much after I came out of hospital.'

Our data did not support the existence of a link between client satisfaction with services and life satisfaction expressed in terms of morale. That a client might have been happy with their home help, meals, or walking aid did not necessarily mean they were satisfied with their own lives. Unfortunately we were not in a position to measure what impact service provision had on morale. What we can say is that the packaging of the available departmental services was not related in any systematic way to levels of morale of elderly clients. This finding is hardly surprising given our earlier reporting of the failure of conventional team responses to identify subjective felt needs in the first place. What we are left to ponder is the relative importance to clients of subjective felt needs on the one hand and satisfactions with services on the other, for both have very different implications in the measurement of the effectiveness of social work intervention.

Service provision

In discussing with team members ways of mobilizing support for the rural elderly, problems were generally defined in terms of bringing clients to services or services to clients rather than in terms of harnessing care latent within the community at large. The following was typical of many comments: 'There is a difficulty meeting problems because of distance and size and the small communities served. The transport problem is big here in providing services for clients . . .'

One worker gave an example of organizing transport for a day care client who lived in a village that could only conveniently be reached by taxi: 'Her need for day care is acute . . . five days a week so that means 28 miles five days a week by private taxi.'

A colleague gave a graphic example of the dilemma of uprooting a person from his home community to find a suitable residential placement:

'There is an old man. I've been involved with him for the last twelve months. . . . He's very frail and I've been suggesting to him that he might like to go into an old persons' home. I said to him, "Well look, I haven't got a place in A but I can offer you a place in C" [20 miles away]. He looked at me with hurt in his eyes . . . he wouldn't consider going to C for all the tea in China. Here was I, a bureaucrat, looking for a bed to slot him in. In town A he has friends, everything. I was doing my best as far as I could see but because of the availability of resources we are having to coerce people.'

The imputation is that scarce, dispersed services in rural areas create inevitable problems of logistics for social workers. We were left with the impression that smaller scale residential and day care facilities would certainly improve service distribution and therefore access, if at the risk of increasing unit costs incurred by agencies. Recognition of this problem did not however force workers to think of alternative strategies like harnessing support from the community. Whilst most workers acknowledged that neighbouring and informal care had declined over the years, many of the communities in Aber were still nevertheless regarded as integrated and self-supporting. One worker summed it up as follows: 'Where I was brought up there was no need for social work. People were so close. It's still the same in some villages. The chapel is still the centre of the community, but it's declining.'

The typical response of the team however was to distance social work from neighbouring and other social networks for fear of disrupting them. Evidence of efforts to develop some community-oriented methods of working with elderly people came unexpectedly from the home help service.

In fact, the availability of home help resources was a major factor enabling many elderly people with physical disabilities to remain in their own homes. Despite the size of the area and its scattered population the team was rarely faced with difficulties in organizing home helps for clients. This was a direct consequence of the home help organizer's ability to recruit women as casual helpers in almost every community. Advertising was unheard of and new helpers were usually sought by word of mouth and personal contact. This reflected a commitment to locate home helps close to the clients whom they would need to support. The organizer herself expressed it simply thus: 'If the need is there we've just got to get there. I don't think we could improve on that.'

With low numbers of women in employment, the Aber area was one which was able to sustain a large pool of casually employed home helps, though the organizer was keen to point out that in the tourist areas where summer work was available recruitment was more problematic. Scattered throughout the whole area, the 159 casually employed helpers were responsible directly to the home help organizer. It was most unusual for these women to be utilized in any other way except, very occasionally, as good neighbours. Social workers had little direct contact with them. However the home help organizer was only able, for obvious logistical reasons, to have occasional review visits with them. Given that the helpers were distributed throughout nearly all communities in Aber their role could have been expanded if they had been more integrated into the social work team. Their presence seemed to offer consider-able potential for identification of community need, assessment of informal care networks, and long-term monitoring of elderly people already in receipt of alternative community services. As we have seen, however, workers' views were not inclined in this direction.

Given a primarily service-oriented social work strategy there were still potential problems of accessing services to clients and clients to services. Once a referral had been made geographical remoteness of the client did not affect the frequency of visits, range of activities, or services provided by the social worker. From the client interviews evidence could be gleaned of clients' abilities to make themselves known to helping agencies. They appeared to be capable of substantial levels of adaptation and there were factors which mitigated the worst effects of geographic isolation for them. To take the example of access to GPs, whether or not old people possessed such means of access as a car or telephone made no impact on the frequency of visits to surgeries, the extent to which GPs actually called at the patient's address, or the high level of satisfaction expressed about family practitioners.

Even in this sparsely populated area, 29 per cent of elderly clients were still able to walk to the surgery. Indeed walking was the single most popular mode of access. Although cars were widely used by those who possessed them, 14 per cent still typically relied on someone else to call round to the GP, usually to pick up prescriptions. Public transport was used by only 7 per cent but another 6 per cent were able to obtain lifts from relatives or neighbours. All this was made possible by the existence of both village and town-based surgeries even though some only operated on a sessional basis during the week. Thus, health care out-reach was important in putting personal social services within reach of scattered populations.

Direct access to social services told a different story. Asked how they normally got in touch with social services, 72 per cent of clients interviewed said they would either phone themselves or get someone else to do this on their behalf. A further 15 per cent said they would write but only 2 per cent mentioned the possibility of actually calling at the social work office. It has to be remembered however that over 60 per cent had no regular arrangement for seeing a social worker and another 27 per cent claimed that they had no social worker so contact with the area office was not a matter of great moment. These findings suggest the existence of a social as well as geographic distance between elderly clients and the social work team. Primary health teams appeared to be more readily available in areas of scattered population but when they were not so easy to reach informal networks of support were clearly relied upon.

In objective terms service deprivation in rural communities is plain to see but it is easy to overlook the part played by family and neighbourhood networks in enabling old people to sustain a reasonable quality of life and cope with day-to-day needs. This was strongly indicated when talking to respondents about the manner in which they would cope with common problems and crises. *Table 3(8)* summarizes these findings.

The outcomes are diagnostic in at least three respects. First, in times of personal stress those living alone were more likely to look for support from neighbours and friends than from relatives. Second, primary groups such as kin, friends, and neighbours accounted for the overwhelming majority of initial sources of help upon which old people would call, despite the fact that all of the respondents had been or still were in contact with social services.

Table 3(8) *Elderly clients: sources of help with common crises*[1]

	illness		money problem		feeling 'down'	
	living alone (n = 51)	living with others (n = 49)	living alone (n = 51)	living with others (n = 49)	living alone (n = 51)	living with others (n = 49)
	%	%	%	%	%	%
primary source of help						
spouse	0	68	0	26	0	33
other in household	0	19	0	16	0	15
relative outside household	28	4	49	13	17	13
(total family)	(28)	(91)	(49)	(55)	(17)	(61)
friend or neighbour	37	2	11	3	63	33
home help	6	0	0	0	0	0
district nurse	2	2	0	0	0	0
social worker	0	0	2	0	0	0
solicitor/bank manager	0	0	16	18	0	0
clergy	0	0	2	0	0	0
other	16	0	4	8	15	3
don't know	12	4	16	16	6	3

[1] Abstracted from leading questions about who would be asked for help if the respondent:
(a) was ill and could not leave the house;
(b) wanted advice about money problems;
(c) was feeling down and just wanted someone to talk to.

Indeed there were only a few respondents who turned to professional workers. Third, there were small numbers of clients, mostly those living alone, who simply did not know who to look to for help, either because they were unable to make a considered choice or because there was in fact no one they could suggest.

Despite the vulnerability of this target group the signs were that informal networks of care were highly valued by the elderly and a principal means by which the demands of daily life in scattered areas were tackled. Although the social work team paid lip-service to this, our data did not support the notion that workers were acting as brokers, enablers, or facilitators between clients and carers. As front-line workers they were subject to wider influences which constrained practice as we shall see later.

The younger physically handicapped

Nearly two-thirds of the younger physically handicapped in the referral group were aged forty-five to sixty-four and only 5 per cent were children. In the long-term group 16 per cent were children. The range of disabling conditions therefore was enormous. Some of the children were multiply handicapped, needing support from a wide variety of agencies, whilst many adults had milder conditions which, though chronic, required little more than provision by social services of aids to daily living and orange car badges. However, some of the older adults had medical conditions which could be severely incapacitating. Details of the sort of work undertaken by the team are given in *Table 3(9)*.

Overall, social workers singled out health and self-care as the major pressing problem, with finance, housing, and transport problems often linked with them. However, there were some differences between the referral and long-term group which influenced social work activity. For referrals it turned out that workers were dealing with little more than applications for car badges, telephones, or various aids to daily living. Consequently the mainstay of social work activity was investigation and assessment, advice-giving, and some amount of resource mobilization; essentially the provision of aids and adaptations.

With the long-term group things were entirely different. A greater variety of problems were being tackled, especially those concerned with mobility of all kinds. Although nearly nine out of ten cases were living in households with an able-bodied person mobility both within and outside the house was a common problem. Though help was available from family members, transport difficulties appeared more prevalent in this rural area than in urban areas. Coping in the home was frequently mentioned as creating tensions between family members and accordingly social workers placed considerable emphasis on general family support work and case-working was much more evident with this group than with the elderly and elderly disabled. Given the quite extensive range of services mobilized for long-term cases the indications are that this group were more incapacitated than newly referred

Table 3(9)   Summary of help given and problems tackled: younger physically handicapped social work cases

	referrals (n = 39) %	long-term cases (n = 32) %		referrals (n = 39) %	long-term cases (n = 32) %
social work activities[1]			*problems tackled*[1,2]		
investigating/assessing	78	55	health/self-care	39	44
giving information/advice	51	93	loneliness	5	6
mobilizing resources	35	34	family relationships	8	18
advocacy	5	10	education	3	9
educating/developing skills	0	0	employment	3	13
problem-solving	8	45	finance	21	56
supervising/reviewing	0	7	housing	18	31
supporting/sustaining	16	55	transport	8	25
providing group activity	0	14	other	37	3
			none	8	6
visiting frequency			*major problem*		
monthly or more	19	67	health/self-care	44	28
monthly to quarterly	16	0			
less than quarterly	65	33	*other agencies contacted*[1,2]		
			general practitioner	38	45
service provided[1,2]			health visitor/district nurse	30	29
aids	59	75	psychiatric services	5	16
adaptations	26	25	other health	11	16
home help	8	22	education	3	10
meals on wheels	0	9	housing	5	32
clubs	8	28	employment	3	6
day care	3	13	DHSS	11	39
adult training centre	3	13	voluntary agencies	5	16
residential care	3	9	none	32	13
holidays	5	25			
financial/material	13	28			
craft instruction	0	22			

[1] More than one category could be used so figures do not necessarily sum to 100.

cases. The majority of long-term cases were visited monthly for purposes of reassessment and continuing support whilst of the referral group a large number were seen only once, after which cases were closed. The team did not possess an occupational therapist. It was perhaps to be expected therefore that directed educative or rehabilitative programmes was not a feature of work.

Many specialist services for the younger physically handicapped, blind, or deaf, were not available in the area. Provision was mainly in the form of clubs in the larger towns. Problems were identified when such social facilities would have benefited clients. For example, the young person returning to the area at the age of eighteen following special schooling was identified as being in a particularly isolated position and needing special help in readjusting to village life. It was, however, difficult for workers to organize clubs because of the dispersion of clients. The social worker for the deaf explained it this way: 'They come back ... they don't mix in the evening ... they've been used to meeting kids from all parts of the country and then when they finish school the population is too spread out. The kids can't get together.'

A colleague, though addressing the more general problems of rural children who come into the hands of the department, portrayed the entire area as being deprived:

'There is so little offered to anyone around here in the way of services and facilities that the smaller communities do not miss out that much apart from the obvious transport difficulties, buses being infrequent and that sort of thing, but you are not really looking at a situation where you have a major town in the area with all sorts of facilities so basically everywhere has got nothing.'

Thus one way in which workers measured relative deprivation in the area was in terms of its inability to support the kinds of specialist services that they saw as typical of the large conurbations. There was no immediate way for social workers to compensate for missing resources like schools for the physically handicapped, orthopaedic centres, employment rehabilitiation centres, and so forth. Hence work could involve a good deal of counselling in order to help clients to make decisions about or come to terms with the idea of using out of county or out of district facilities. This was especially prevalent in cases involving the hard of hearing and partially sighted or blind.

In view of the apparently straightforward nature of many of the

newly referred cases it was no surprise to find that nearly one-third
needed no contact at all with outside agencies. Liaison with primary
health teams was a prominent feature but in long-term work recur-
rent problems with welfare benefits necessitated a good deal of
contact with the DHSS. The need for ramps and other, mainly
minor, types of adaptations to council houses meant approaches to
the housing department. Despite representing and protecting the
clients' interests in this way, social workers did not talk about their
activities in this field as anything approaching advocacy.

The mentally ill

Dealing with new referrals represented a small proportion of the
mental health work undertaken by the team. Furthermore, crisis
intervention, identified in terms of compulsory admission under
the Mental Health Act, was needed in only five cases in the six-
month period. Hence work with this client group was essentially
concerned with long-term cases, no obvious division being
apparent between 'short' and 'long-term' work to the three workers
involved. A summary of the details of the problems tackled and
help given is reported in *Table 3(10)*.

Not surprisingly, social workers identified health/self-care as the
predominating problem to be tackled. The effects that mental ill-
health had on the family and in long-term cases on their financial
security were singled out as supplementary difficulties, often
exacerbated by problems of loneliness, housing, and employment.

One worker had been instrumental in developing a group for
mentally ill clients which met weekly in the northern town. However social workers saw activity with this group as directed
towards individuals, a tendency evident in data from the case
review form. Problem-solving, supporting, and advice-giving were
major activities, with little reliance on practical services. The team
were typically involved in the use of their own skills working
directly with clients and liaising with other agencies. Two workers,
one qualified and one unqualified, touched on what they thought
was a central aspect of this activity:

'I try to help people find a purpose in life, it's what many people
have lost.'
'My idea is to encourage people to help themselves, to work out a
problem, to see things in a different light. I try to help them
change their way of coping with things.'

	referrals (n = 18) %	long-term cases (n = 17) %
social work activities[1]		
investigating/assessing	41	18
giving information/advice	41	82
mobilizing resources	41	29
advocacy	18	29
educating/developing skills	0	12
problem-solving	71	82
supervising/reviewing	12	23
supporting/sustaining	65	88
providing group activity	0	18
visiting frequency		
monthly or more	93	88
monthly to quarterly	7	12
less than quarterly	0	0
service provided[1,2]		
aids	0	18
home help	0	30
meals on wheels	6	6
clubs	11	18
day care	6	12
sheltered housing	0	6
holidays	0	12
financial/material	11	29
craft instruction	0	12
other	28	6

	referrals (n = 18) %	long-term cases (n = 17) %
problems tackled[1,2]		
health/self-care	82	76
loneliness/isolation	41	35
family relationships	71	65
child behaviour	6	6
education	0	6
employment	24	6
finance	18	65
housing	24	23
transport	0	12
other	0	12
none	6	0
major problem		
health/self-care	38	33
other agencies contacted[1,2]		
general practitioner	67	71
health visitor/district nurse	17	35
psychiatric services	78	77
other health	22	12
child guidance	0	6
marriage guidance	0	6
education	6	0
housing	17	41
employment	17	6
DHSS	33	71
probation	0	12
voluntary agencies	0	6
other	6	6
none	11	0

[1] More than one category could be used so figures do not necessarily sum to 100.
[2] Categories which accounted for less than 5 per cent of cases in both the referral and long-term group have been excluded.

With average case-loads of fifty-two (including mentally handi-capped cases) workers were able to maintain programmed visiting. In contrast to work with mentally handicapped clients most clients were visited at least monthly and no cases in our long-term sample had been visited less than quarterly.

Thus, from the data we have available, it emerges that mentally ill clients known to the Aber team received a remarkably high level of social work support. However, the workers involved were faced with a number of problems. The most difficult of these was their isolation from the region's psychiatric hospital, 80 miles away. They seemed unable to develop collaborative work with GPs to a point where they could encourage new referrals. Neither did they have much opportunity to forge links with the hospital.

A recent expansion of community psychiatric nursing into the area made the team even more conscious of their marginal role within mental health services in the county. Nurses were seen to be in an advantageous position, having ready access to psychiatric consultation and being able to provide continuity of contact with patients by making regular visits to the hospital. The senior social worker in charge of the team saw these nurses as usurping the tradi-tional role of the area-based social worker. The team had made some attempts to overcome these problems. Regular meetings had been set up with the nurses involved so that duplication of effort could be minimized and there was some evidence that collaboration on cases was taking place. For instance, the weekly group in the northern town was run jointly by a team member and an area nurse. Furthermore, a social worker attended the one out-patient clinic, run monthly in the area, to liaise with the psychiatrist involved.

It was, however, at the level of role confusion between social work and community psychiatric nursing that the team seemed unclear. Workers were threatened when, having made every effort to provide information on clients who were admitted to hospital, they discovered that a community nurse had been asked to follow up their client on discharge. It was evident to both the team and their nursing colleagues that no simple division of labour could be worked out and what was required was collaborative effort. The senior social worker, aware that the team was dependent on health services for referrals, suggested that they received referrals from psychiatric services only if the community nurse had suggested redirection at the point of referral: 'for instance financial problems,

CPN's don't like things like that . . . they are seeing us in the light of a welfare agency . . . practical things, aids and adaptations.'

Compared with his previous role as a mental welfare officer, the senior social worker saw a definite change in attitude towards social work by the medical profession. He feared that in the light of these changes community-based social work in the area would be relegated to a peripheral service. These problems seemed difficult to resolve at area level without clear policies which attempted to integrate the contribution of the two disciplines.

The mentally handicapped

Unlike other client groups served by the Aber team the mentally handicapped and their families were typically seen as long-term cases. New cases were rare, re-referrals of old cases more common. The main details of help given and problems tackled are reported in *Table 3(11)*.

The range of problems tackled for this client group was greater than for the younger physically handicapped. In nearly a quarter of the long-term cases no one problem was given priority. Problems of education, finance, self-care, and transport emerged as the most prevalent followed inevitably, in nearly one-third of cases, by family problems.

Social work activity was conceived mainly in terms of general support work, advice-giving, problem-solving, or case-work, and continuing mobilization of various needed resources. In conjunction with other professionals the team were constantly seeking ways of integrating this group in the community and of exploiting leisure, employment, and further education outlets on their behalf. As will be seen this did not necessarily mean outcomes were successful.

In only one out of the thirty-four long-term cases examined was education and skill development tackled directly. Development of habilitation programmes was usually left to clinical or educational psychologists. The social work role was more one of co-ordination and for families the social worker was very much the gatekeeper to other agencies or services rather than a teacher. Whilst most of the handicapped children and adults attended either special schools or the one adult training centre in the area, group-work was not a feature of activity. Though perceived as desirable for parents, the sheer size and population sparsity of the area were seen as the

Table 3(11)   Summary of help given and problems tackled: mental handicap social work cases

	referrals (n = 6) %	long-term cases (n = 34) %		referrals (n = 6) %	long-term cases (n = 34) %
social work activities[1]			problems tackled[1,2]		
investigating/assessing	★	15	health/self-care	★	39
giving information/advice	★	74	family relationships	★	30
mobilizing resources	★	35	child behaviour	★	21
advocacy	★	18	education	★	46
educating/developing skills	★	3	employment	★	18
problem-solving	★	53	finance	★	42
supervising/reviewing	★	9	housing	★	12
supporting/sustaining	★	68	transport	★	33
providing group activity	★	3	other	★	9
			none	★	6
visiting frequency			major problem		
monthly or more	★	50	combination	★	23
monthly to quarterly		9			
less than quarterly	★	41			
service provided[1,2]			other agencies contacted[1,2]		
aids	★	15	general practitioner	★	24
adaptations	★	9	health visitor/district nurse	★	15
club	★	27	psychiatric services	★	35
adult training centre	★	47	other health	★	12
residential care	★	9	education/school	★	47
holidays	★	24	housing	★	9
financial/material	★	24	employment	★	6
craft instruction	★	15	DHSS	★	47
			other	★	9
			none	★	12

[1] More than one category could be used so figures do not necessarily sum to 100.

[2] Categories which accounted for less than 5 per cent of cases in both the referral and long-term group have been excluded.

obvious inhibiting factors, not only for the social worker but also for working or car-less parents. Consequently specialist workers focused mostly on individual families by offering support, advice, and case-work. Some of the social work activity, however, was intermittent with more than 40 per cent of the families in the long-term group visited less than quarterly. Occasional monitoring was as typical as intensive support.

Besides furthering the integration of clients in the community the provided services were perceived as a major source of support and relief to families. The special schools and adult training centre clearly gave most parents respite from the daily grind of care and positive assistance with habilitation. The ATC, however, served the entire district so inevitably transport difficulties arose. The only available minibus had to be shared between various social services establishments causing some curtailment of time available for day care and training. As there were some communities inaccessible to the minibus, reliance on private hire was necessary for one or two clients.

At the time of the study the ATC was only four years old and still some way short of its maximum occupancy level. Workers were aware that an economically marginal rural area like Aber offered few employment prospects for the mentally handicapped so it was imagined that unless alternative strategies were sought the ATC would soon be filled by those due to leave special schools.

In respect of employment habilitation the workers seemed rather unsure of their role whilst also expressing some scepticism of the ability of disablement resettlement officers and the Department of Employment to do anything positive in furthering the employment and work training prospects for this client group. That social workers were not actively seeking alternative places of work or training indicated this was a grey area that was not the clear responsibility of any one agency. The isolation of Aber from major centres where specialist vocational guidance and employment habilitation courses were available was another factor which complicated co-ordinated service delivery approaches in this field.

Social workers were involved in arranging periods of relief for families in the summer by providing special holidays for the handicapped. Families were also encouraged to become involved in club and local society activities as this was seen as a way of assisting them to share their problems whilst opening up new social horizons for their handicapped offspring. This in fact was the nearest that the team got to group-work.

The mental health senior social worker maintained a register of mentally handicapped persons in the area but admitted that the team was unaware of all cases in the community. Migration patterns and the involvement of other agencies made comprehensive knowledge impossible in the absence of a closely monitored case register.

One worker highlighted the position of incomers to this area: 'I've a thing about mental handicap. Those who live round here live in massive houses with wealthy parents. I think it's an area they have retired to and mentally handicapped people have to "retire" with them.' However, the cultural assimilation of these English families in traditional Welsh communities was never raised as an issue, perhaps because social integration *per se* for the mentally handicapped and their families presented more immediate problems. The social work team dealt with this matter by matching the ethnic characteristics of workers to those of families. Both English and Welsh families were supported by qualified workers.

Workers were above all else engaged in supporting families and acting as gatekeepers to other agencies. The team kept in close touch with the special schools in the area and in nearly half the cases the DHSS had been contacted, usually about attendance allowance problems. Otherwise workers were spending their time liaising with primary health teams, community mental handicap nurses, and psychiatrists. The emergence during the previous three or four years of community nurses made available more support to families, but according to members of the team, caused some blurring of the various professional roles.

Families and children

The work of the child care workers in the Aber team comprised a wide range of activity. Statutory work involving children in care or on supervision constituted over 66 per cent of long-term cases. Much of the referral work required workers to address presenting problems of child behaviour and family stress which were perceived as being rooted in the social and economic deprivations faced by the communities in the area. A summary of the details of the help given and problems tackled by the team is presented in *Table 3(12)*. Referrals and long-term cases will be considered separately.

Out of forty-five referrals taken by the team one child was taken into care, eight children were placed on supervision orders, three

referrals (n=45) and long-term cases (n=47)

	referrals (n=45) %	long-term cases (n=47) %
social work activities[1]		
investigating/assessing	27	27
giving information/advice	61	49
mobilizing resources	7	21
advocacy	7	17
educating/developing skills	2	13
problem-solving	23	36
supervising/reviewing	39	72
supporting/sustaining	52	55
providing group activity	0	0
visiting frequency		
monthly or more	64	64
monthly to quarterly	12	23
less than quarterly	24	13
service provided[1,2]		
residential care	9	19
fostering	0	36
adoption	6	0
holidays	0	6
financial/material	18	19

	referrals (n=45) %	long-term cases (n=47) %
problems tackled[1,2]		
health/self-care	13	17
loneliness/isolation	4	5
family relationships	49	57
child behaviour	36	48
child abuse	7	26
education	16	43
employment	4	10
finance	40	29
housing	29	24
other	9	17
none	9	14
major problem		
family relationships	27	
child behaviour		28
other agencies contacted[1,2]		
general practitioner	27	31
health visitor/district nurse	24	24
psychiatric services	11	11
other health	13	13
child guidance	11	20
education/school	29	62
housing	24	22
employment	7	9
DHSS	31	22
probation	7	13
voluntary agencies	0	7
other[3]	9	33
none	11	0

[1] More than one category could be used so figures do not necessarily sum to 100.
[2] Categories which accounted for less than 5 per cent of cases in both the referral and long-term group have been excluded.
[3] Includes mainly police, courts, and fuel agencies.

adoption cases were processed, and three cases were identified as having children at risk of abuse within them. Thus it can be seen that statutory work was not a major element of the new work coming to the team. Half of the referrals were described as family cases in which a principal client as such could not be identified.

Problems tackled in these cases seemed to fall into two main areas: delinquency and child behaviour on the one hand and finance, housing, and family conflict on the other. Referrals were equally divided between the two groups. The existence of multiple problems was more a feature of these clients than any other group on the Aber team case-load. Hence it was not surprising to find major activity described in such diffuse terms as providing advice and supporting the families concerned. Such support was relatively intense; two-thirds of cases were visited monthly or more often.

Whilst resource mobilization was not a significant feature of work with referrals, financial and material aid provided directly through the department or more usually through the local office of the Department of Health and Social Security characterized work in approximately one-third of cases. The DHSS was seen as the primary source of money and relationships were seen as satisfactory, especially because workers had developed personal contacts with supplementary benefit officers. While some housing problems were presented by clients, these usually involved rent arrears. Problems of homelessness were minimal and were usually redirected to the district housing department. The negotiation of fuel debts was not presented as a problem by the social workers interviewed.

For cases involving the provision of residential care, the area had a small community home in the north of the area. However, most facilities for children in trouble were outside Aber. There was considerable resistance to use of such establishments, given the geographical distance this would place between children and their families. One worker identified a particular problem for Welsh-speaking children placed in establishments out of county:

> 'I would say children taken into care lose out very much. They will be taken away because of lack of resources to an English-speaking area. Some, when they come back, have adopted English ways. A child can be so mixed up – he will never be able to read either Thomas Hardy or Daniel Owen!'

The team preferred to use supervision orders or a network of foster parents if long-term placements were needed for children.

The absence of group-work stemmed in part from the difficulty of developing intermediate treatment in the area, since it was difficult to overcome the problems of bringing children together. As one worker keen to develop this activity put it:

'We hope to get a group of four or five boys soon but one lives in [a town in the south], one in the north, one in [a village on the coast] and one [in a small town in the east]. It's all very well, you've got to get these boys together somehow, which takes time. What can you do with one person in isolation from an IT point of view?'

While workers seemed aware of their inability to resolve some of the structural problems presented to them by families, they were active in liaising with a wide range of agencies in attempts to identify and ameliorate the problems presented at referral. However, advocacy was not perceived as a central activity, workers preferring to encourage clients to pursue this role themselves.

There was little pressure on the team to close cases that did not involve statutory work. However, the long-term cases held by the team mirrored, albeit on a smaller scale, the typical features of child care case-loads held by their urban counterpart. Given that so many of these cases involved children who were in care (45 per cent) or subject to supervision orders (21 per cent) it was to be expected that over 60 per cent of cases had been active cases for at least two years. It was a common feature that multiple problems were being tackled by workers. Where child behaviour or child abuse arose, problems of family relationships were also mentioned. Problems of schooling were much more prevalent in this long-term group. In cases where a child was not the main focus of activity, difficulties faced by families turned on marital conflict, home-making, budgeting, and poverty. It was however these cases which often presented to the team 'crises', on which much time and effort were expended. In such cases, social workers were pessimistic about the outcomes of their work.

Social work activity with the long-term sample reflected the proportion of statutory cases being worked. Reviewing was the dominant activity, often alongside advice-giving, problem-solving, and general social work support to clients and families. Team members, one qualified and two unqualified, talked in similar terms about their work and tackled cases of equal complexity.

Activity was described as 'case-work' but it was difficult to encourage workers to talk in the abstract about their role or methods of work. Concrete case examples were usually presented, illustrating complex family breakdown or child behaviour. However, compared with other Aber team-workers the child care team saw both family dynamics and the effects of structural environmental factors impinging on their work with individual clients. Predictably, education departments and schools appear to be the most popular contact points for these cases. However, a wide range of other agencies were involved.

While these workers seemed unanimous that much of their work emanated from or involved them in trying to ameliorate the effects of wider economic and social factors, they did not see their role as encompassing community development strategies. It was not social work as they or the department understood it. How they came to such an understanding is our next consideration.

3.4   SOCIAL WORKERS' PERSPECTIVES

In Aber the interviews were informed by a number of specifically local issues, from the specialist team structure to the special nature of social work in an area that was not only rural but ethnically distinct. Social workers were conscious of these issues if not always in ways we had anticipated. For example, it was felt that too extensive a provision of welfare services in rural communities would undermine their established networks of support. Typical of many comments were the following:

'I don't think it is the role of the social services to step in and take over what these communities are doing. In fact we should be kept out as much as possible.'

'I feel that [social] services that are available here damaged a great deal of this [informal care]. We pay good neighbours, we pay the home help, and people are reluctant to do things. You can have a family living next door to an elderly person who over the years has been caring for them day and night . . . now they hear that someone down the road is doing exactly the same but getting paid for it, say under the Good Neighbour Scheme, and they say, why should we do it unless we get paid for it?'

These views were further supported by team members. Aber workers stereotyped certain communities as being self-sufficient on the evidence that few referrals came from them. Referrals filtering through were usually interpreted as coming from people unable to accept help from informal networks or who presented behaviour that was beyond such help. The dilemma was to be able to serve these stereotyped communities without contaminating them with the values of 'the welfare state'. Views about the need to distance social work provision from the community were unrelated to whether workers were professionally qualified or indigenous to the area. Sensitivities about the unintended consequences of state intervention could be seen as a convenient scapegoat to avoid engaging the community but for the workers concerned it was a live issue presenting risks and uncertainties, even threats to the established social work role. Set in this context it was not surprising that Aber workers seemed limited in their ability to draw on informal sources of support in their work. For the majority informal care 'existed' in communities. The central problem was how to preserve that strength which was perceived as beyond their sphere of control.

Allied to these perceptions were workers' views of volunteers and voluntary associations. The team relied on volunteers for the delivery of meals on wheels and the development of Good Neighbour Schemes whilst also encouraging their involvement in social and craft clubs. However, it was the responsibility of individual social workers to recognize problems within their own case-load which could be met through voluntary effort. Limited evidence was presented of help mobilized from this source, for the elderly and handicapped. Workers did not perceive a role for volunteers in their work with children and the mentally ill. Specialist workers for the blind and deaf seemed alone in maintaining contact with national and local voluntary organizations and were more geared to looking outside the department for service provision than their colleagues. While team members who were lay ministers saw chapel and church groups as potential sources of voluntary support, there was no evidence to suggest that attempts had been made to foster social care partnerships with them.

The interest and ability of both volunteers and voluntary organizations to involve themselves in social service work were questioned. Working from a centralized office base made it difficult for the team to identify local groups who could contribute to social care. Furthermore, they were not actively encouraged by senior management to recruit such help. In this respect the area manager's view of the team's ability to mobilize voluntary effort was illuminating.

'I don't think we ever have learnt to use either volunteers or the community. But it's difficult to maintain any service just with volunteers. They have their own personal and family commitments so you can be let down at the last moment. Maybe we should be looking to voluntary organizations but they don't exist!'

Thus, Aber workers seemed constrained in working to harness care from the community as a result of both their own perceptions of the brittle nature of informal care and the boundaries set by agency policy. The prevailing system of work in which team members responded reactively to individual referrals limited their ability to identify and use sources of help beyond those organized by the department. Hence workers found it difficult to consider a view of practice in which they acted in a more proactive resource creation role at the community level. By contrast the home help organizer not only recruited from the community but also had less anxiety that she might 'interfere' with informal networks.

Both organizationally and culturally, social workers felt disqualified from intervening where communities appeared able to solve their own problems. Paradoxically, however, they also felt disqualified from intervening where communities were manifestly unable to solve major problems besetting them. In describing the presenting problems of clients, workers pointed to processes of social disorganization such as unemployment, economic marginality, depopulation, and retirement migration as affecting the whole area and therefore many of their clients. For most workers, born and brought up in the area, cultural values were affected by these changes and a traditional Welsh way of life was under threat but there was little they felt they could do as social workers about these underlying causes of clients' problems. Social work was essentially concerned with activity based on work with individual cases. The development of strategies aimed at tackling these wider problems was not only beyond workers' perceptions of their agency remit but also beyond their conception of social work. Consequently activities based on a community action or development perspective did not arise. These were elements of 'community work' which was seen as a specialism. As a result the majority of the team expressed a feeling of powerlessness in the face of these social changes.

It was apparent also that team dynamics contributed to members' formulated conceptions of their role. Workers attempting to innovate beyond the boundaries of accepted practice faced strong group pressures to conform. The two most recent recruits, being comparative strangers to the area, seemed to be aware of the passivity of other team members in questioning both policy and team practice. One such worker had very different views from those of her more established colleagues: 'Sometimes I just burst, how *can* you accept that! They say you'll never get that through, but they won't stop me getting what I want, but it's difficult to be enthusiastic in a vacuum.'

For the majority such deviance seemed to be accepted as part of the passage from novice to established team member. New members were just unaware of the constraints placed upon them.

It was this boundary set by departmental policy and operation which legitimized day-to-day work. These factors and the influence of management on social work practice are considered in the next section.

3.5   THE INFLUENCE OF MANAGEMENT

Supervision

Supervision in the Aber team had undergone a number of recent changes shortly before our contact with them. As with many other features of area teamwork, county headquarters had developed guidelines to regulate it. At the time of our study, supervision was set in the context of a case review system operated by the three seniors. This had the effect of formalizing the whole process and emphasized the monitoring and managerial role of the senior social worker. The reasons for such policy guidelines to be developed were complex. However, the desire by headquarters to promote uniformity in operations across the county extended to this attempt to regulate the relationship between the senior and his team members. Each senior social worker was required to review all the cases held by his team members every three months. The objectives set by county policy were to monitor the quality of work, decide on matters such as frequency of visiting and closure, and last but not least provide a framework for consultant advice.

As a first step senior social workers had been asked to review existing case-loads and to close down cases which had not been visited in the previous three months, unless there was a statutory duty or other good reasons for the department to remain involved. This resulted in some significant falls in case-loads held. Apart from the specialist worker for the blind whose work remained untouched and who continued to hold a case-load of 154, average case-loads ranged from sixty-six in the elderly physically handicapped team and fifty-two and forty-seven in the mental health and child care teams respectively. The three seniors had accepted the system and acknowledged its emphasis on their managerial role in monitoring work. One senior expressed a view shared by his colleagues:

> 'You have to try and work it through the middle, helping social workers to do the best job they can, but work by departmental policy. . . . I think there is an element of control in it, if there is no control things can get out of hand, not that social workers are irresponsible, they just don't know what their limits are.'

While this system of regulated review was seen as central to supervision, each senior stressed that 'informal supervision', comprising consultation, advice, and decision-making, took place outside these more formal meetings. In this respect each varied in the way they supported and monitored an individual social worker's work. The senior in charge of the elderly sub-team viewed the system as an exercise to facilitate case closure, with consultation and advice being available on an informal basis day to day. His two colleagues, on the other hand, met with their workers individually every three weeks, reviewed briefly all cases, and discussed in depth those presenting particular problems. The child care senior also made a point of being present in the team room every morning so that he was available if advice was needed.

Workers' views about this type of case inspection varied. For some the new system was seen as a positive help in organizing their work. A minority, being more sceptical of anything emanating from headquarters, saw it as an administrative chore which had been imposed on their own individual way of organizing their case-load. However, little overt criticism was evident from those interviewed.

As with allocation, supervision was seen as a joint exercise between the senior social worker and the individual concerned.

While informal discussion on cases took place between team members, workers turned to their seniors for advice and guidance on departmental policy and practice. Noting the inexperience and level of competence of some team members the seniors encouraged this kind of consultation which provided further opportunities to 'keep a finger on the pulse' of their workers' case-loads. Occasionally they felt the need to do more than monitor work. One senior described situations in which he needed to direct work with individual cases because of a worker's inexperience. This active role in day-to-day decision-making was possible because of the lack of referral pressure on the Aber team.

Anxiety concerning the inexperience of some workers did not result in senior social workers setting up development meetings through which practice skills could be shared and developed. The absence of such a team approach might be explained by virtue of the fact that the specialist structure was a relatively recent feature of the team. However, neither the senior social workers nor the majority of social workers suggested that such meetings would be of benefit.

The furthering of professional development and individual practice skills did not emerge as issues in interviews with workers. In-service training was organized by the training section at headquarters and those workers who had attended these events often questioned the relevance of the contribution these made to their own practice. Hence they were heavily dependent on their senior and team colleagues in this respect.

Two team members aptly summed up the dominant view held by the whole team of the regulation of the supervision process:

'You have the expectation at the back of your mind that you'll get backing from your department – but it doesn't quite work like that.'

'There is always somebody looking over your shoulder all the time wanting to know what's going on. ... I'm able to develop [my own style] but I am not allowed to develop it on my own.'

The development of bureaucratic controls over practice, rather than the promotion of individual autonomy where workers were both trusted and supported in taking the appropriate decisions, seemed central to these developments.

Managerial control and worker autonomy

How far did Aber workers see the department as an enabling or
constraining influence on their own view of social work practice?
We have seen that for the majority their view of practice seemed
set within the taken-for-granted routines of the area, and their
freedom to exercise their own discretion over decisions was viewed
in terms of the ability to pursue work with individual clients.
Similarly, constraints were perceived in terms of shortfalls in
agency services and the problems of meeting individual clients'
defined needs. Our discussion of the supervision process has
identified that management at headquarters had implemented
procedural guidelines to monitor the quality of work and that this
attempt to regulate the work of team members was not questioned
by senior social workers. For social workers also this encroachment
on their autonomy was not questioned. In this respect, the area
officer's conception of his role is illuminating: 'We are area officers,
not area directors. We are expected to conform to county policy,
our priorities are determined by them. Staff are given the
opportunity to comment [on policy].'

However, the ability of team members to contribute to such
policy development was limited, given the physical and psychological distance between themselves and headquarters staff. While
regular staff meetings took place in the area they were seen as
meetings in which information was channelled down via the area
officer from headquarters. This is not to say that team members
were unable to put their points of view across. What was important
was whether the area officer felt able to take an issue up with
headquarters management. For the majority, there seemed a tacit
acceptance that any innovation seen to affect work beyond the
individual case had to be sanctioned by reference to headquarters.
One illustration of this was in the move towards specialization of
work by client group. A number of workers commented that at the
time this change in team structure was under discussion the team
had been united in its view that the generic system then in operation was best suited to the rural area they served. However, area
management had not been able to convince county headquarters,
and the specialist team structure had been implemented across the
whole department. With such experiences in their minds, team
members were, not surprisingly, rather sceptical of their ability to
participate in policy creation.

Given these perceived constraints, to what extent did team members draw a boundary between decisions which could be taken by the area team and those which needed to be sanctioned by head-quarters? To solve this, workers turned to procedural guidelines rather than their conception of 'the professional social work role': 'I've seen it written down somewhere that headquarters staff, whoever they are, are not to interfere with case-work decisions.' However, case-work decisions requiring financial expenditure or use of 'county' rather than 'area resources' needed the involvement of headquarters. Some attempt had been made to delegate certain decisions to area management in this respect, including operational responsibility for area residential homes for the elderly, the provision of telephones for the physically handicapped, small budgets for emergency payments under section 1 of, the 1963 Children's Act, and provision of holidays for the handicapped and more were under consideration. However, social workers were aware that where headquarters involvement was necessary, their own case-work decisions, taken in conjunction with their senior, could be called into question. For example, decisions on the placement of children requiring residential care often brought a response from headquarters management which questioned the competence of the worker to take the appropriate action. For workers the boundary between their area of discretion in such cases was unclear.

Time spent negotiating with headquarters placed workers in a position in which they saw themselves faced not only with delays in meeting pressing needs but also with having to explain what they saw as delays in quite simple and non-problematic decisions to clients: 'There's nothing more frustrating than working with a client and having to make excuses for your own department, telling your client "It isn't me".'

Team members saw a need for more delegation of authority, especially in matters involving financial expenditure. Where this was not possible, they wished to present their decision on the needs of an individual client to staff at headquarters who would then enable and facilitate this decision, respecting the judgement of the worker involved. It was evident, however, that this mutual trust was lacking. Further resentment was expressed at plans to extend the case review system to include the monitoring of workers' case-loads by headquarters staff.

One senior, commenting on his relationship with headquarters, seemed to suggest that their failure to communicate their ideas and involve the team in policy formation was central to this mistrust:

> 'I'm sure they are very honest people, hoping that they are helping the client and ourselves. . . . they've now got this thing on case-load management. I don't know whether it will improve what we are doing, but I can't see the real need for it. What they need to do is come to the area, and see how things work. You can't do it all from sitting at a desk at HQ.'

With authority and control over practice vested so far up the vertically arranged hierarchy it was hardly surprising that the Aber team was not promoting innovative working. For most members of the team county headquarters was seen as setting the policy framework through which their role was legitimated and regulated. Those few workers who were openly critical seemed to be looking towards other agencies in which to pursue work, seemingly feeling powerless to change the *status quo*. For the Aber team, management was a distant group of people, rarely seen and little understood. This perception that management had an enigmatic quality only served to reinforce feelings that policy decisions failed to take into account local needs and conditions.

4

Dereham

4.1 REFERRAL TO THE SOCIAL SERVICES DEPARTMENT

In the six-month period considered for the study there were 481 cases allocated for social work or occupational therapy help, nearly a third of which were for the occupational therapist alone. The elderly, as a client group, accounted for over half of all referrals, the only other prominent client group being those falling into the category 'family and child care' (23 per cent). Some of the basic characteristics of the elderly referrals are set out in *Table 4(1)*. This clearly shows the extent to which the very elderly make considerable demands for social services. As would be expected, given the prevailing age structure of these clients, there were more women than men, a factor also true of long-term cases. Marital status and residence were variables discriminating cases that were quickly closed and those that received long-term support. Larger percentages of the long-term cases lived alone and were widowed than was the case among referrals – presumably a reflection of greater need or risk. Unlike family and child care cases, but in common with the other client groups, owner-occupation was the major form of housing tenure for the elderly. Our interviews with elderly clients showed that whilst a third of the elderly born in Norfolk were owner-occupiers, twice as many of those born elsewhere lived in homes they owned outright. The large numbers of bungalow developments built over the previous ten years in many of the small villages throughout the area had presented appealing prospects to many retired people, particularly those from London, the south and south-east, where property prices were considerably higher than Norfolk. With nearly a third of elderly clients coming from these relatively affluent areas, the fears of social workers about emerging demands on scarce departmental resources could be understood. Coupled with the general ageing of the population at large, this had been taking place at a time when the local service infrastructure was declining, making the prospect for many of these 'in-migrants' potentially difficult. The comments of two workers illustrated this problem well:

> 'Some in-migrants, particularly pensioners, when they move up here they're fine; they've got their motor cars; they've got their pensions and they've got a bit of money put aside; but ten years on they can't drive any more, they're not mobile; their savings are gone and they [are] cut off from the outside world.'

> 'They don't stop to think that in ten years' time the situation isn't going to be the same and they are all going to be on walking aids and needing buses that aren't there.'

The lack of foresight and unrealistic expectations of those moving into the area to retire were seen as increasing the level of need.

Table 4(1) also summarizes the biographical details of persons referred for home help services. From this it would seem that age is a major factor in determining whether a person receives the service, for nearly two-thirds of the individuals referred were over seventy-five years of age, although 16 per cent of referrals for the service were aged less than sixty-five. Taking all home help referrals, a higher proportion were women in comparison to referrals for social work. Amongst long-term home help cases it can be seen that there was not a higher ratio of women to men. One reason which might account for this is the greater dependence of elderly men upon outside sources for help with domestic tasks due to entrenched gender roles. Far more of the long-term home help clients, compared to those newly referred were living alone, suggesting that the service is indeed meeting the needs of a very vulnerable section of the community.

Among family and child care cases it was found that children were the largest single area of concern, representing some 40 per cent of referrals and 60 per cent of long-term cases. A much greater proportion of these family and child care cases were living in council-rented accommodation in comparison to other client groups. Though the team recognized the significance of the elderly in terms of the weight of service provision, family and child care cases made up the majority of long-term cases. However this was regarded as a quirk of the area compared with other rural areas of

Table 4(1) *Characteristics of elderly people referred to social workers and the home help service*

	social work referrals (n = 279)[1]	home help referrals (n = 71)[1]
	%	%
aged 75 plus	61	59
female	62	77
widowed	51	67
living alone	37	51
in council accommodation	32	30
in owner-occupation	49	47

[1] n values differ for each response.

Norfolk. That problems of a complex and serious nature such as child abuse frequently arose was considered to challenge the notion of the rural area as a place where social workers are concerned mostly with the provision of practical services to elderly people. Indeed the structure of the area case-load was such that it prompted one worker to describe it as a 'microcosm of an urban area'.

'If you take child care, again there are a hell of a lot of child care cases that we take on. And we're not in the luxurious position of saying "OK under normal circumstances we wouldn't but we'll get involved in this family". They really are pressured situations in families that affect children. The abuse of children; we don't have a clean sheet on that one either. I would imagine the abuse of children in terms of, well sexual abuse, is fairly high here and I would think probably in Norfolk higher than in many parts of the country.'

Despite being one of the smallest client groups, the mentally handicapped covered a broad range of ages. There were slightly more males than females on case-loads and overall most remained unmarried and lived with their immediate family or in residential or hostel accommodation.

Whilst most mentally ill clients were either young adults or middle aged nearly a third of the referrals were aged over seventy-five years. Few elderly mentally infirm clients became long-term cases. Indeed only 16 per cent of the mentally ill were

aged between sixty-five and seventy-five and none aged over
seventy-five. As we have come to expect with mental illness most
of the sufferers were women, a large proportion being divorced or
separated.

Considering finally the younger physically handicapped, our
data showed that a substantial percentage of referrals were
individuals of older working age, whereas with long-term cases the
age distribution was more balanced. This is explained by the
considerable number of referrals for aids for persons with developing chronic illnesses and disabilities. Social work intervention was
more likely to be provided for the family supporting a physically
handicapped child or young adult.

The question of access to social services was not simply a matter
of where a person lived in relation to the area office. Of equal
importance was the question of who actually made the initial
referral. *Table 4(2)* shows the major sources of referral for the
different client groups. Formal sources, mostly statutory agencies,
were responsible for the majority of referrals and as can be seen a

Table 4(2)   *Social work and home help referrals: sources of referral*

	elderly (n = 262)	younger physic. h'capped (n = 43)	mentally ill (n = 32)	mentally h'capped (n = 24)	children and families (n = 109)	home help only (n = 76)
	%	%	%	%	%	%
informal sources						
self	10	23	12	13	28	3
other informal	25	12	15	8	8	19
total all informal sources	(35)	(35)	(27)	(21)	(36)	(22)
formal sources						
primary health	36	30	18	17	18	50
other health	7	16	33	8	6	13
SSD worker	14	14	15	42	6	12
police, probation and juvenile liaison officer	0	0	3	4	21	0
other statutory source	3	5	0	4	9	1
other	5	0	4	4	4	3

large number of these emanated from primary health teams.
While the primary health teams were the most significant sources
of referral for the elderly and younger physically handicapped, for
other client groups referral sources seemed to reflect the specific
nature of problems arising. Family and child care cases stood apart
in so far as self-referrals were more in evidence, as were 'social
control' agencies like probation departments and the police. For the
elderly the importance of family, friends, and neighbours as
originators of referrals can also be seen. Home help referrals
provided an even more extreme example of the dependence of the
social services department upon the medical profession for
referrals, with over 60 per cent coming from this single source.

Variations in referral sources came to light when comparing the
two patch teams with each other. The team covering the patch
more distant from the area office received fewer referrals from
informal sources. Since this team had no physical base in the patch
there is a suggestion that geographical factors in such rural areas
militate against direct referral contacts from families and
neighbours.

Questions about where referrals came from, and the degree to
which the various referral agents were aware of the department,
were put to the workers in interview. Most readily recognized the
significance of medical sources. Given the dependence of the social
services department upon these medical sources, the relationship
between the two agencies is obviously a crucial one. However,
GPs, along with other agencies, were often considered to make
inappropriate referrals. A major area of concern for workers was
the tendency for agencies to pass to the department problems which
they could not, or were not, prepared to deal with.

One worker's response to the question of how well agencies
understood social services was as follows:

'On the whole . . . not particularly enlightened. Having said that,
medical services provide one of the largest groups of referrals. I'd
say that their perceptions are very limited, or their perceptions of
what limitations we've got are, and I get the feeling very often it's
a means of them unloading their worries and responsibilities as
much as meeting a specific need that they've identified.'

Another agency with which the department had considerable
contact was the DHSS. Frequency of contact did not necessarily
lead to quality of contact. Many workers were critical of that

department and in particular the local sub-office. As one worker commented:

> 'I think DHSS are the least enlightened. They push everything our way. They'll even push financial problems our way which we have to push back to them. I don't know what on earth they think we can do, but if they can't make a payout they send them up here assuming we've got coffers of money down in the cellar.'

This confusion over roles between the two agencies extended to the client as well. A common problem was that of people calling into the social services office when they ought to have been contacting the DHSS. Comments such as these raise questions about the extent to which the social services department ought to be attempting to improve the nature of its relationships with other agencies. At the time of the research contacts between agencies were typically informal, *ad hoc*, and based on individual cases; although in the case of referrals for the housing department a liaison structure had recently been established which the workers welcomed.

Details of the means by which social work referrals came into the office are summarized in *Table 4(3)*. If social work and occupational therapy referrals are considered together, it will be seen that nearly a half came by telephone. While this was partly the result of different referral sources it was indicative of access problems encountered by clients in remoter parts of the area. Although the figures are not separately reported here, the team whose patch included the area office had four times as many referrals through

Table 4(3)   *Social work referrals: method of referral*

	elderly (n = 231)	younger physically h'capped (n = 32)	mentally ill (n = 32)	mentally h'capped (n = 22)	children and families (n = 101)
	%	%	%	%	%
telephone	55	44	56	50	45
letter	20	16	16	36	28
office visit	19	31	22	9	19
other	5	9	0	5	8

personal office visit as the more distant patch. The indications are that ability to gain personal access to an office is especially important for informal referrals. While the rate of referral from formal agencies will be maintained by telephone or letter, it may be that informal referrals are deterred by limited access. This may also apply to self-referrals, half of which were made through office visits.

Clearly, office location is a major factor influencing the means by which a person contacts the department. This raises important questions for the agency. Does the relative inaccessability of the office to so many people in the area reduce not only knowledge and awareness about local social services but also the probability of using services? Our data were only concerned with expressed needs so we cannot directly answer this question. What is clearer is that distance heightens dependency on the telephone and written communication as methods of referral and there are clear indications that both methods and channels of referral vary sharply by client group.

It should be noted that the area office was located in the largest centre of population, a situation common to that in many other rural areas. Nonetheless there was an awareness of the difficulties posed for enquirers and clients living to the west, for whom a visit to the office could entail a round trip of some 40 miles. Given the poor frequency and high cost of the available public transport in this sparsely populated area it was surprising that as many people came to the office as was the case. One means of responding to this access problem that had been considered was the establishment of a sub-office in Swaffham for the team covering that area. Such a structure had not, however, been put into practice because of problems to do with administrative back-up and lack of financial resources.

The case review exercise also identified the clients' parish of residence in order that some analysis of the geographical distribution of referrals could be undertaken. This showed that the largest percentage of the social work and occupational therapy referrals came from the two major towns in the area, roughly in proportion to their populations. Apart from these two towns only one other parish produced over 5 per cent of the total referrals. This was a village to the south-west of Dereham which workers in the patch correctly identified as being a common source of referrals: this they attributed to the rapid growth of new development.

In order to gain some idea of the influence of parish population upon referrals all parishes were grouped into three categories by population size. Only four parishes fell into the largest population category of 2,000 plus. While this group comprised nearly half of the total population of the area, it only accounted for just over a third of all referrals. The middle category, parishes with populations between 500 and 2,000, contained almost a third of the total population and an equal share of the cases. This left a third of the cases originating from the smallest parishes, which contained less than a quarter of the total population. This inverse relationship between referrals, as an indicator of demand, and population size probably more accurately reflects social needs in the community which are not related to any simple notion of community size. One of the reasons put forward by workers was the differential effects of the changing structure of many Norfolk villages and the concomitant decline of the old rural communities. Several comments highlighted this issue in different ways:

'I mean one would expect rural communities to have extended families in the same village and be able, somehow, to cope with lots of problems.'

'You'll get a very caring village and you'll get a very uncaring village. But when you go to what I'd call the older established villages where there hasn't been a great deal of building, this is where the old community spirit is still alive.'

'What seems to have happened is that some of the more out of the way villages, where the community is far more as it was, seem to manage their own better. Where there's been a large influx of development and in-migration I think we seem to get much higher referral rates.'

It would appear that many social workers believed there to be something distinctive about the ability of the inhabitants of rural areas to look after their own social casualties. This manifested itself in the notion of 'problem' villages, paradoxically engendered by the lettings policy of the district council:

'But if you do get moved into a house out in the country where you are more than a mile from a bus stop, the house has got half a dozen broken windows and wallpaper peeling off the walls . . . there's no way of heating the water in the summer because the only way you've got of heating the water is coal, and apart from farm work, there's no work around . . . you know there's no way that a family . . . is going to cope with that problem. And I do think that some agencies need to be more intelligent about how they treat some of these families.'

4.2 RECEPTION, INTAKE, AND ALLOCATION

A number of screening processes and filters were in operation which affected whether, or how, referrals were allocated to social workers. In contrast to the position in Aber, the receptionist was the first point of contact with the agency. She would either redirect a caller to the appropriate agency or pass on the enquiry to the duty officer. The duty system was operated by the two teams on an alternating daily basis. In theory only qualified social workers manned the duty desk, but because of staffing constraints it was often carried out by unqualified social workers, and occasionally social work assistants. This became legitimated as part of their informal training but it was pointed out by the area officer that the decision to use unqualified workers was also a perceived need to conserve the use of qualified workers. There was a wish to avoid having them tied to a desk for long periods, whilst retaining the advantages of allowing a more skilled evaluation of referrals. Such evaluation made, the duty officer could redirect to another agency, take action on the spot, or pass on the referral, via the area officer, to the relevant team leader for allocation.

Concern over the point of intake and the duty system centred around two issues. First, the physical arrangements for callers to the office left much to be desired. The waiting area was small and uncomfortable, the interview room itself tiny with inadequate sound insulation and the duty officer was required to be present at a desk located in the central client records filing room which had a regular flow of people in and out. (Since the research took place the physical arrangements for interviewing clients have been improved.) Second, there was dissatisfaction amongst social workers with the insufficient time and effort devoted to the role of the duty officer. For many workers this resulted in the job being seen as a chore rather than a crucial, and even critical, element in social work practice. As a consequence of this underpinning attitude, referrals would sometimes be passed for allocation without a full initial assessment, in the knowledge that visiting social workers were there as a second line of defence.

The inherent complexity of differentiating between problems which could be dealt with on the spot and those requiring allocation was thus exacerbated by prevailing attitudes towards the duty system. Some form of in-service training might have helped, though social workers tended to see the requisite skills as dependent more upon intuition and experience than formal skills.

If duty was not felt to be entirely satisfactory, neither was emergency cover. During the study period the department operated an area-based emergency standby system. Anyone telephoning the office after hours would be redirected by answering machine to the number of the social worker who was 'on call' at that particular time. The system was a voluntary one among professionally qualified workers only, who would work evenings and weekends for one week at a time. Changes did occur, however, during the researchers' contact with the area. Some dissatisfaction with the system stemmed from the extra burdens it placed upon the workers. The extra financial rewards associated with duty working were rarely sufficient to mitigate the occasional stresses and strains on workers. These pressures were keenly felt when other agencies became unnecessarily demanding or manipulative, or when standby was used for non-emergency work.

All these issues surfaced with the decision of the Social Services Committee to change the county-wide organization of standby work due to financial constraints. The proposed 'long-stop' system, as it came to be called, operated in such a way that all emergency calls would be routed from the police, GP, or other agency via an independent answering service to a county service co-ordinator who had a list of all social workers participating in the scheme. If a case was considered to warrant social work involvement the nearest available social worker would be contacted and requested, though not obliged, to deal with the problem.

These proposals were unpopular with social workers, many of whom questioned not only the effectiveness of such a system but also the additional responsibility it placed upon participating officers. Social workers in the Dereham area therefore adopted a modified, and purely local, standby system where calls to the county co-ordinator would be passed to the social worker who happened to be on the area rota. Although the system essentially remained the same as far as the workers were concerned, clients no longer had direct access to them by telephone.

How then were these referrals distributed to workers? *Table 4(4)*

Table 4(4) *Social work referrals in the study period[1]*

	all (n = 481)	elderly (n = 279)	younger physic. h'capped (n = 47)	mentally ill (n = 33)	mentally h'capped (n = 26)	children and families (n = 113)
cases referred (%)	100	58	10	5	7	23
number of referrals per 1000 population	10.4	6.0	1.0	0.56	0.7	2.4
number of referrals per 1000 population pensionable age		36.2				
referrals to patch teams Dereham (%)	100	62	6	10	8	20
Swaffham (%)	100	55	13	4	3	27
number of referrals per week (area)	18.5	10.7	1.8	1.3	1.0	4.3
number of referrals per worker per week	1.7	1.0	0.2	0.1	0.1	0.4

[1] Dual classification of client group means that some cases have been counted twice.

sets the entire picture in perspective and shows the overall rate of referrals and their distribution within and between the two patch teams. *Table 4(5)* shows how these referrals were reflected in caseloads following case allocation. Case allocation took place during the two, weekly, team meetings. Referrals were first summarized by the team leader and discussed by the team as a whole. Although allocation decisions rested, in principle, with the team leader, group decision-making was more the norm. This allowed social workers to bid for those cases towards which they might wish to gravitate, but also enabled the team leader to distribute cases fairly equitably among the members of the team. The approach was felt to be democratic and met with approval.

The allocation procedure therefore allowed individuals in these generic teams considerable scope to develop specialist interests.

Table 4(5)   *Social work case-loads*

	all	elderly	physic.[1] h'capped	mentally ill	mentally h'capped	children[2] and families
case-loads held by team at end of 6 months	482	140	51	50	45	196
average case-load per worker	43.8	12.7	4.6	4.5	4.1	17.8

[1] Includes those defined as being physically handicapped as a primary category.
[2] Includes fostering cases.
Note: Information taken from client record information system, June 1979 (excluding occupational therapy cases).

Day-to-day demands did not always allow allocation of work to be neatly dispatched in this way, but working to the strengths and interests of individual workers was held to provide clients with a more effective service. The one client group considered to have benefited directly from this policy was the elderly, who were allocated to all grades of worker, qualified, unqualified, and social work assistants alike. This however was due largely to the sheer volume of demand from the elderly which required that all workers take on elderly cases. It was not the result of widespread or spontaneous clamour from the social work teams.

Table 4(6) shows referral allocation within the teams and gives some idea of this informal process at work. Although at least a quarter of the referrals received by each worker were elderly, differences nevertheless occurred between the two teams. Allocations to the two social work assistants in the Swaffham team resulted in 60 per cent and 70 per cent of their respective referrals coming from the elderly.

The following comments from social workers illustrate the way this pattern of case allocation operated. The first is from an experienced, qualified worker:

'You start off going with social workers visiting, just to be able to learn how to enter a person's house and you take on the elderly and handicapped ... not necessarily because that work is any easier to do, or less complicated to do, or that it requires less skills, because if you're doing work with the elderly the skills are

Table 4(6)   *The distribution of social work referrals at allocation*

	eldery (n = 278)	younger physically h'capped (n = 47)	mentally ill (n = 32)	mentally h'capped (n = 25)	children and families (n = 111)
	%	%	%	%	%
allocated to:					
qualified social worker (n = 217)	33	19	82	52	69
unqualified social worker/social work assistant (n = 138)	26	26	18	44	31
specialist worker (OT) (n = 143)	41	55	0	4	0

as important ... but the cases do tend to get allocated to social work assistants or new staff, almost to practise on I suppose. So I find I do very little work with the elderly now.'

Another worker saw the issue slightly differently:

'Now the elderly isn't the most glamorous group to attract people to specialize in, which is why it ends up with the assistants being involved. But of necessity we have to accept cases outside our own particular interest and I think that gives us the range, and by and large we give those cases the same emphasis as the ones within our discipline.'

In the Dereham team a greater balance between client groups existed with around 40 per cent of all social workers' referrals involving elderly people. Even so, one of the qualified workers specialized in work with this client group. Despite some differences between the two teams, mental illness and family and child care cases tended to be allocated to qualifed workers. Social work assistants and unqualified workers however took on a disproportionately large share of cases involving the younger physically handicapped and mentally handicapped.

The extent to which any case allocation policy allows the development of informal specialism can be better gauged from an examination of the long-term cases. Looked at in this way, over 50 per cent of the long-term cases held by two of the qualified workers in each team were found to be in the family and child care category. Other qualified workers either had mixed case-loads with a slight bias to family and child care or with a weighting towards cases with a mental health element.

Thus a number of factors were at work in the allocation process. We saw a desire by both team leaders and workers to encourage the development of areas of interest or specialisms. This was tempered by the practicalities of referral demands and to some extent by prevailing agency expectations of who does what type of work. Finally we observed the existence of a form of on-the-job, *ad hoc*, training for social work assistants and unqualified workers which resulted in their being given a gradually increasing variety of cases besides the elderly and physically handicapped.

4.3   SOCIAL WORK PRACTICE AND SERVICE PROVISION

The elderly

Team activity with the elderly is summarized in *Table 4(7)* which draws contrasts between referral and long-term social work cases. The case review data show that nearly all problems tackled are defined in terms of a health or self-care element. Besides housing and financial needs, which sometimes accompanied health problems, other needs, notably loneliness and transport, were conspicuous by their absence. However, in long-term work the picture was rather different with loneliness, social isolation, and family problems appearing in at least a quarter of all cases. The indications are that socio-emotional or interpersonal problems are much likelier to need longer-term commitments from social workers. There was a recognition in the social work team that some of the most pressing problems existed for the elderly supported by their family, as well as those who were estranged or living alone. Commenting on some of the critical aspects of caring for old people in the community, one worker identified the main difficulties in the following way: 'I would say it's problems in the care of these people by their relatives, the continuous nature of caring for someone and the burden that puts on the carers.'

Loneliness and isolation were problems for many elderly clients, but our interviews with these elderly people suggested this was

	referrals (n = 279) %	long-term cases (n = 75) %
social work activities[1]		
investigating/assessing	88	71
giving information/advice	36	32
mobilizing resources	69	63
advocacy	7	11
educating/developing skills	0	1
problem-solving	3	11
supervising/reviewing	2	8
supporting/sustaining	16	64
group-work	0	8
visiting frequency		
monthly or more	38	42
monthly to quarterly	51	31
less than quarterly	11	27
service provided[1,2]		
aids	40	22
adaptations	19	4
home help	9	44
meals on wheels	1	12
clubs	2	8
day care	5	16
residential care (long term)	2	11
residential care (short term)	12	37
financial/material	3	7

	referrals (n = 279) %	long-term cases (n = 75) %
problems tackled[1,2]		
health/self-care	83	83
loneliness/isolation	9	32
family relationships	8	24
finance	11	21
housing	21	13
transport	3	11
other	6	3
major problem		
health/self-care	75	64
other agencies contacted[1,2]		
general practitioner	34	71
health visitor/district nurse	7	6
psychiatric services	4	11
other health	12	14
housing department	8	18
DHSS	7	19
voluntary agencies	9	19
others	9	11
none	42	6

[1] More than one category could be used so figures do not necessarily sum to 100.

[2] Categories which accounted for less than 5 per cent of cases in both the intake or long-term group have been excluded.

more widespread than social workers were prepared to admit. Of our interview sample 40 per cent stated that they felt lonely at least some of the time. Administration of the Lawton (1975) morale scale showed that a third were facing problems of low morale. In their simple aggregate form morale scores were not correlated with residence patterns and indeed only two of the seventeen scale items discriminated significantly between those who lived alone and those who lived with others. This suggests that we are dealing with a subjective condition which is difficult to equate with objectively defined determinants or correlates. We return to the question of how well social services dealt with such felt needs later.

Elderly clients were also asked how they felt about being referred to the social services department for help. The overwhelming majority stated that they were either glad or had felt relieved that such contact had been made. Indeed only one person interviewed expressed annoyance that the department had been contacted on their behalf. Even the few who expressed some reservation about the initial contact appeared to have been won over by their subsequent experiences with the department. The following were typical comments:

'I didn't want a home help. I thought I could manage on my own and I didn't want a lot of women looking after me. Now I see that I can't manage without women. And I'm very pleased.'

'I was very pleased. I like to be independent as much as possible but I don't mind accepting help when I need it.'

'I felt dreadful about it, but now I see that it was right to accept help. I had no alternative.'

If there is some initial reluctance to ask for help, no stigma is felt for receiving it. As is evident from *Table 4(7)*, most of such help was of a practical nature, especially aids to daily living, minor adaptations to property, home help, and, for a small number, short-term care. Although around 40 per cent of the elderly referred also had physical handicaps of some kind our client interviews suggested that a surprisingly large proportion, also 40 per cent, were able to perform, without assistance, personal care tasks based on the Harris (1971) inventory. Thus many of the disabilities suffered even by elderly clients presented only minor handicaps. Only bathing and cutting toenails presented significant problems, to over 25 per cent and nearly 50 per cent respectively.

Unfortunately there was often little that social workers could do to organize chiropody on a systematic basis and this does seem to be a much-needed service. Only a third of the clients had had a visit from a chiropodist in the previous six months and half of these felt they received the service too infrequently.

Long-term cases received a wider range of services than referrals. Most noticeably a much larger proportion were in receipt of domiciliary services. Amongst this group were home help clients, two-thirds of whom lived alone. Clearly the socially isolating position of living alone is an important criterion in service provision. However there was a substantial increase in the use of short-term residential care in the team's long-term work, as relief for permanent carers.

Cases held exclusively by the home help organizers differed in several ways. For a start they were defined almost exclusively in terms of health and self-care problems. Whether this arises from the way organizers define their role or whether it accurately reflects the more limited scope of need, we remain unsure.

Despite these surface differences, the home help service was very much an integral part of departmental provision. The attachment of a home help organizer to each team increased integration. Although home helps and the organizers were immediate monitors of clients, there were signs that this intermediary role was under-played and even, sometimes, abused. Occasionally the home help service was expected to maintain in the community elderly clients whose physical or mental disabilities would otherwise have necessi-tated institutional care. Though recruitment of home helps was unproblematic, since female employment opportunities were restricted, limitations had been placed upon the service at the time of our study in the form of financial constraints and cutbacks. For some clients hours had been cut, for others the service withdrawn altogether. Organizers considered that this placed unfair burdens on home helps, who often carried on doing the work for clients in their own time. Many clients interviewed verified this by mentioning the unpaid tasks their home helps often did for them.

Home help organizers were also responsible for providing liaison for meals on wheels, although not all referrals came through the office, some bypassing the system and going direct to the organizers of the schemes. Their responsibilities also included the organization of night-sitting services for the terminally ill, staffed mainly by home helps, and a laundry service in the Swaffham patch. Despite this commitment to a broadened domiciliary role the area team recognized the need for an expanded unsocial hours service to provide care for those people who would otherwise be left alone and at risk during the evenings, weekends, and at holiday times.

The client interviews left us with many impressions of their views of services. In more than 80 per cent of cases the elderly people expressed their overall satisfaction. However, when asked about the specific services over a quarter made some form of critical comment. Thus while the home help service was unanimously appreciated, the hours available and charges made were often objected to. Typical of many client views were the following:

'It's better. But the home help used to come twice a week and now they've cut out the Thursdays, and you have to pay a pound now. They can't do much in an hour.'

'It's made a lot of difference. Once you've met a social services worker you really regard them as friends. I'd know what to do if things really got bad again.'

'Well I don't have the home help any more. I went into hospital in February for my hip and just before I went they said the home help was going to be cut to one hour a week and I'd have to pay a pound for it so I dropped it altogether. I need help in the house but I manage.'

Questions were also asked about unmet needs and improvements to services. Some clients were concerned with needed improvements in practical services like more regular and available transport and chiropody services. Others talked about income worries and the need for increases in state pensions to offset the effects of inflation and the difficulties of being on fixed incomes. Yet others advocated the need for regular visits to elderly people to keep a surveillance on their mental and physical well-being and improve their quality of life. Unfortunately the social services department had no routine way of identifying these feelings, so we remain very unsure about the ability of the agency to act on them. This seemed to spring out of seeing clients as passive recipients of services rather than as persons who participate in decisions about the packaging of needed services and support.

Interventions by social workers with newly referred cases were typically based around initial investigation and assessment work, advice-giving, and a considerable amount of resource mobilization. Whilst these remain important activities in long-term work, greater emphasis ultimately has to be placed on supporting and sustaining clients over quite extended periods. This is evident from *Table 4(7)* and parallels the position in both Aber and Selly Oak. Group-work, advocacy, and problem-solving were only rare features of work. Activities seemed very much dependent upon the prevailing view of the status of work with the elderly. As one worker put it: 'the elderly are treated as the recipient of services not as individuals.' Social work with the elderly was not seen as an area where qualified workers had much interest as it was not 'glamorous' enough to attract specialization. 'It's perhaps a rather undervalued work because it's not seen as important as work with the mentally ill or children and families.' Thus the position arises where: 'One gets an elderly person referred and one either provides short-term care or a home help or aids. I mean, very rarely does one provide ongoing social worker support as such for an elderly person.'

This, as we have seen, led to a tendency for unqualified social workers and social work assistants to be allocated these cases. Only in circumstances where the client was living alone without family or neighbourhood support did the workers consider it appropriate to carry on visiting. Because of the pressure of other work the 'tea and sticky bun visits', as one social worker called them, were not possible. However, with their less demanding case-loads, the social work assistants were considered to be in a position to do more routine visiting of the elderly and in that sense it was felt that clients received a good service. Given client responses to questions about morale and loneliness we were left to question whether even these visits were enough and what alternative interventions might be possible.

This rather undervalued view of the status of the elderly percolated to other areas of the department's work, manifesting itself in views about use of volunteers: 'I think you use a volunteer in a pretty straightforward situation where they're having a cup of tea with granny or letting granny off-load.'

Paradoxically we have a situation where this type of 'case-work' is deemed suitable for volunteers but the obverse obtains with all the other client groups. It has been noted that there seems to be a quite substantial disjunction between needs as assessed by workers and needs as felt by the clients. This divide, also reported in the Aber study, might understandably receive reinforcement from the weight of satisfied consumer opinion about practical services. The fear is that this has allowed the importance of practical services to obliterate recognition of more intangible, but still real, felt needs. Moreover, expectations about provision of a fragmented service have been realized and accepted as appropriate by clients and workers alike. It remains to be understood how far problems of poor morale and loneliness might be tackled, now they have been identified.

The weight of referral demands from the elderly necessitated, as we have seen, much of this work to be shared between practitioners. This had some spin-offs as the following comment reveals: 'If you had all family and child care cases you'd have to have a much reduced case-load because the pressures from that can be quite incredible. So when you just nip out for a casual part three assessment it is a bit of light relief, if you like.'

Although the allusion to 'light relief' was real enough, this did not prevent workers from forming views about welfare shortfalls and alternative strategies for social care. For example, feelings about the perceived lack of residential resources and the assumptions underpinning the low status of work with the elderly went some way towards explaining the dominant view that this client group, more than any other, could benefit from the development of much more community support. The mobilization and support of informal care networks for the isolated or 'at risk' elderly was a strategy which many workers believed could alleviate some of these problems.

Our client interviews touched on this and there were indications of possibilities to be pursued. *Table 4(8)* gives some indication of the importance which elderly people placed upon different potential sources of support in a series of hypothetical situations. It is clear that for both those living alone and those living with other members of their family, informal sources are perceived as the mainstay of continued support, even for those receiving services from the department. A higher proportion of the elderly living alone could not suggest who they might turn to in times of crisis, but most have relatives or neighbours to whom they can turn. This would seem to be a major resource to be built upon.

Among the referrals, a surprisingly high proportion did not require social services to contact any other agency. For those that

Table 4(8)   *Elderly clients: sources of help with common crises[1]*

	illness		money problem		feeling 'down'	
	living alone (n = 49)	living with others (n = 52)	living alone (n = 48)	living with others (n = 52)	living alone (n = 48)	living with others (n = 52)
	%	%	%	%	%	%
primary source of help						
spouse	0	37	0	31	0	44
other in household	0	17	0	17	0	19
relative outside household	14	4	44	14	19	14
(total family)	(14)	(58)	(44)	(62)	(19)	(77)
friend or neighbour	39	12	13	2	48	8
home help	10	8	4	0	4	0
district nurse	2	0	0	0	0	0
social worker	0	4	2	6	0	0
solicitor/bank manager	0	0	8	10	0	0
clergy	0	0	2	0	0	0
other	27	17	6	6	4	2
don't know	8	2	21	15	25	14

[1] Abstracted from leading questions about who would be asked for help if the respondent:
  (a) was ill and could not leave the house;
  (b) wanted advice about money problems;
  (c) was feeling down and just wanted someone to talk to.

did, the overwhelming importance of the health services was clearly evident. With long-term cases the position was quite different, with few cases capable of being dealt with by the department alone. While contact with health services continued to be of paramount importance, long-term problems of finance and housing for the elderly showed up in the larger proportions requiring contact with the DHSS and the housing department. Home help cases produced a contrasting picture with very few cases requiring any degree of collaboration with other agencies. Where this occurred it was most noticeably with GPs.

Thus the pattern of services provided to elderly clients was practical rather than 'case-work' oriented, though interviews with clients suggested that some case-work at least might have been appreciated. The elderly were, in short, seen *en masse* as the recipients of services rather than individuals with quite a high level of emotional problems.

The younger physically handicapped

Though cases dealt with by the occupational therapist have been included with social work cases for the purposes of this analysis, the division of labour in the team resulted in different practices. Despite sharing an office with members of the area teams, the occupational therapist worked separately from the social workers by providing a specialist service to both teams. Referrals for occupational therapy services could come either direct from external, primarily medical, sources or from internal requests via a social worker, or home help organizer, for an existing client.

The occupational therapist was responsible for assessment and distribution of personal aids and liaison with headquarters about adaptations of property. All such cases were retained on the client record information system and given the status of non-active (unless also active to the social worker) until the aids were returned.

Workers' activities with the younger physically handicapped are summarized in *Table 4(9)*. Given the nature of this client group, problems of health and self-care dominate as would be predicted. The only other problems appearing to any great extent amongst referrals were those of finance and housing, which were mainly related to the nature of the client's disabilities. Services were restricted almost entirely to the provision of aids and adaptations. The nature of the social work task is similarly seen in a narrower way than for other client groups, and reflects a concentration upon mobilization of mainly practical services. In consequence it is of shorter duration and workers anticipated that only a few younger physically handicapped clients were likely to become long-term cases. Only 2 per cent were expected, for example, to have a case duration in excess of one year. This reflected the strategy of the occupational therapist who normally put them into the a 'non-active' category.

Long-term cases were few. However, our data suggest that these clients presented problems additional to that of health and self-

social work activities[1]	referrals (n = 47) %	long-term cases (n = 17) %
investigating/assessing	91	65
giving information/advice	44	67
mobilizing resources	71	33
advocacy	7	27
educating/developing skills	0	7
problem-solving	4	27
supervising/reviewing	0	7
supporting/sustaining	11	80
group-work	0	0
visiting frequency		
monthly or more	36	29
monthly to quarterly	56	29
less than quarterly	8	43
service provided[1,2]		
aids	62	33
adaptations	24	7
home help	2	27
clubs	2	20
temporary accommodation	0	7
residential care (long term)	0	7
residential care (short term)	2	7
fostering	0	7
adoption	0	7
holidays	0	13
financial/material	4	7
craft instruction	2	7
other	2	7

problems tackled[1,2]	referrals (n = 47) %	long-term cases (n = 17) %
health/self-care	78	82
loneliness	4	20
family relationships	4	27
child behaviour	2	27
education	2	20
employment	2	7
finance	22	7
housing	15	13
transport	9	20
other	4	20
major problem		
health/self-care	67	38
other agencies contacted[1,2]		
general practitioner	16	40
health visitor/district nurse	5	0
psychiatric services	2	20
other health	16	27
education	5	33
housing	16	13
DHSS	14	33
voluntary agencies	11	20
none	50	20

[1] More than one category could be used so figures do not necessarily sum to 100.
[2] Categories which accounted for less than 5 per cent of cases in either the intake or long-term group have been excluded.

care. Issues being tackled by the social workers hinged around the 'knock-on' effects of coping with physical disability. Practical services provided were likewise more varied than the referrals, with home help, clubs, and holidays figuring more prominently. From the social workers' reporting of activities, it appears that these cases called into action more particular social work skills of problem-solving and advocacy. However, it was in the provision of long-term support attendant upon pressures faced by families in caring for the physically handicapped that the focus of long-term work was found. This resulted in over a half of these cases being open for longer than two years.

Only a small proportion of the referral group were allocated to qualified workers and among the long-term cases only the elderly were less likely to be allocated to qualified staff. In terms therefore of team priorities, physically handicapped clients seemed, like the elderly, to have an implicitly low status. Thus whereas the departmental response to the provision of aids through the occupational therapy service was mostly efficient, investment in terms of social work, or perhaps case-work, was limited.

In comparison to other client groups, work with substantial numbers of the younger physcially handicapped did not require any form of liaison with outside agencies. The issuing of car badges was carried out by the administrative section of the department where the responsibility for liaison with GPs and the distribution of the badges actually lay.

Besides departmental resources there were also available a variety of voluntary schemes in the area. Clubs for the disabled which met monthly were located in both the major towns in the area. A resource much valued by the social workers, from the standpoint of supplementing departmental resources, was the Crossroads care attendant scheme. This provided an alternative source of help to the relatives and carers of physically handicapped people.

The mentally ill

The most frequently cited problems of this diverse client group predictably revolved around health and self-care needs. However, we are only too aware that the global categorizations used in the case review study militated against greater precision in our understanding of their needs and problems. Nevertheless, amongst both referral and long-term cases loneliness and isolation figure as prominent problems, these often being intertwined with difficulties in family relationships. Coupled also with these interpersonal and socio-emotional stresses we also saw practical difficulties arising in the finance and housing domains. Indeed it was common for referrals to be associated with practical problems of day-to-day living.

Social workers described their activities with the mentally ill as much more indicative of the 'case-work' approach than with other client groups, as can be seen from *Table 4(10)*. In both referral and long-term cases the emphasis was upon supporting and sustaining the client and attempting to solve clients' personal problems. Straightforward mobilization of resources was of lesser relevance.

As has been noted elsewhere, mental illness, along with family and child care cases, were most often dealt with by qualified social workers. This predisposition was even more extreme in one of the patch teams with a qualified worker specializing in mental health work. It is not clear whether such specialization accounts for the finding that almost twice as many mentally ill and family and child care cases received visits on a monthly, or more regular, basis than the elderly or physically handicapped. Although a small percentage of mental illness referrals had an expected case duration of over one year, they nevertheless made up a much larger percentage of long-term work than incoming referrals. Workers usually had a clearer idea of when they would be able to close cases down (usually after particular obstacles or relationship problems had been cleared) than with other client groups where closure could be difficult to determine.

Predictably, with admissions to and from hospitals to arrange, the most frequent contacts with outside agencies were those with primary health and psychiatric workers. In a very considerable proportion of cases, both referrals and long-term work also involved contact with voluntary agencies. This was indicative of the considerable dependence of the social services department upon organizations such as MIND in the provision of care of the mentally ill.

The mentally handicapped

Only twenty-six referrals were received from this client group during the six-month study period. This however is largely

Table 4(10) Summary of help given and problems tackled: mental illness social work cases

social work activities[1]	referrals (n = 33) %	long-term cases (n = 48) %
investigating/assessing	76	68
giving information/advice	41	40
mobilizing resources	31	30
advocacy	15	23
educating/developing skills	6	4
problem-solving	25	36
supervising/reviewing	6	21
supporting/sustaining	47	79
group-work	3	11
visiting frequency		
monthly or more	62	32
monthly to quarterly	28	32
less than quarterly	10	36
service provided[1,2]		
home help	0	8
clubs	9	15
day care	9	19
residential care (long term)	3	10
residential care (short term)	3	6
financial/material	6	15

problems tackled[1,2]	referrals (n = 33) %	long-term cases (n = 48) %
health/self-care	76	67
loneliness/isolation	36	34
family relationships	36	53
child behaviour	6	13
child abuse	3	11
education	6	6
employment	9	4
finance	18	38
housing	21	17
other	9	8
major problem		
health/self-care	42	47
other agencies contacted[1,2]		
general practitioner	41	70
health visitor/district nurse	6	15
psychiatric services	66	66
other health	13	2
child guidance	3	11
education	3	13
employment	3	6
housing	13	19
DHSS	9	36
voluntary agencies	16	30
others	16	15
none	13	2

explained by the department's policy of maintaining mental handicap cases as open cases warranting support and reassessment over quite extended periods. Having reached the point of becoming a long-term case, the expected duration of nearly three-quarters of the cases was indefinite. Referrals were usually received at an early stage in the clients' life, much earlier than other client groups. Whilst many were referred as children the department tended not to become involved until they had left school. Despite this practice of early referral and lengthy periods of case activity, the actual frequency of visits was lower than for any other client group. Over a quarter of the cases were visited less than once every six months. There was, nonetheless, a realization among workers of the apparent need for a fuller range of support for the parents of handicapped children.

In common with the elderly and younger physically handicapped, health and self-care were the dominant problems although a variety of other needs were being tackled. For cases receiving long-term social work support nearly a half involved problems of family relationships. This was considered to be the major problem in long-term work as *Table 4(11)* shows.

For newly referred cases, services were largely restricted to day care provided through voluntary organizations and to provision of places at local authority adult training centres. Long-term cases were similarly served, though club activities and home help support were more in evidence. The lack of facilities for mentally handicapped people was frequently mentioned by social workers, in particular the need for an adult training centre closer to hand. Clients had to make journeys to centres up to 20 miles away.

Although social workers expressed their dissatisfaction with existing community services, social work with this client group was not popular. This conflict was compounded to some extent by prevailing public attitudes which were considered to be obstructive towards development of care in and by the community yet which is, after all, the stated government policy (DHSS 1980).

As is evident in the table, long-term social work covers a predictably wider range of activities than it does for referrals. In addition to a greater emphasis on supporting and sustaining clients in the community, stress was put on educating clients and families, problem-solving and review visiting. Other agencies contacted tended to be related to the specific requirements of the clients, though for long-term cases over a third required contact with the

Table 4(11) Summary of help given and problems tackled: mental handicap social work cases

social work activities[1]	referrals (n = 26) %	long-term cases (n = 34) %
investigating/assessing	65	44
giving information/advice	42	36
mobilizing resources	42	61
advocacy	12	24
educating/developing skills	0	15
problem-solving	4	18
supervising/reviewing	4	30
supporting/sustaining	27	61
group-work	4	6
visiting frequency		
monthly or more	45	33
monthly to quarterly	27	24
less than quarterly	27	43
service provided[1,2]		
home help	4	12
club	4	15
day care	8	18
adult training centre	19	24
temporary accommodation	4	9
residential care (long term)	0	9
residential care (short term)	8	15
fostering	4	9
holidays	8	9
financial/material	15	9
other	0	6

problems tackled[1,2]	referrals (n = 26) %	long-term cases (n = 34) %
health/self-care	62	70
loneliness/isolation	0	6
family relationships	19	49
child behaviour	12	33
child abuse	0	6
education	12	27
employment	4	27
finance	19	21
housing	15	15
transport	4	9
other	15	3
none	4	3
major problem[1,2]		
health/self-care	54	41
family relationships		
other agencies contacted[1,2]		
general practitioner	19	52
health visitor/district nurse	0	12
psychiatric services	19	39
other health	8	9
child guidance	0	6
education/school	23	30
housing	15	12
employment	0	12
DHSS	4	36
probation	0	6
voluntary agencies	15	12
others	19	9
none	35	9

DHSS. Indeed in only very few cases were contacts with other agencies not required.

Families and children

The heterogeneity of this group contributed to a diverse range of problems tackled and to varied interventions, as *Table 4(12)* confirms. Problems of family relationships occurred in over half of the cases and the team confirmed this to be the single major problem in their experience. While child behaviour difficulties occurred in a third of all cases, the practical needs associated with housing and low income also figured significantly. These patterns were even more accentuated in long-term work.

For the referral group only a limited range of practical services were provided. Section 1 monies were readily accessed as a preventive and supportive measure but apart from this the only other service provided was that of informal supervision, which clearly relates to those child behaviour cases referred through the juvenile liaison system.

The broad spectrum of problems tackled is more readily reflected in the way the team worked with the long-term cases. Whilst assessment, information, and advice-giving were all well represented, hardly any resource mobilization was actively carried out. The crux of work with this client group lay however in the area of advocacy, primarily with DHSS and housing agencies, the solving of personal problems, supervising offenders, and supporting and sustaining families.

One of the most striking factors in long-term work was the fact that family and child cases comprised nearly 40 per cent of the total case-load. This was manifestly a reflection of departmental policy, for as one worker pointed out, the team was all but forced to make family problems a priority in social services. As one worker put it: 'A lot of child care problems are just that much less tangible but because of this they are, therefore, more threatening if they're not got hold of and worked through and modified.'

A significant feature of long-term work was that child abuse figured in over a third of these cases, and family problems, virtually by definition, were present in every four out of five cases, whilst child behaviour difficulties arose in one out of two cases. So much for the romantic idyll of peaceful life in the countryside. The problems of contemporary society seemed only too pervasive. In

Table 4(12) Summary of help given and problems tackled: family and child care social work cases

social work activities[1]	referrals (n = 113) %	long-term cases (n = 115) %
investigating/assessing	74	69
giving information/advice	53	54
mobilizing resources	28	43
advocacy	26	33
educating/developing skills	3	24
problem-solving	27	48
supervising/reviewing	15	63
supporting/sustaining	33	61
group-work	6	7
visiting frequency		
monthly or more	67	42
monthly to quarterly	19	31
less than quarterly	14	27
service provided[1,2]		
home help	1	10
club	7	11
residential care (long term)	0	11
residential care (short term)	2	5
fostering	5	37
holidays	5	20
financial/material	14	36
other	0	6

problems tackled[1,2]	referrals (n = 113) %	long-term cases (n = 114) %
health/self-care	23	27
loneliness/isolation	9	16
family relationships	51	81
child behaviour	30	53
child abuse	5	34
education	8	22
employment	7	16
finance	34	36
housing	22	21
transport	2	5
other	7	6
none	5	1
major problem		
family relationships	27	52
other agencies contacted[1,2]		
general practitioner	29	65
health visitor/district nurse	13	25
psychiatric services	8	14
other health	6	8
child guidance	4	11
education/school	21	52
housing	24	21
employment	1	10
DHSS	20	31
probation	7	13
voluntary agencies	11	9
others[3]	30	25
none	10	6

addition to financial and material help to alleviate problems of
daily living, one of the most common features of long-term work
was that of fostering. Three times as many children were being
fostered as were in long-term residential care, indicating the
importance attached to fostering as a supportive or preventive
resource. The emphasis of work with juvenile offenders was upon
statutory rather than voluntary supervision.

Given that long-term cases seemed to be those presenting greater
dysfunction within the family, the social workers' response was
predictably to place more emphasis on case work approaches. As a
result these cases usually embodied greater emphasis on education
and development of skills and on problem-solving than with any
other client group. Although some workers suggested community
work as an alternative strategy, only one was overtly critical of the
case-work approach:

'Case-work is designed to deal with individual problems. It's
designed to deal with those problems that wider problems are
throwing up. There's no way that you can get at the root of
things through case-work. It's not that sort of job. But I do think
the social services department ought to be involved in the
solutions that are necessary for those wider problems.'

There was generally perceived to be a need for more community-
oriented solutions to existing problems. As a means of achieving
this a patch-based system of service delivery was a frequently
stated alternative to the existing one. Thus as one worker observed:

'I tend to think it would promote more community-based
solutions to the problems and obviously it would be much better
for communication, because you would get that much more
personal links in the community. Ultimately there have got to be
very wide-ranging changes really to provide a decent service to
all of the people who need it. But the amount of money and
people that have got to be involved in that, at the moment, just
means that you work on a case-work basis and you do what you
can with the problems that get referred.'

Comments of this kind confirm the view that although many
workers accepted the need for change, the problems of instituting
this change and the disadvantages of the lessened security of these
new roles together caused considerable inertia. Some indication of
the uncertainty with which social workers approached any new

technique could be seen in the case of group-work. The use of group-work as a technique for working with certain types of client was an area that had been developed to a small degree by one of the teams through the instigation of an intermediate treatment group in the major town. IT groups provided one way in which volunteers could become involved in such cases but generally this client group was not one thought to be amenable to the use of volunteers as part of the social work strategy. It was felt inappropriate to involve non-professionals in these cases because of attendant risks as the following observations illustrate:

'I would never put a volunteer into a multi-problem family . . . I think you use a volunteer in a pretty straightforward situation.'

'You sometimes find that they come back with more anxieties than the client's got. Consequently you're spending more time propping up the volunteer than you are propping up the clients.'

Nevertheless, volunteers were used to help run the weekly drop-in sessions for single parents initiated by one of the teams in the major town.

Given the existence of child abuse and child behaviour problems it was only to be expected that a good deal of liaison was required with schools and education authorities. However, primary health teams and specialist workers were usually involved in case conferences or when care proceedings were set in motion, and in this sense the social worker was frequently acting in a gatekeeping or co-ordinating role, collating information and advice from a variety of sources.

4.4   SOCIAL WORKERS' PERSPECTIVES

Working with the community

Our discussion of practice in relation to client groups has highlighted some central ambiguities. For example, development of the informal care of clients was held to be an aspect of work which ought to be encouraged, but workers did not pursue this in any positive way. The elderly in particular were identified as the client group most able to benefit from this type of informal support. But even here, and in spite of many workers pointing to the need for greater community involvement, little activity was noted.

Contact with voluntary agencies was mainly with those

providing services of a practical nature like aids, clothing, transport, and furniture, such as the Red Cross and the WRVS. However, local voluntary organizations who ran clubs and day care facilities for particular client groups also figured. Individual volunteers were used only to a limited extent and in a similar way to voluntary agencies, especially for assistance with transport. While some volunteers had a part to play in the various clubs supported by the department, few were used as additional input to a case on a client-matched basis. One reason for this was related to concern about the extra organizational and support demands this would place on social workers. The answer was seen to lie in the appointment of a specialist worker to recruit and maintain a group of volunteers.

The need for more emphasis on supporting informal carers was tied up with a view accepted by many team members of the need to develop a 'patch' philosophy. This view maintained that 'area' problems needed 'local' solutions. This, however, was contingent on latent community support being there to be tapped and the ability to develop suitable methods of mobilizing it. The level of decentralization implied by this was considered to offer advantages in improving the visibility, understanding, and image of the department to the community at large. Despite these aspirations and a departmental policy aimed at involving the informal volunteer network, there was little evidence that this could be transformed into practice.

It seems clear from our study that the reasons for this lay in a lack of commitment on the part of social workers and their managers towards implementing a new and uncertain strategy. Such a strategy would have demanded a change in attitudes on the part of the social workers, the way in which the area was organized, the way in which social workers specialized, and perhaps, above all, a belief that community involvement was a realistic way of undertaking social work.

Working with other agencies

On the whole the social workers seemed critical of the way in which other agencies related to them. We have seen that a great deal of liaison took place between agencies, but these relationships were defined more by the needs of the individual client than by any long-term formalized strategy. Hence the quality of referrals passed between agencies reflected relationships with specific individuals in those agencies rather than inter-agency policy dictates. This however was considered to lead to isolationist tactics and the separation of professional roles. Typical of this was the key area of liaison with GPs. Talking about the issue of joint work one social worker commented: 'I'll share goals with the doctor, but in fact more often it's a separation of roles rather than a sharing of goals.'

Relationships with some agencies were more systematized. Meetings with the housing department and the juvenile liaison scheme and with the liaison officer from the DHSS were cited as examples. These meetings allowed social workers not only to discuss particular cases with representatives of the agencies concerned but also to enable both sides to gain insight into the way in which the other operated. Both sides were bound to benefit, as were the clients.

Working to specialize

As already mentioned implementation of a patch-based system was a frequently suggested alternative to the existing structure as a way in which community initiative might be harnessed. This had been discussed amongst workers in the past but the concept never materialized, primarily, it was felt, because of the massive reorganization and redeployment entailed. However it was also felt that patch-based work might undermine the developmental specialisms, which most workers valued:

'Specialism from a generic base I think is a good thing.'

'I'd certainly be unhappy working as a generic worker working in a generic team. I'm quite happy being a specialist worker in a generic team.'

'Well yes, I would say it is the best way to function, providing that specialization is recognized. In other words, if a member of the team would like to have their case-loads slanted in a particular direction then that is acknowledged.'

Although the two teams were ostensibly organized on a generic basis, in reality the opportunity existed for the social workers, including those who were qualified, to develop their own specialist interest. In practice, then, they were operating a system of client specialism, or as near to it as the referral structure would permit, within the context of a generic team. In the end, it appeared to be against this client-oriented specialism that the workers effectively judged any other method of team organization and work.

The generic team was felt to be a useful learning enviornment for non-qualified workers who could develop skills both through the development of their own case-loads and also from their more experienced colleagues, but the role of generic worker was not favoured because of the wide range of knowledge required to carry out the full range of tasks. The prevailing system was thus a compromise between a principled approval of patch-based generi-cism and a practical preference for specialism within the team.

4.5 THE INFLUENCE OF MANAGEMENT

In 1978 Norfolk social services department undertook a major reorganization of its management structure involving a shift of emphasis from functional assistant directors at the county head-quarters to divisional management teams with overall responsibi-lity for the provision of residential, field, day and community care.

One of the main aims of this restructuring was to achieve a management structure which was more responsive to local needs and demands and had greater control over the resources to meet such demands. Thus a divisional tier of management was introduced to co-ordinate activity over a number of areas within the county. Although this was an attempt to decentralize resources, many field-workers saw it as strengthening the control of managers above area officers and thereby weakening the area tier. Since the majority of our interviews were with social workers and team leaders, who did not regard themselves as part of that management structure in its fullest sense, it was perhaps inevitable that views expressed would mirror this distancing. For example one team leader observed: 'I don't really think we come into contact with many people from the higher echelons of the management structure; not directly, not personally. I suppose that is what the management structure is all about.'

Here the team leader was also making a comment, which the area officer was to reinforce, about the need to 'use' the management structure rather than cut across it either horizontally or vertically. This must have been a temptation for members of the area team, since both divisional and area staff were located in the same building and therefore, at least physically, very accessible.

The outline management structure is shown on page 30. The communication links with senior management were either on a direct personal basis or through a hierarchy of management meetings. At the bottom were the weekly team meetings which took place separately for both teams. This was the principal method used by the team leader to pass to the team information from area management meetings which were held separately. The area management team comprised the two team leaders, the area officer, and the area administrative officer. The area officer was the common denominator between this meeting and the divisional management team. This team was the means by which policy decisions taken at the county level were disseminated to areas. Above this level existed county-wide management teams where divisional matters were represented by the divisional manager.

Thus formal communications followed a predictable system of vertical hierarchical organization. Given the administrative complexities of this arrangement and the number of management layers involved, we were not surprised to hear workers say that the system often failed to communicate at all. Being in a key pivotal position, the area officer bore much of the brunt of this criticism. Having to operate from the middle of such a structure, he found himself in an extremely sensitive gatekeeping role, exerting considerable control over information and resources. He had responsibility for a specific budget, was frequently party to 'confidential' decision-making by higher management or committee, yet also supposed to be loyal to his area team who voiced the need for more resources or information. Informal channels were often used to access needed information and this tempted workers to by-pass the immediate manager and go direct to the resource provider such as a head of home or someone higher up the management structure. In fact, the area officer made it clear that this tendency caused him some headaches. The rationale for the organization of management tiers in Norfolk, like Aber, may have been understood by management but was seen as unnecessarily complicated by social workers.

More intimacy was involved in the supervision of case-loads by the team leader. In the Dereham teams this took place on roughly a weekly to fortnightly basis, and served a variety of different functions for the personnel involved. First, it was considered a means 'to help social workers develop their own expertise, confidence and ability'; second, it fulfilled a monitoring function, being 'a way of keeping an eye on the work that's being done'. This permitted assessment of the individual social worker's performance as well as observation of how cases were being managed. In this respect the team leaders commented that they considered it part of their task to know something about all the cases on their social workers' case-load. Finally, the team leader's role in supervision contained some elements of case-load management. One team leader summed up this role in the following way:

'I consider myself to be providing as much of a service to the client as the social worker. That's partly because I have control over the work that comes in and the way it's allocated and the way that it's carried out and also because I should have the knowledge about my social workers which means I know, let's say, who can cope with a certain situation and who can't ... But I think the fact that they are responsible to you doesn't mean that they are answerable to you for their work, but that they have the right to expect something of you.'

The majority of social workers indicated that the degree of autonomy or control they had in determining methods of work with individual cases was quite adequate. Thus, face to face contact with the client was subject to very little direct control by management. On the other hand, where workers were mobilizing resources for clients they often complained of coming up against communication barriers and the organizational constraints of large bureaucracies. These two conflicting attitudes are exemplified by the following statements of two social workers:

'... once you have been given that referral you have total control over how you handle it and consequently if anything goes wrong you are answerable to whoever.'

'But obviously working in a local authority influences what you do because you gradually find yourself being absorbed in the department, accepting the limitations.'

Indeed the only factors mentioned as preventing workers from carrying out their job as they would have wished were related either to lack of specific resources, or to organizational constraints or conflicts, rather than to any lack of individual freedom in their contact with the client.

This broader administrative effectiveness was perceived as hinging very much on the pivotal position of the team leader between the worker at the 'coal-face' and the upper echelons of the management structure. The team leader acted as a filter between these upper and lower strata, passing information up and down. The team leader also acted as a kind of sponge by taking up social workers' anxieties and frustrations. As one team leader saw it:

'I was putting myself in a position almost between the devil and the deep blue sea. I was standing between management and social workers and I was very much a middle man and I knew that management and social workers would throw things at me. I'm in the middle carrying both to some extent.'

Decisions about case closures were also taken during supervision sessions. Theoretically, all closures were determined by the team leader but in practice it was seen as either a joint decision or, with more experienced and qualified workers, a decision they themselves took which the team leader simply 'rubber stamped'. At times it was valuable to have the team leader involved in the process to tell workers how to set their limits and to avoid hanging on merely to satisfy their own needs and curiosities rather than the needs of the clients. Although the process of case closure was straightforward, the actual administrative act frequently did not happen for some considerable time after the social worker had psychologically made the decision. This, however, sometimes meant that there were extra hiatuses caused by the fact that case notes were not always written up. This vital recording work had to be completed before cases were closed. Nevertheless case closure was often perceived as a risky business and far from straightforward as one worker explained:

'Some cases I can close very happily because they really do seem to be completely resolved from the point of view of anything the department can do. But I'm definitely talking here about the distinction between what the department can do ... [in] providing specific services and what I, individually, can do as a supporting person. That's the distinction.'

In the view of the social workers a distinction could be drawn between higher management, including the area officer and above, and their most immediate management, the team leader, in terms of relevance to immediate needs. The greater the physical, functional, or administrative separation, the less relevance managers were perceived to have for day-to-day practice. It was difficult to know whether this represented mutual misrepresentations by management and social workers or a natural and understandable reflection of the way in which authority in large organizations is exercised.

5

Selly Oak

5.1 REFERRAL TO THE SOCIAL SERVICES DEPARTMENT

Our examination of the work of the Selly Oak team begins by asking, 'Who were the clients?' During the six months of the study period, Area 12 recorded 384 social work referrals to the team. Forty-five per cent involved elderly people, 35 per cent families and children, about 10 per cent each mentally ill and younger physically handicapped people, and 2 per cent mentally handicapped people. Just over a half were not previously known to the department, although this figure was rather lower for the elderly and mentally handicapped client groups. These two groups can thus be seen as relatively more likely to be the subjects of cases opened, closed, and re-opened.

The other three teams on Area 12 (two operating from the same office, one from a sub-office) did not experience the same proportion of elderly referrals, which is thought to be one of the highest in the city. *Table 5(1)* illustrates how a distinctive profile of these elderly people can be constructed: six out of every ten were over seventy-five; eight were female; six were widowed; five lived alone and five in council accommodation.

Meaningful comparisons can be made on some of these indices with other client groups. A fifth of the mentally ill were over sixty-five and a further fifth between forty-five and sixty-five. Of the younger physically handicapped, more than half were in the forty-five to sixty-four age range, indicating an association of debilitating disease with advancing age. These two client groups also have a preponderance of women. If widowhood was the most common marital status of the elderly, being single was a significant characteristic of a quarter of the younger physically handicapped clients, half of the mentally ill, and all of the mentally handicapped. The

Table 5(1)   *Characteristics of elderly people referred to social*
             workers and the home help service

	social work referrals (n = 174)	ḥome help referrals (n = 114)
	%	%
aged 75+	65	75
female	76	87
widowed	62	56
living alone	53	70
in council accommodation	47	★
in owner-occupation	32	★

★ Too little information was available for useful comparisons on this variable.

only group to live alone anything like as frequently as the elderly were the mentally ill (47 per cent), so these two groups share a position of physical, and thus potentially social, isolation without the kind of immediate family involvement available to many other clients. The elderly had the widest spread of housing tenure. The proportion in owner-occupied accommodation was exceeded only by the younger physically handicapped (54 per cent); only a few elderly of all the clients lived in privately rented accommodation; though half lived in council accommodation, the figures for families and children (84 per cent) and the mentally ill (74 per cent) were much higher. The elderly were thus differentiated from other client groups not only by their age but by a distinctive pattern of gender, marital status, household composition, and tenure – they were more likely to be female, to have lost their marriage partner, and to live alone in their own homes than other client groups.

Elderly clients were also the most dispersed geographically and least concentrated in the distinctive sub-areas of Selly Oak identified by social workers. In contrast, 40 per cent of families and children referrals came from one post-war council estate. Conversely, this client group and the mentally handicapped and mentally ill were relatively under-represented in the 'respectable' owner-occupied areas of Selly Park and Bournville.

Old Selly Oak – nineteenth-century terraced housing – and Weoley – part of an inter-war council estate and some substantial owner-occupied semis – were more mixed in the kinds of resident clients. This distribution matched quite closely social workers' perceptions of the area they served. It was an administrative creation: the Ley Hill council estate area in particular had recently been transferred from a neighbouring team to equalize the team work-loads within the area.

Sources of referral

Analysis of referral sources and methods illustrates the variety of initial routes to becoming a social work client. The importance of informal referral networks is highlighted in *Table 5(2)*, particularly for the elderly, whose relatives are responsible for contacting the

Table 5(2) *Social work and home help referrals: sources of referral*

	elderly (n = 174)	younger physic h'capped (n = 36)	mentally ill (n = 33)	mentally h'capped (n = 7)	children and families (n = 136)	home help only (n = 114)
	%	%	%	%	%	%
informal sources						
self	33	27	33	★	37	11
family/relatives	22	21	10	★	5	11
neighbours/ friends	4	0	7	★	2	1
other members of the public	1	0	0	★	1	1
total all informal sources	(60)	(47)	(50)	★	(45)	(24)
formal sources[1]						
primary health	12	15	17	★	4	24
other health	4	15	7	★	3	
other SSD worker	16	6	17	★	12	52
education	0	6	0	★	5	0
housing	0	0	0	★	6	0
juvenile liaison officer	0	0	0	★	6	0

[1] Only categories accounting for at least 5 per cent are listed; hence column percentages do not sum to 100.

★ Referrals for the seven mentally handicapped cases came via other SSD personnel (4), a psychiatrist (1), another member of the public (1), and (1) was self-referred.

department in nearly a quarter of the cases. The health services are a critical source of referrals for all but families and children, many of whom came to social services through contact with the police or the education and housing departments.

The social workers did not feel that some referral sources were more credible than others. The referral was after all only a trigger for social workers to make their own assessments. However, our observation of team meetings did identify what might be called referral resistance, especially where it was felt that social services were being used as the department of last resort, for example, as a means of disposal (a difficult old lady); an agent of social control (a problem council tenant); or where unrealistic expectations were held of what social work intervention might achieve (a child causing 'difficulties' at school). At least one interviewee felt that a crucial element determining the nature of social services response was the degree to which the referrer was able to spell out precisely what was being requested in terms acceptable to the social work team. The importance of this factor is difficult to determine; it may suggest that some potential clients referring themselves might have been at a disadvantage.

Of course gaining access to the services of a social worker is not just a question of being referred by the right person. Clearly for many of the formal sources of referral contact by telephone or letter would be the norm. It serves as comment on the physical accessibility of the area office that for only two client groups, families and the mentally ill, was referral by means of a visit to the office in more than 10 per cent of the cases (*Table 5(3)*).

Table 5(3) *Social work referrals: method of referral*

	elderly (n = 174)	younger physically handicapped (n = 36)	mentally ill (n = 33)	mentally handicapped (n = 7)	children and families (n = 136)
	%	%	%	%	%
telephone	65	77	47	★	35
letter	25	13	20	★	34
office visit	9	7	33	★	31
other	1	3	0	★	0

★ Methods of referral for the seven mental handicap cases were telephone (4) and letter (3).

The home help service had its own area office and the meals on wheels service (sometimes provided by voluntary organizations) was administered from a central office in the city centre. The question therefore arises as to what extent the clients referred to these services had the same characteristics as those referred for more general social work support.

Unfortunately difficulties of accessing records and their sparse nature means there is too much missing information for comfort. Both home help and meals service clients tended to be older than elderly social work clients and meals on wheels recipients were nearly all over seventy-five. More women appeared as home help than social work cases but relatively many more men were referred for meals on wheels. It is also true that home help and meals clients were more likely to be living alone than social work clients in general. If these are taken as indices of vulnerability, then the most vulnerable elderly are being supported and monitored by the domiciliary services. Yet 70 per cent of the home help clients had no current social work support.

Self and other informal means of referral decline proportionally for the home help service and disappear altogether for meals on wheels. The main routes were through the health services and, for home helps especially, medical social workers who provided over a quarter of all new referrals to that service. To consult a doctor or spend some time in hospital are clearly important ways clients gain access to these social services – a very different picture from that for the social work clients.

Given the high level of vulnerability of the clients of domiciliary services we are left puzzled by their geographical distribution. Why were there proportionately less referrals than to the social work team from Old Selly Oak, where our area profile identified a concentration of vulnerable elderly, and yet more in Weoley? Is it because the social work team is more in touch with Old Selly Oak than other parts of the patch or does the reliance on formal sources of referral to the domiciliary services exclude some groups of isolated elderly people?

RECEPTION, INTAKE, AND ALLOCATION

Requests for help to social services departments bring a variety of responses, from redirection of the initial enquiry to another agency to acceptance and allocation of the enquiry as an active social work case. For the agency, the main objective is to ensure that only those seen as legitimately requiring long-term social work achieve the status of a case. In Area 12 at the time of our study this was achieved through the operation of a series of filters, any of which could prevent further progress of the enquiry. Each filter or stage in the case process required the exercise of discretion by an individual acting alone or in consultation with colleagues or supervisors. These key personnel were the receptionist (or in the case of correspondence, the administrative officer); the duty social worker; the ward team leader; and the social worker to whom a case might potentially be allocated.

The receptionist servicing all three teams on the area had three kinds of responsibility: for the switchboard, for responding to personal callers (who rang a bell at a wooden window-shaped partition by her desk), and for some routine clerical duties. The switchboard was extremely busy, up to a hundred calls being taken on some mornings. Her strategic importance for potential clients was that she was the first point of contact and did a lot more than just put them through to a social worker. She would check that they did want social services (and not, for example, the DHSS); that they wanted the social work teams (and not the home help office); that they lived in the right catchment area and weren't already an open case. The importance of these activities for initiating the processing of a case was highlighted by a remark from a member of the administrative staff: 'I don't know if social workers realize that three-quarters of their work is done for them by the receptionist before anyone gets through to them.'

Once passed through from the receptionist to the duty team, another set of discretions became operative. In simple terms this was a question of distinguishing between those callers who could be dealt with on the spot as a 'miscellaneous enquiry' and those meriting further investigation, to be passed on to the relevant team leader. This decision was almost universally agreed to be unproblematic especially for elderly clients:

Q. 'What about the elderly; I'm just trying to find out if that judgement is even more difficult with the elderly. If a relative of an elderly person, or an elderly person themselves rings up, seeking a specific service, whatsoever this might be, how do you decide [if] this is an elderly person at risk?'

A. 'Well you know I would tend to say it's simpler with the elderly because a very high percentage of the requests from elderly people are for a specific service and they know what they want. They want this and nothing else and many elderly people, the one thing they don't want is their privacy invaded. They are asking for X and they don't want Y or Z, thank you. But the concerned social worker usually asks a number of questions which are based on us assessing the degree of support that they have in that field, in cross-checking this request, i.e. are they living alone; if they're living apparently happily with relatives or friends and then they ask for a bath aid, one tends to accept that they want a bath aid and not a social worker.'

The response to referral pressure

In practice, the decision to treat something as a 'miscellaneous enquiry' disguised a wide variety of responses from complete inaction to comprehensive advice (see *Table A*).

Table A*   *Characteristics of miscellaneous enquiries (%)*

elderly person involved	30	one client contact only	85
family and child care problem	45	information given	74
self-referral	71	closed after direction to	
referral by office visit	56	another agency for	
qualified social worker		resolution	38
involved	73	financial problem involved	35
no contact made with other		housing problem involved	29
agency	79		

* The tables labelled alphabetically in this chapter are those for which comparable tables are not presented in Chapters 3 and 4.

A clear pattern emerges: self-referrals, particularly by office visit, often ended as miscellaneous enquiries. Most clients were only seen once, though generally by a qualified worker. The problem was likely to be a financial or housing one but only rarely did social services intervene on the client's behalf – the usual procedure was to offer advice and direct the client elsewhere. Miscellaneous enquiries were more likely to involve families and children and less likely to centre on an elderly person. However, with the exception of a small cash payment to a family, the only practical services facilitated for these 110 clients went to seven elderly people who,

Social work in context

while their social work request didn't result in further work, became clients of the meals on wheels or home help service. The team leader was the recipient of cases passed through from the duty team. By no means all such cases were actually allocated to team members; a number of other options were available. A case might be closed if a client did not respond to a written invitation to make contact or if the case was regarded as legitimate but of low priority. Another agency, perhaps already involved and even the referral source, might be persuaded to monitor the case and contact the team if the situation deteriorated. Very rarely a case might be left open but not allocated. A particular strategy adopted by the Selly Oak team leader was to allocate some cases to himself, personally make an assessment visit, and then have an OT or social work assistant work under his supervision. These various strategies were self-consciously adopted by the team leader to protect his team from bombardment at a time when they were well below strength. *Tables 5(4)* and *5(5)* indicate the pressures on the team during the study period.

Table 5(4)   *Social work referrals in the study period*

	all (n = 418)	elderly (n = 174)[1]	younger physic. h'capped (n = 36)	mentally ill (n = 33)	mentally h'capped (n = 7)	children and families (n = 136)
referrals per client group (%)	100.0	45.0[1]	9.0	9.0	2.0	35.0
number of referrals per 1000 population	11.1	4.6	0.95	0.87	0.19	3.6
number of referrals per 1000 population pensionable age		36.2				
number of referrals per week	16.7	7.0	1.4	1.3	0.3	5.4
number of referrals per individual worker per week	1.9	0.8	0.2	0.1	0	0.6

[1] Client group figures based on 384 referrals for which CRFs were completed.

Table 5(5)   *Social work caseloads*

	all	elderly and physic. h'capped	mentally ill	mentally h'capped	children and families
case-loads held by team at end of six months	437	240	12	26	159
average case-load per worker	48.6	26.7	1.3	2.9	17.7

Source: Area 12 returns to social services department headquarters.

The style of allocation

The amount of discretion exercised by the team leader was inevitably a subject of some controversy. It was not that team members felt that they would necessarily have disposed of cases in different ways but that the process was, in its prevalent form, hidden from them. This related very closely to differences of opinion about the allocations procedure itself. The previous team leader had operated a system of bringing all new referrals to the team meeting for open discussion. This had been continued up to and including the period from which our case sample was taken. In the subsequent period of observation, however, the team leader instituted a system of direct personal allocations outside team meetings. Apart from one exception, who felt that the previous procedure had been boring and wasteful of time and was quite happy for the team leader to see allocations as part of his managerial function, the new system was not appreciated. Team members did not feel they would now have foisted upon them cases they could previously have avoided; the space for negotiation and discussion was still felt to be there. It was more that the system of allocations at team meetings gave members an insight into the overall work-load of the team which they did not feel could be easily obtained in any other way.

If the allocation system was seen by some team members as an issue of principle, as against the team leader's stress on efficiency, the actual practice of allocation reflected the division of labour in the team. Since only qualified social workers could take on statutory work with families and children, they had to divide this work between them, topping up their case-loads from other client groups. Conversely, social work assistants were largely restricted to work with the elderly and physically handicapped. The presence of the area mental health specialist on the team accounted for most of the referrals in that client group (*Table 5(6)*).

Table 5(6)   *The distribution of social work referrals at allocation*

	elderly (n = 136)	younger physic. h'capped (n = 31)	mentally ill (n = 26)	mentally h'capped (n = 6)	children and families (n = 87)
	%	%	%	%	%
allocated to:					
qualified social worker	28	29	19	0	36
social worker assistant/ unqualified social worker	32	19	4	17	5
specialist worker	9	23	23	69	1
team leader	32	29	54	17	59

Note: This does not include all study referrals. Others were left unallocated, became miscellaneous enquiries, or were allocated to members of other teams.

Discretion in the distribution of the services of the department continued, after the filters of reception, duty, and allocation had been passed, in the determination of how long a case stayed open. The characteristics of our sample of 246 long-term cases were different from those of the six-month sample of referrals (see *Table B*).

Clearly some client groups were more likely to become long-term cases – only the elderly in fact figured in a smaller proportion of long-term cases than in our sample of referrals. Comparison with the corresponding figures for the previous six months showed this to be a stable pattern. Indeed the elderly occupied a unique intermediate status in being more likely to filter past the duty stage and become the subject of an allocated case but less likely to become long-term clients. This can be confirmed by looking at the duration of cases (see *Table C*).

Most of the elderly cases had been open for less than a year and a

Table B *Long-term cases by client group*

	elderly (n = 94)	younger physic. h'capped (n = 36)	mentally ill (n = 25)	mentally h'capped (n = 14)	children and families (n = 114)
	%	%	%	%	%
cases in each client group	38	15	10	6	46
referrals in each client group	45	9	9	2	35

Note: Some long-term cases fall into more than one client group category so percentages sum to more than 100.

Table C *Length of current case episode*

	elderly (n = 94)	younger physic. h'capped (n = 36)	mentally ill (n = 25)	mentally h'capped (n = 14)	children and families (n = 114)
	%	%	%	%	%
up to 1 year	51	43	16	21	14
1–2 years	25	29	24	36	35
2–4 years	18	20	28	36	35
over 4 years	6	9	32	7	15

smaller proportion were open for more than two years than for any other group. The clearest contrast is with the family and child care cases, half of which had been open for over two years. The biographical details we collected give little clue as to differences between those who became the subject of long-term cases and those who didn't. Elderly long-term clients were more likely to be widowed (70 per cent) and living in council accommodation (55 per cent) but the overall client profile is largely the same. The exception is in the considerably higher percentage of elderly clients living alone (67 per cent) – not surprisingly it appeared the most discriminatory factor in determining the need for long-term social work help. The critical differences between long and short-term work were revealed by examination of the way that social workers characterized their practice.

5.3   SOCIAL WORK PRACTICE AND SERVICE PROVISION

The elderly

Problems of elderly clients tackled by social workers were largely contained by the health/self-care category. Loneliness as a problem to be worked on occurred only once in every eight referrals, a frequency almost matched by housing problems, with financial problems the other major area of new work (the 20 per cent figure for other problems is mostly accounted for by telephone applications for which no suitable category existed). Whilst the long-term cases produced an increase in tackling problems of loneliness, finance, housing, and transport, the elderly as a client group had the narrowest range of defined problems (*Table 5(7)*).

Typically social work intervention with referrals took the form of assessment, the provision of information and advice, and the mobilization of resources, with some more limited work on personal problems and longer term support. Whilst there was increasing diversification in long-term social work with the elderly, it was less obvious than with other client groups. Supporting and sustaining is a major feature of this diversification but what form this took was not clear. Less likely than other client groups to receive no or just one visit, they were more likely to be visited at one to three monthly intervals. A somewhat higher proportion (81 per cent) of the elderly clients that we interviewed who were receiving social work help estimated the frequency of visits to be less often than monthly. GPs, housing, voluntary agencies, the DHSS, and health visitors were the key points of external contact in order of priority.

Once beyond the duty stage, the bulk of work with the elderly consisted of providing services from within the department. Indeed it was the provision of these services, and the needs underlying them, which characterized cases open for longer than six months. The mobilization of all the main services more than trebled in long-term as opposed to 'new' cases. Their appropriateness, adequacy, and speed of delivery were thus of crucial importance to the social work team and any analysis of their activity.

Aids (in 48 per cent of long-term cases) and adaptations (28 per cent) were two of the key services provided for elderly people in Selly Oak. It was generally acknowledged that Area 12 as a whole had not yet been able to come to terms with their provision, though

	referrals (n = 174) %	long-term cases (n = 94) %
social work activities[1]		
investigating/assessing	75	81
giving information/advice	51	56
mobilizing resources	39	66
advocacy	2	12
educating/developing skills	1	8
problem-solving	5	14
supervising/reviewing	1	10
supporting/sustaining	13	32
providing group activity	3	4
visiting frequency		
weekly or more	3	14
monthly or more	14	20
less than monthly	22	28
less than 3 monthly	4	15
less than 6 monthly	n/a	20
once off	37	n/a
never visited	20	3
services provided[1,2]		
aids	15	48
adaptations	5	28
home help	22	41
meals on wheels	8	26
clubs	5	10
day care	2	11
long-term residential care	1	5
short-term residential care	4	11
holidays	1	7
financial/material	1	6

	referrals (n = 174) %	long-term cases (n = 94) %
problems tackled[1,2]		
health/self-care	70	91
loneliness/isolation	12	30
finance	7	17
housing	11	17
transport	2	5
other	20	6
none	5	1
major problem		
health/self-care	63	75
other agencies contacted[1,2]		
general practitioner	19	45
health visitor/district nurse	8	13
other health services	8	21
housing	5	27
DHSS	3	23
voluntary agencies	9	23
other	4	8
none	59	29

[1] More than one category could be used so figures do not necessarily sum to 100.
[2] Categories which accounted for less than 5 per cent of cases in both the referral and long-term group have been excluded.

considerable improvement was evident with the inception of an intake team system after the study period had ended. The problems were essentially organizational. Area 12 operated a system where every applicant had to receive an initial visit from a social worker who subsequently had nominal responsibility for the case. This was to ensure that any other potential needs were assesed. So few results were yielded, however, that this system was thought to be wasteful of social workers' time and damaging to the clients, since hopes were raised of an immediate response when in fact none might be forthcoming for weeks or even months. This delay was caused partly by the case processing system. Even when at the point of allocation, aids cases were rarely classed as urgent and therefore only when the social worker had time to visit and subsequently write up the file would it get passed to the occupational therapist. Since for most of the six-month period only one occupational therapist was available to service three teams, further delay was inevitable. All adaptations cases were processed through head office which would instruct the housing department or a contractor to carry out the work. The regulations governing the financial limits which could be approved within the area were constantly changed by the social services committee. Hence the provision of adaptations was measured in months, even years, rather than weeks.

Further domiciliary services

A fifth of all new elderly social work clients and 40 per cent of long-term clients were provided with a home help. Social workers perceived this as one of the most efficient and supportive of the services they could provide, especially as they could mobilize it through one phone call to the home help office. This was in every way separate from the main Area 12 office. It was housed in a separate building some three miles away (on the Selly Oak team's patch and once their working base): it operated its own system for processing referrals and it was responsible to its own district home help organizer. To help supervise the 260 home helps the area organizer had four assistant organizers, one for each ward.

Referral sources for the home help service were much more heavily weighted towards the health service than for social work cases. GPs, medical social workers, district nurses, and geriatric social workers were the main working contacts. Nearly all the referrals were by phone, one reason it was notoriously difficult to get through to the switchboard. Details were taken and assessment visits, including, where relevant, assessment for meals on wheels, undertaken within forty-eight hours.

The major problems faced by the home help organizer were distributing amongst clients the 3.2 hours *per capita* currently allocated to her, matching home helps' preferences and personalities with those of clients, and covering for sickness and leave. She acknowledged that home helps provided more varied support for, and spent more time on, their clients than they were paid for, a point endorsed by the social work team. The home help service was seen to occupy a pivotal position in the provision of services to the elderly. It enabled elderly people to be supported in both a practical and psychological sense in the community; it effectively was left to monitor some of the most dependent clients on a regular basis; it was seen as potentially much wider in scope especially with family cases.

One in four long-term elderly clients had been provided with meals on wheels. Social workers perceived this as a reasonable service, the only reservations being about the inflexibility of the rounds owing to shortage of transport, the quality of some of the pre-packaged frozen meals, and a fear that price increases might deter some potential recipients. But such criticisms were also seen as in part the product of unreasonable expectations by the clients of what such a service could provide.

Clubs, day, and residential care

For lunch clubs, day care, and short or long-stay residential care the picture was more uneven. While there was not felt to be a particular shortage of such places, the quality of care was thought to be variable in both the statutory and voluntary sectors. Questions about the adequacy of these services were often answered in terms of the merits or otherwise of this or that club, centre, or home. One social worker in particular did, however, make some strong observations about the quality of life in old people's homes in general and the failure of social workers to maintain contact once clients had been placed:

A 'I don't think RA [Residential Accommodation for the Elderly] is okay really, I'm very strongly against some things in RA.'

Q. 'What, the quality of it?'
A. 'The quality. Yes, I mean it's all spit and polish but what about the poor old people that sit in their chairs for half a day and they're not spoken to. They're too big a lot of the homes. I think they've made a lot of mistakes . . . So there is something wrong in the homes, I think, when we get an old person into a home, that's it for us, we don't visit any more. That is when we should start visiting, we should be the liaison between the old person who really got to know us, visiting in their own home, and the staff in the home.'
Q. 'So it's really just a cut-off point once they're inside?'
A. 'Because if they hadn't got any relations or friends to visit, I think, and I've heard this, old people go into a home and that's it, it's curtains for them, they just sit in a chair and nobody bothers about them. The staff are kind and they are very good, but they haven't got time to sit and talk to some of the old people. And suddenly to go into a home of about sixty people, it's a bit traumatic isn't it really? So I don't know, I think their whole concept of a home is wrong. Some of them are split into two and they're smaller groups, that is perhaps better. I know they do have handicraft people going in, don't they, trying to get them to do things. But there is not nearly enough, you know, contact with the outside world, or perhaps with the social worker for a bit, to keep an eye on them. They're not happy, they just sort of go like cabbages.'

Whether the range of provision that can be called social support – particularly through day care and social clubs – was adequately catering for need was impossible to judge given the information available either to the team or ourselves. We do know that some of the workers in the voluntary sector we interviewed expressed doubts about whether these needs were being met and often could not see that social services departments were geared to providing social or emotional support to clients on a long-term basis. Furthermore, the client interviews showed considerable indications of isolation and loneliness.

Thirty-seven per cent of the respondents gave low morale responses on at least eight of the seventeen items on the Philadelphia Geriatric Centre Morale Scale and independent probes produced similar results. Twenty per cent said they had no one in whom they felt able to confide; 22 per cent that they had no one from whom they could ask small favours and 35 per cent wished they had more friends.

The provision of telephones for the isolated and vulnerable elderly was a frequent request, though few applications progressed beyond the duty stage. In mid-1980 the regulations affecting social service department provision of telephones were tightened up considerably so that effectively only the chronically sick housebound living alone could have them paid for. This was not seen by workers as a deficiency in the range of services available or as an aspect of unmet need. The acknowledgement of delays or inadequacies in service provision did not appear to extend to considerations of policy over which the workers themselves had no control.

Services to the blind

Working twenty-five hours a week to cover all four teams on the area, the area blind specialist had thirty-four active cases on the Selly Oak patch at the time of study though many more were technically open. She estimated 70 per cent of her clients to be elderly. Blindness was a special handicap for the elderly coming at a time when they were often disabled in other ways, possibly living alone, and almost certainly less adaptable than the young. The specialist drew on services generally available to the elderly: the home help service she considered especially important. Meals on wheels were used as a last resort, since relearning to cook for themselves was an important part of rehabilitating the blind. A wide range of special blind aids could be drawn on but again with discretion since they too could encourage over-dependence. These were often provided through the local branch of the Royal National Institute for the Blind whose activities underlay much of her work. Volunteers were used both for individual visiting and for helping with two weekly clubs, one specializing in handicraft run jointly with an adjoining area. She alone of all the social workers had no problems with transport: the department did not question her bills for minibuses and taxis.

Inadequacies in the service perceived by this worker at the time were a shortage of skilled personnel, a disinterest amongst other social workers in working with the blind, a single overworked mobility officer for the whole city, and a general need for more trained workers.

Different service 'packages' for different elderly clients

Analysis of characteristics of elderly clients living alone compared to those living with their spouse or other members of the family revealed clear differences. Those living with families were less capable on all the thirteen self-care tasks we monitored and, not surprisingly, were more likely to be receiving aids or adaptations. In contrast, those living alone were more likely to receive the assistance of a home help, meals on wheels, financial and material support, or a holiday. They also got more frequent social work visits. Indeed, almost all those in receipt of long-term support were living alone.

Table 5(8) illustrates another set of differences between the two groups – their sources of help with common crises. Obviously the proportions of help from within and outside the home were different but remarkably similar sources of help were quoted, especially for money problems. Illness and 'feeling down' would see a heavier reliance by those living alone on friends and neighbours and their home helps. Otherwise few would look to statutory services or acknowledged voluntary sources such as the clergy and a quarter of those living alone were unsure where they would seek help if they were 'feeling down'.

The very range of services available to the elderly tended to structure social workers' perceptions of clients' problems and their own activities. Thus, though loneliness was recognized as a problem and though a good part of work with the elderly did consist of personal support, this was swamped by the concern with providing tangible services. In many cases, of course, the clients only required specific services but the differentiation of service packages between our two broad client types seems to exemplify the problem. Specific services are requested. Often the response is appropriate but why do elderly people living with families and spouses rarely receive longer term social work support? Do they not have similar emotional and social needs to those living alone; are there not complicating problems of coping with each other? Certainly in terms of their satisfaction or dissatisfaction with services and in their expressions of morale and loneliness our study showed the two groups to be remarkably similar.

The views of the elderly clients

It is the genuine difficulty of moving beyond specific service provision in work with the elderly which has led some commenta-

Table 5(8) *Elderly clients: sources of help with common crises*[1]

	illness		money problem		feeling 'down'	
	living alone (n = 84)	living with others (n = 33)	living alone (n = 80)	living with others (n = 30)	living alone (n = 84)	living with others (n = 32)
	%	%	%	%	%	%
primary source of help						
spouse	0	46	0	23	0	41
other in household	0	36	0	17	0	22
relative outside household	31	12	50	13	17	13
(total family)	(31)	(94)	(50)	(53)	(17)	(76)
friend or neighbour	41	3	8	3	51	13
home help	18	0	1	0	5	0
district nurse/ health visitor	0	0	0	0	0	0
social worker	1	0	4	7	0	0
solicitor/bank manager	0	0	13	13	0	0
voluntary visitor	2	0	0	0	0	0
clergy	0	0	1	0	0	0
other	1	0	4	0	2	0
don't know	6	3	20	23	25	13

[1] Abstracted from leading questions about who would be asked for help if the respondent:
  (a) was ill and could not leave the house;
  (b) wanted advice about money problems;
  (c) was feeling down and just wanted someone to talk to.

tors to argue for separating out straightforward service provision from general assessment and long-term supportive work. One check upon this whole issue we used was the perception of clients: the extent to which they felt that there were problems in their lives that social workers did not recognize, that they recognized but could do nothing about, or that were assumed to be covered by the elaborate package of services available.

Our interviews with 122 elderly people revealed them to be largely willing clients of the department. Only 8 per cent had experienced apprehension or irritation at being referred to the department and 72 per cent expressed overall satisfaction with the services they had received at the time of the interview. Furthermore 76 per cent would have, or had, recommended the services of the department to other people in similar situations to themselves.

Examining the views on particular services showed that all of those who had received a telephone or adaptations from the department felt them to be essential or of great benefit to them. At least 80 per cent felt the same about a wide range of other services including meals on wheels, home helps, aids, and day centre attendance.

The home help service was often singled out for particular praise:

'Well, my home help looks after me. I don't know how I'd manage without her – she's more like a daughter to me.'

'We can't speak too highly of the home help. She even takes washing to do at her home.'

'[She has made a] great difference. She does the things around the house I can't manage. She'll help out with shopping as well if I need it.'

The interpretation of the broad satisfaction about the majority of services should be made with care. Twenty-four per cent did express dissatisfaction with at least one specific service. Furthermore our data showed a considerable disjunction between genuine appreciation or recognition of the essential nature of a service and areas of specific criticism. This was true even in relation to the home help service, where the degree to which client and particular home help were compatible was clearly vital. There were also reservations expressed about the scope of the service:

'When I had a home help two mornings a week it was a great help. I'm satisfied but with reservations. One and a quarter hours just isn't enough.'

'Home helps can't do windows and lights. I can do the rest. It's climbing and bending I need help with.'

Delay in the provision of aids and adaptations was another problem: 'I wish I had been told the shower would take time [two years]. I found waiting and not knowing what was happening very worrying. I didn't know whether to save – should we try to fit one or wait?'

Another interviewee, who had waited two years, felt she couldn't complain because the aids she had received were so good.

One of the most common additional causes of clearly expressed dissatisfaction was if a service was refused or unavailable. Chiropody and the provision of a telephone were most frequently mentioned. One otherwise satisfied client: 'I rather fell out with them over the telephone.' Others accepted the limitations on what could be provided: 'I suppose they haven't got enough manpower and facilities to accept everyone who needs them.'

The greatest degree of ambivalence expressed was about the help provided by social workers. Only 54 per cent felt them to be essential or of great benefit to them and 10 per cent saw them as no benefit at all. Partly this could be attributed to not understanding what the social workers were doing:

'I don't know what they [social worker and district nurse] come for. I don't need any interference.'

'She was very pleasant but you only get what you ask for – you're not told what is available.'

A bigger problem seemed to be that social workers couldn't always provide for their central needs or at least did not communicate an interest in these. 'I sometimes feel shut in. Can't they help with transport so I can get out?'

Many clients talked about needs for social contact but didn't see that as what social services were about. For instance, one client adjusting to the problems of living alone for the first time was no longer being visited by a social worker: 'I can't make friends. I always had them [husband and her friend who lived in]. My sons call but I would like to go out, to have an activity.' Several clients similarly expressed severe anxieties, about the neighbourhoods in which they lived, changes in their life that had occurred and about the future, that were not current social work concerns. It would be unfair to give the impression, however, that social workers were consistently unappreciated. 'It's a nice surprise when she comes [about once every three months]. I enjoy her visit. It's a new face.' Some clients particularly specified help with the problems of adjustment to disability, bereavement, or early retirement. 'I was greatly relieved. They've helped me cope [with my disability] better. They've told me about other people who can help.' There was, in particular, praise for the social worker for the blind: 'Couldn't say a word against them. They've all been marvellous. She doesn't come often enough for me.'

A final problematic area for many clients was the problem of regularity in visits by social workers and other visitors. Only 25 per cent of those with social workers expected a regular visit and, to many, worrying about whether they would get a visit, or when, upset their routine. Two clients claimed not to have had promised assessment visits and even home helps occasionally did not come when expected, which could be unsettling.

This was exacerbated by the distant (in every sense) nature of the area office. Whilst 49 per cent could have phoned directly and 23 per cent said they could get someone to phone for them, whether in fact they would have done either of these was open to doubt. Only 2 per cent would visit the office or get someone else to do so.

Clearly most clients were glad of the services provided by the department though they were not uncritical. Many, however, remained unsure of the role of the social workers themselves. Our interviewers reported direct and indirect expressions of tension, especially from clients living with spouses or families. Such problems of social isolation and adjustment were seldom the subject of sustained social work involvement, though whether it is desirable or possible to release social work personnel from the provision of practical services to enable them to intervene significantly in these areas remains an open question.

The younger physically handicapped

The profile of the perceived problems, delivered services, social work activities, visiting frequencies, and agency contacts for the physically handicapped under 65 (*Table 5(9)*) bore a remarkable resemblance to that of the elderly. Without finer instruments of discrimination than we have managed, it is impossible to know whether this similarity is consistent, or why. It may be no accident that this group, with the elderly, provides almost all the social work assistant case-load. It may also be that, as with the elderly, the scope of social work intervention is determined by the services available. A check on the clients' perspective to help clarify this issue was not available for this group. All that can be done here is to note the main similarities – and the few differences – between the social work response to the elderly and that to the younger physically handicapped.

Though the major problem for the younger physically handicapped was, as in the case of the elderly, the 'health/self-care' category, this also tended to go along with a greater range of other problems. Housing and finance, if marginally, were greater

social work activities[1]	referrals (n = 36) %	long-term cases (n = 36) %
investigating/assessing	71	86
giving information/advice	46	83
mobilizing resources	51	66
advocacy	0	11
educating/developing skills	3	20
problem-solving	9	34
supervising/reviewing	3	9
supporting/sustaining	6	28
providing group activity	11	11
visiting frequency		
weekly or more	3	6
monthly or more	17	21
less than monthly	23	21
less than 3 monthly	6	41
less than 6 monthly	n/a	9
once off	26	n/a
never visited	26	3
services provided[1,2]		
aids	23	57
adaptations	14	26
home help	6	14
clubs	9	6
day care	3	14
adult training centre	3	6
long-term residential care	3	6
short-term residential care	0	14
holidays	3	9
financial/material	6	9

problems tackled[1,2]	referrals (n = 36) %	long-term cases (n = 36) %
health/self-care	75	92
loneliness/isolation	14	8
family relationships	14	31
child behaviour	0	8
education	0	14
employment	0	14
finance	8	25
housing	14	22
transport	11	8
other	6	8
none	6	3
major problem		
health/self-care	64	72
other agencies contacted[1,2]		
general practitioner	17	49
health visitor/district nurse	6	9
other health services	43	43
education	3	20
housing	11	26
employment agencies	0	11
DHSS	6	9
voluntary agencies	9	20
other	6	11
none	49	17

[1] More than one category could be used so figures do not necessarily sum to 100.

[2] Categories which accounted for less than 5 per cent of cases in both the referral and long-term group have been excluded.

problems than for the elderly. Not unexpectedly, handicap at an early age was seen to cause problems in family relationships and child behaviour. Finding employment opportunities and education problems emerged as significant for this group amongst the long-term cases and this produced a consequent broadening of social work activities and agency contacts. It is amongst this group, too, that only partially resolvable problems of transport occur, a point attested to in interview.

Q. 'Are there any problems in the things that you can help them with?'
A. 'Transport, yes, we've come up with transport, it's very difficult to get transport for them.'
Q. 'Why is that, do you think?'
A. 'Well, for the simple reason they [the social services committee] have cut back on transport and we can't get it you see. Most of the time we can't transport them. One off, if we are not that busy we will, but we just can't keep it up ourselves, and we have to attend to something else. It is, the difficulty is, transport.'

Aids and adaptations, day and residential care and clubs dominated practical service provision, with a lesser though not insiginificant use of home helps, particularly for those living alone. Social work activities showed a common emphasis to the elderly on assessment, service-giving, and resource mobilization, though group activities and personal problem-solving were consistently more prevalent. There was noticeable broadening of social work activity on long-term cases, with considerable emphasis on education, problem-solving, and advocacy. There was even more contact with members of the health services, though less with the DHSS than in the case of the elderly. Finally, visiting frequency was markedly similar to that with the elderly, though long-term cases were visited slightly less frequently.

It is not clear what status work with the physically handicapped had. In an area still using pre-Seebohm categories it was classified with work with the elderly under the 'welfare' heading. There were certainly indications in team discussions of a feeling that the health services might have taken more responsibility for some additional services, such as transport. Given that half the physically handi-capped were middle aged and nearly two-thirds women, it may be that their demographic characteristics and the service package available for them reinforced their status as prematurely aged.

The mentally ill and handicapped

The seven mentally handicapped and thirty-three mentally ill people presented as new clients during the period (and fourteen and twenty-five long-term clients respectively) showed the greatest diversity and intensity of problems tackled of all the client groups. Health and self-care again predominated yet loneliness (particularly amongst the mentally ill) was greater than for any other group, as were the (slightly smaller) figures for financial difficulties and housing problems. Family relationships particularly and difficulties with education and employment reinforced this broad pattern of problems amongst the long-term cases. Diversity was again evident in the range of services provided. Day and short-term residential care (particularly for the mentally ill), financial or material support, and holidays predominated, though clubs, aids and adaptations (for the mentally handicapped), and home helps were also in evidence. The emphasis of social work activity shifted somewhat. Though assessment, advice-giving, and mobilizing resources were clearly important, group activity, personal problem-solving, and skill development were more frequent than for any other groups. That liaison with health services, and psychiatrists in particular, should have figured so largely in contact with other agencies is not surprising; that the housing and social security departments were contacted more frequently than any other group, even family/child cases, reveals the material deprivation consequent on mental illness or handicap. A good deal of social work assessment was apparently conducted in the absence of the client, nearly half of the new 'clients' never seeing a social worker. Once taken on as a longer term case, however, the mentally ill or handicapped were more likely than any other group to be visited at least monthly (*Tables 5(10)* and *5(11)*).

It is doubtful whether our research instruments were sophisticated enough to measure the particular difficulties posed by this group. The looseness of the health/self-care category has been noted. This consideration must be extended to that of 'helping solve personal problems': what problems, how, and with what degree of success are the obvious questions begged here. More detailed description was made available through interview with the area's mental health specialist who was attached to the Selly Oak team. She felt that for a number of reasons of varying degrees of legitimacy, work with the mentally ill or handicapped was not given a very high priority. She quoted the example of notifications

Table 5(10) Summary of help given and problems tackled: mental illness social work cases

social work activities[1]	referrals (n = 33) %	long-term cases (n = 25) %	problems tackled[1,2]	referrals (n = 33) %	long-term cases (n = 25) %
investigating/assessing	67	50	health/self-care	63	88
giving information/advice	38	63	loneliness/isolation	38	32
mobilizing resources	16	71	family relationships	28	68
advocacy	3	29	child behaviour	9	24
educating/developing skills	3	33	child abuse	9	24
problem-solving	19	58	education	6	20
supervising/reviewing	3	54	employment	6	28
supporting/sustaining	9	58	finance	28	40
providing group activity	9	33	housing	22	28
			other	9	12
visiting frequency			major problem		
weekly or more	6	13	health/self-care	34	56
monthly or more	9	30			
less than monthly	9	22	other agencies contacted[1,2]		
less than 3 monthly	3	26	general practitioner	16	63
less than 6 monthly	n/a	9	health visitor/district nurse	6	21
once off	21	n/a	psychiatrist	34	71
never visited	52	0	other health services	13	38
services provided[1,2]			child guidance	0	13
aids	0	13	education	6	25
adaptations	3	8	housing	13	29
home help	9	13	DHSS	9	50
meals on wheels	3	13	employment agencies	0	8
clubs	3	13	voluntary agencies	3	17
day care	13	50	other	0	8
adult training centre	3	4	none	47	8
long-term residential care	0	16			
short-term residential care	0	16			
holidays	6	16			
financial/material	6	32			
craft supplies	6	8			
temporary accommodation	6	4			

social work activities[1]	referrals (n = 7) %	long-term cases (n = 14) %
investigating/assessing	★	50
giving information/advice	★	79
mobilizing resources	★	71
advocacy	★	29
educating/developing skills	★	36
problem-solving	★	64
supervising/reviewing	★	43
supporting/sustaining	★	50
providing group activity	★	29
visiting frequency		
weekly or more	★	31
monthly or more	★	31
less than monthly	★	0
less than 3 monthly	★	31
less than 6 monthly	★	8
once off	★	n/a
never visited	★	0
services provided[1,2]		
aids	★	50
adaptations	★	21
day care	★	29
adult training centre	★	29
long-term residential care	★	14
short-term residential care	★	29
holidays	★	43
financial/material	★	43
craft supplies	★	7
temporary accommodation	★	14
fostering	★	7

problems tackled[1,2]	referrals (n = 7) %	long-term cases (n = 14) %
health/self-care	★	86
loneliness/isolation	★	0
family relationships	★	57
child behaviour	★	29
education	★	43
employment	★	29
finance	★	36
housing	★	36
transport	★	29
other	★	7
major problem		
health/self-care	★	43
other agencies contacted[1,2]		
general practitioner	★	64
health visitor/district nurse	★	7
psychiatrist	★	50
other health services	★	50
education	★	29
housing	★	29
DHSS	★	36
employment agencies	★	7
voluntary agencies	★	43
others	★	7
none	★	7

[1] More than one category could be used so figures do not necessarily sum to 100.
[2] Categories which accounted for less than 5 per cent of cases in both the referral and long-term group have been excluded.
★Percentages omitted as small number of cases would distort figures.

received in the area of sections under the Mental Health Act, which – as observational material confirmed – were simply recorded and filed unless they concerned a current client:

Q. 'I was just wondering whether because the area has a mental health specialist the number of mental health cases they take depends on how many you can handle. Whether it worked like that?'

A. 'They don't even let me know. I'm sure there are a lot more sections done than I ever hear about and I would have liked to have kept account, you know to say, well that is the number that was admitted on section from Area 12 last year, but you don't get that.'

She felt that in addition to such organizational embodiment of priorities there was a genuine uncertainty amongst social workers about what could or should be the form of social work intervention. Her own emphasis was on individual therapy and especially on group-work, the latter being difficult to achieve for lack of staff support, suitable meeting places, and transport facilities. But of all the services which might have been provided for this group it was the provision of hostels that was most in short supply:

Q. 'What about the resources you've got. I mean the places in hostels, group homes and so on. Are there enough of those?'

A. 'Oh, no. Not enough at all. Not enough at all of hostels ... Take the one at Alwold Road [for the mentally handicapped]. There has been no movement in that since I had a fellow out for the group home four years ago. There are still twenty-five beds, twenty-four occupied, one rota bed for short term and that goes for every hostel in Birmingham, they are chock-a-block full. There are 107 on the waiting list. I think it's forty-five women and the others –'

Q. 'What, these people are living at home, are they?'

A. 'They live at home and must be on the waiting list and really and truly I could add another twenty to that waiting list so there aren't enough hostels.'

It was not all pessimism; the appointment of a district mental health liaison officer was improving the co-ordination of information and a mental health lobby had developed within the department. An experiment with a specialist mental health team in an adjacent area, though it had foundered on the rocks of social work radicalism, at least showed some management awareness of the problems. Nevertheless other social workers also agreed that the department did not give sufficient priority to this client group, nor provide adequate services and resources. No doubt part of the explanation of this lies in the political arena: the mental health lobby is still some way behind those for other groups. But there may have been some organizational reasons as well. First, for the mentally ill especially there was no established package of services comparable to those available for the old, the younger physically handicapped, or even the mentally handicapped. Nor were there the kind of statutory responsibilities evident in child care work. Second, there was considerable overlap with the health services. The professional dominance of psychiatry and the shift of responsibility once hospitalization occurred meant that neither the health nor the social services had any consistent overview of individual cases. Third, there was the problem of social workers' attitudes – though in this, as in all such generalizations, there were individual exceptions. Social workers appeared to be less prepared and trained for, less sure of their skills and competence in, dealing with this group than any other. Deficiencies in policy, resources, and staffing were compounded by uncertainties over the social work principles which should underlie practice with the mentally ill or handicapped.

Families and children

Social work with families and children threw most sharply into relief the complicated interrelationship of social behaviour and material environment. Thus the most frequently occurring problem amongst new work was that of finance (37 per cent) followed by child abuse, housing, family relationships, and child behaviour. Minor but impinging influences were health/self-care, education, and employment. Whilst the material problems retained their significance in the long-term cases, they became overlaid by a cluster of more behavioural problems – family relationships, child abuse, child behaviour, and education. Tangible services available for new cases were limited in number and kind. No service was provided in more than 5 per cent of cases and only financial or material help and residential care in more than 1 per cent. Alternative home environments to the family and material provision dominated a range of practical services that was still restricted, if more widely used, in the long-term cases. Social work activity was initially restricted: assessment and advice were the early stresses, with some resource mobilization and advocacy. A much wider range of activities was generated by the long-term cases, with an emphasis on supervision and review. Liaison with other agencies was diffuse: in those 59 per cent of new cases where it occurred at all, health, education, resource distribution, and social control agencies were all involved. That most of this work was specific and short-term is evidenced by visiting frequency. Forty per cent were never visited at all and only 16 per cent received more than one visit. Eighty-two per cent were closed within six months. In contrast, the long-term cases were amongst the most frequently visited of all clients. They also generated the greatest variety of contact with other agencies (*Table 5(12)*).

The fact is that social work with families and children is not easily measured. Outside the provision of advocacy for financial and material resources, the provision of residential care and the execution of supervision orders, we are quickly into problems of human relationships:

Q. 'Let's take the example of children in care. Do you see care as a last resort; would you do your utmost to keep a child out of care if you possibly could?'
A. 'Oh yes, I think I would. Yes, as a general statement I think I would. Once they're in care, I would then see my priority as getting them out again, back home, or if that doesn't work then finding an alternative placement for them.'
Q. 'So with cases like that, with a child for instance, and it may not be possible to generalize, in which case you must say, are you working with the child or are you working with the family or the child within the family, where is the problem in your experience located?'
A. 'Well, I think it depends where the case is at. If the child is at home, you have to make a decision as to whether you see the problem as the child or the family as a whole, or perhaps one or other parent. I like to work with family groups. I like to try not to scapegoat any particular member of the family because I think families are such complicated groups . . .'
Q. 'So are you trying to correct malfunctions within the family?'
A. 'Well, I like to think that, yes. I think I'm trying to do that. How successful I am at doing it is quite a different matter. But I like

	referrals (n = 136) %	long-term cases (n = 114) %
social work activities[1]		
investigating/assessing	63	56
giving information/advice	57	60
mobilizing resources	8	41
advocacy	9	20
educating/developing skills	4	25
problem-solving	4	37
supervising/reviewing	7	68
supporting/sustaining	4	38
providing group activity	3	14
visiting frequency		
weekly or more	4	4
monthly or more	4	31
less than monthly	5	32
less than 3 monthly	0	24
less than 6 monthly	n/a	4
once off	47	n/a
never visited	39	6
services provided[1,2]		
aids	1	7
day care	2	12
long-term residential care	1	32
short-term residential care	3	18
holidays	1	6
financial/material	4	27
fostering	2	16

	referrals (n = 136) %	long-term cases (n = 114) %
problems tackled[1,2]		
health/self-care	10	30
loneliness/isolation	2	7
family relationships	21	70
child behaviour	20	49
child abuse	31	35
education	5	27
employment	3	10
finance	37	32
housing	23	23
other	6	6
major problem		
finance	29	
family relationships		32
other agencies contacted[1,2]		
general practitioner	7	36
health visitor/district nurse	9	14
other health services	12	34
child guidance	3	7
education	7	53
housing	8	32
employment agencies	0	6
probation	10	25
DHSS	10	37
voluntary agencies	8	30
other	13	14
none	41	5

[1] More than one category could be used so figures do not necessarily sum to 100.
[2] Categories which accounted for less than 5 per cent of cases in both the referral and long-term group have been excluded.

to try and get at the sort of family dynamics a little bit and
work out where the difficulties are. The problem with children
in care is that once the situation has got to that stage – where
you might well not have been involved before – once they're in
care they then are the scapegoat immediately. They're the
problem and they've been removed. I think that that brings a
whole new light on the thing really. You might feel it's quite
inappropriate for the child to have been removed: at least
inappropriate in that the child wasn't perhaps the cause of the
problem although everybody was under the impression that he
or she was.'

Q. 'So is the process of social work as you describe it a question of
a kind of unit called the family in which things have gone
wrong into which a social worker was introduced in order to
put things right?'

A. 'Yes. I think put simply that is the case with a lot of family
work.'

There was one resource available to the Selly Oak team without
consideration of which their work with families and children could
not be understood. 870 House was a joint education and social
services project, funded by those departments but with an independent management committee. This unit, providing a specialist
youth club, day education unit, and drop-in facilities for children
relieved much of the referred pressure on the team.

Q. 'In fact, that unit does almost take referrals off your hands
doesn't it, as I understand, if you think it's appropriate?'

A. 'If we think, yes there are many cases where we feel they can
deal with the needs of the clients as appropriately as we could,
in some cases more appropriately, and'will virtually hand it
over lock, stock, and barrel. Other cases we are not able to
hand over completely, for example a supervision order. But
where a lad is already a member it may be that the administration of the supervision order, i.e. the practical work with his
parents and with the child is best done by the unit and we take a
secondary position. We have to remain involved by virtue of
the order but at the same time our contact tends to be with the
unit who in turn have contact with the family. This is done by
agreement with the family and the child, at the start of an
order.'

It may be significant that to provide this service package for children – part youth club, part school, part counselling centre – an organization had to be set up outside the existing administrative structure. A similar scope of activities was envisaged for a new IT centre to be opened in a particularly notorious part of the Ley Hill Farm Estate, which a qualified social worker on the team was subsequently appointed to lead.

Otherwise work with families and children was framed by the one-to-one relationship between social worker and family or child, bounded by statutory obligations. Sixty-nine per cent of the long-term cases were characterized by the existence of a supervision or care order. Such work was individualized, invisible, and infinitely variable. Of all the client groups this one is least amenable to conceptualization, measurement, or evaluation as 'service delivery'.

5.4 SOCIAL WORKERS' PERSPECTIVES

Social workers' views of their practice – the relationship between clients' problems, the services and resources which could be provided by the social services department or other agencies, the active forms which their social work intervention took – were by no means uniform. The essential division was between a self-consciously radical group who took a 'political' view of their activity and those who were more conservative in style and more concerned to achieve 'efficiency' and co-operation. But all were aware that many of the problems besetting their clients were beyond the solving capacity of social work. Problems of housing, poverty, inadequate community facilities, and social isolation could have their effects mitigated by social services but more radical changes were the responsibility of other arms of the welfare state and those who controlled them politically.

Social workers were thus less concerned with the policies and systems of resource-distributing agencies than with their flexibility over individual clients on whose behalf the social worker approached them. This was seen as almost entirely dependent on the quality of personal contact. Having a name, knowing who to ask for, having had previous contact – these were the mechanisms for circumventing bureaucratic systems. In the case of the housing department this had been formalized with regular liaison meetings, where a representative of the local housing management team would meet social workers to discuss particular cases. With the DHSS, staff exchanges had been set up but these were of less immediate use than having the names of strategically placed supervisors. With other agencies, the quality of day-to-day contact again depended upon perceptions of the competence and understanding of social services departments held by particular individuals: headmasters in schools, GPs in the health service. It seemed to be the case that, outside housing liaison meetings, contact on the ground (as opposed to long-term high level planning) was left very much up to the worker or team to cultivate at an individual level.

Informal networks

Community facilities of any kind were scarce, especially on the newer council estates, where informal support was almost non-existent. Elsewhere it was little better, except where neighbours had taken it upon themselves to act as substitute relatives for the elderly. The most social workers felt able to do to mobilize such informal networks was to ask clients, neighbours, and shopkeepers to get in touch if they were aware of crises – but this required the precious commodity of social workers' time:

Q. 'So what's the relationship of social work to those kinds of community networks?'

A. 'I think we should be very involved. I should have the time to go round and find out what's going on so that I can tap into those resources. I don't see myself as a community worker in setting them up. I've made the mistake of trying to be a community worker in the past. But I think a social worker needs to know about them and have a relationship with the people who run them so that they're tuned in to an area. Which we don't – partly because we spread out too far and partly because we're never given the authority.'

To an extent the low level of community support could be compensated for by the use of voluntary agencies. Some church groups were active, especially in providing lunch clubs and voluntary groups for the elderly. But more often the voluntary groups called upon were branches of national organizations – WRVS, CAB, National Institute for the Blind – or city-wide agencies: the Birmingham Association for Mental Health, the Visiting Service for Old People, or the Birmingham Council for Old People.

Officially, as part of an agreement negotiated between management and unions, volunteers could only be used if provided through a voluntary organization. Since few existed for families and children, this group were particularly short of non-statutory support. More than one worker cast envious eyes at the probation service's use of volunteers.

Informal care networks and locally-based groups were two important features of social workers' definitions of unmet needs. But more often this term was interpreted fairly narrowly as a problem of deficiencies in existing services: holes were seen in the social work net but extensions were rarely suggested. Hence problems of transport, of hostels for the mentally ill and handicapped or late teenagers, youth and community centres, were all quoted as examples.

Innovation

Given these kinds of problems, contacts, and resources, social workers saw the purpose of social work as to provide relief and support:

'I would say a social worker is a person who tries to help someone else with a problem they can't deal with themselves. And because as social workers you're given resources you can pass them on. You're a relieving service, not always a solving service.'

'I'm trying to get people to cope as best they can with the situation they're in and get the most out of that situation.'

'I see social work in very simplistic terms as supporting people and trying to change their environment ... I accept that sometimes all I can do is to help them cope within the environment they've got even if it's a lousy environment.'

These should not be read as statements of complacency. There seemed to be a genuine desire on the team to go beyond the existing model of individual case-work but this was only rarely achieved. Three kinds of obstructions to this were seen as operative. The first was the strict hierarchical division of labour within the team. Members who scarcely ever worked together on cases hardly had the basis for teamwork of a more ambitious kind. Status divisions between qualified social workers and social work assistants made the latter anxious to conserve their position, because they saw changes, like a proposed patchwork system, as likely to divide the team and erode their autonomy. Second, there was the absence of an adequate physical base. The area office was 3 miles outside Selly Oak. A converted large semi-detached house, there was nowhere suitable for even interviews with existing clients, much less any form of group activity. Reception and duty took place in a converted garage. Attempts to find a supplementary base in Selly Oak foundered for want of a suitable building and uncertainty over whether organizationally this would constitute a sub-office.

Third, there was the problem of the lack of the time and personnel required to undertake initiatives: coping with existing and new work was as much as the team could manage. But for more radical members of the team the emphasis on case-work was not a necessity but an active selection of priorities:

Q. 'Are there obstructions in the department to doing those forms of group and community work?'

A. 'I think there are obstructions; one is finance, second is that somehow these things are secondary to your actual case-work. They don't recognize it as case-work and therefore it seems to have to do that, you've got to do that over and above. It's a bit like IT work isn't it? You know it's great, you know IT works great as it doesn't interfere with your case-work. And exactly the same, you know your grass roots perhaps, community work type of activity, you know you've got to look after your cases that's the important thing. Perhaps if you got to recognize it, perhaps if you get six old dears down to a luncheon club you can see them all at one go; I don't know. That's it in simple terms but it's very much still, my first thing on the tape was this business about the one-to-one case-work. As you know I've tried to get away from that but it's impossible you know, there's this tremendous resistance, that you are responsible for that case. Accountability seems to be the name of the game and you can't go beyond that.'

How such deterrents to innovation worked out in practice was illustrated by a project to run an advice desk for two sessions a week in a new purpose-built health centre. After much protracted negotiation with the health authorities and not a little internal conflict, this project did get under way. But the misgivings were considerable. Its objectives were ambiguous, whether it was to be a walk-in service to the public or a way of picking up health service

referrals more quickly. The centre opened just as the area office had
started an intake team system and it was not immediately clear how
their work would relate to the advice desk. There were also considerable reservations about the motives and understanding of
health personnel; whether they would be tempted to palm off some
of their more awkward patients on to social services. That the
project did eventually get off the ground demonstrates that these
difficulties were not insurmountable. But the amount of time, talk,
and effort involved in instituting what was after all a modest form
of innovation indicated an environment of inflexibility.

Client perspectives

Social workers did not feel that clients had a consistent view of
their function partly because it depended on each individual's
previous knowledge and experience, partly because the function
did vary considerably:

'I don't think they really know what social workers are for in
many respects. I think the role varies so much, well my role
varies with clients anyway so much, from a soft sort of
supporting person right through to a hard nut, a semi-policeman;
through to some sort of family case-work, group-work, therapy.
I think I would be a bit of all sorts and within that I'm not sure
that people really understand. I try and explain what I'm trying
to achieve and sometimes you can't because in fact you're not
quite sure what you are trying to achieve. I try and explain, but I
think probably the vast majority of people see you as "I must
tidy up because the Welfare's coming." Well a lot of the older
people think that you are from the Welfare. They call you the
Lady from the Welfare, and you know to them . . . it used to be
that. They don't really know what you can do; they are amazed
when you tell them about all the aids you can have. Most people
know about home help and meals on wheels. I think that's got
round. They don't know about the aids. But I've never had
anyone query who I am. They just open the door and you walk
in and I just say "Hello, I've come to see you". You don't even say
who you are. I've never been challenged or had to show a card or
anything like that.'

Whatever their view of social services as an institution, clients
did use the characteristics of the individual social worker to

determine their response. Some workers felt it was a positive attribute to be able to talk the clients' language, others that respect should be cultivated. Some felt that clients respected maturity, others that they were unduly prejudiced against youth. But these were short-term rather than long-term effects: extended contact could overcome preconceptions and clarify the nature of the social workers' function.

5.5   THE INFLUENCE OF MANAGEMENT

Irrespective of the official description of the managerial hierarchy, for the social workers it existed at four levels: team management, area management, central management, and political management. The further away these became, physically and hierarchically, from the team, the less intense feelings appeared to be. The emphasis has to be on 'appearances' since it was on this topic particularly that social workers were most guarded in interview, and – which may or may not be the same thing – least willing to generalize. In itself unwillingness to talk openly about management is indicative of the felt vulnerability of the subordinate: despite the interviewer's assurances there was always the risk that something they said in an unguarded moment might be held against them.

At the immediate level of team management, there were fewer such inhibitions. The main forms of routine contact between team and manager were allocation, supervision, and closure. One experienced qualified worker stressed how important supervision was both for effective case-work and protection through and from management:

Q. 'So if you feel you have quite a lot of control over what's allocated to you, do you feel you have a lot of control over how you approach clients and what you do with them? Are you just given complete freedom to go away and treat the case as you see fit and again is that different because of your status and experience?'

A. 'I think within understood departmental guidelines social workers at all levels have a lot of freedom to go away and deal with a case according to their training and experience. The newer entrant to the profession is necessarily and desirably more closely supervised, when their work is discussed with them and perhaps guidance given. The more experienced worker is less closely supervised because supervision is less necessary. But having said that, however experienced or skilled you are with the work, supervision, consultation, – use what niceties you like – is necessary in my opinion. I don't find supervision threatening in any way and consider it a very necessary part of the way we work.'

Q. 'Can you explain a bit why? What role does it have, is it a sounding board for your . . .?'

A. It's a sounding board, yes. Many situations, however experienced you are, I feel you meet with situations you are not sure of and I think you welcome a second opinion; the need to discuss. You also, with some of the more controversial or risky decisions you make, welcome the feeling – well, you have told your team leader and you've got his backing.'

The usefulness of supervision was endorsed by most of the social work assistants, who found the prolonged absence of the team leader through illness had removed an important reference point. Other qualified social workers were more selective in the regularity and intensity with which they participated in supervisory sessions. There was certainly a feeling that the managerial skills necessary for being a good case-work supervisor were very different from those required for administration and policy-making. Some workers saw this as part of a general conflict of loyalties between field-work team and area management:

Q. 'Is it true that the role of the team leader is strategic and contradictory? Does that role as at present constituted seem possible to carry out?'

A. 'I don't feel wholly qualified to answer that. I do feel that the way the team is structured and organized does affect the service offered, regardless of personalities, although obviously they affect it: they've made it part of themselves . . . As far as the team leader's role is concerned, he's in an impossible position. I think that a team leader has to decide which side of the fence he is on and when he's prepared to take risks and in what direction. Are they pro field-work or do they want to keep the administration tidy? Those who are adventurous tend to be administrative disasters.'

But opinion was again far from unanimous. One member who had experiences of the team leader role felt that contradictions were in the eye of the beholder:

'I think a team leader is the jam in the sandwich. He's inevitably
going to be in situations where people feel angry with him
because their needs have not been met as they've perceived them.
However hard a team leader tries I think he's going to find himself
in this position and I think the acceptance of this is part of the
job. In reality terms there will obviously be areas of conflict but I
didn't – looking at it from the side of attempting to do the job – I
didn't find this a major problem. I suppose how far the team
leaders represent line management, represent authority, how far
this is acceptable and easily absorbed by you as a worker
depends a little bit on your philosophy of social work I suppose.
If you are a radical who sees your primary task as changing a
system rather than working with individual clients, then I
suppose it must be very hard coping with idiotic team leaders –
as you would see them – who stand for the system and the *status
quo*. If you tend to see yourself, if your primary interest in social
work, is more working with individual clients and you are
prepared to let society largely change the system as and when the
need arises, and you see yourself as a member of a team of people
doing a job at a specific level, then I think the conflict is
minimal.'

Possibly the least controversial aspect of team management was the
closure of cases. Since the bulk of family and child case-work was
covered by statutory obligations, the point at which a decision to
continue or not with the case had to be made was, to an extent,
predetermined. It was then a question of whether more work would
be productive or whether some form of risk continued to exist. For
all client groups this occasionally amounted to an admission that
case-work was achieving, and apparently could achieve, very little.
The decision to close a case had to be approved by the team leader
and the file initialled, though sometimes social workers would
deliberately allow a case to drift into closure, giving the client time
to reactivate it if they wished. Outside families and children there
was a sense that imposing a clear cut-off point would be neither
understood nor appreciated by the clients.

Pressure to close or keep open cases often came as a result of area
management negotiation. Both the mental health and blind specialists would have liked to retain cases on an open-ended basis but
found this to be in conflict with administrative norms about case
closure. It was also not unknown for teams deliberately to keep

open certain types of cases as a means of bargaining for more resources within the area.

Area management

Bargaining took place at area management team (AMT) meetings where the four team leaders met the area manager and the area administrative officer to discuss matters of policy and practice within the area. Much of the material of team meetings consisted of matters which had been or were due to be discussed there. In so far as the area had discretion over policy AMT took the decisions. AMT had designed and instituted the intake team system. As a result they considered the whole area's staffing position. Posts were reallocated on the basis of statutory work with children, a criterion much resented by the Selly Oak team who were disadvantaged by their relatively greater share of 'welfare' work.

AMT was the real locus of power within the area and its clandestine nature thus became the target for radical workers' resentment. Area management had in fact agreed to the presence of observers representing each team but the proposal had been vetoed by central management.

This kind of limitation on AMT's powers was further illustrated by discussion of the inadequacy of the area office, described earlier. All the possible solutions – a portakabin extension, relocating one team in a sub-office, creating a new area – depended upon resources being made available by central management. The amount of pressure exerted by area management was qualified by the fear that having the building officially condemned might result in relocation of some teams in central office. Whatever the deficiencies of the existing accommodation, this was a fate to be avoided at all costs.

In the eyes of more radical workers central administration and political governance were synonymous. This was especially so over industrial relations. The management was composed of both councillors and senior officers, the employees were the social workers on the ground, with area and team managers as a rather uneasy buffer. The union structure further complicated the issue. All members of the department, both managers and managed, were eligible for membership of NALGO, though the younger and more radical members of the department had joined NUPE, otherwise the union of manual workers in the department. Complications developed, including some heated exchanges as to how far salary negotiations could properly be discussed at team meetings.

The role of the centre

Most contact with central administration was of a routine nature. Every team meeting would include communication from that source: clarification of regulations and procedures, notices and minutes of committee meetings, requests for information. Even some of these, however, provoked antagonistic responses. NAI procedures were regarded as suspect, complaints from the court section about social workers' ignorance treated with scepticism, exhortations to cut down car mileage claims, or the use of taxis treated with disdain. Lengthy reports on such diverse topics as fostering or computer-based record systems were thought impossible to read. More adverse still was the reaction to a request from central administration channelled through the administrative officer for all social workers to record and submit overtime, so that payment or time off in lieu could be awarded. Radicals and non-radicals alike simply suspected the motives behind this request – though not for the first time their reservations were not shared by the team leader. Their responses ranged from the defence of professional autonomy and integrity to an emphasis on formally negotiated procedures, thus indicating the range of possible bases from which to view management activity.

It was not always clear whether initiatives from central management in fact came from political sources though at times this was transparently so. A new Social Services Committee chairperson laid down strict conditions for circumstances under which direct representations to her about individual clients could be made – a move not appreciated by the team. In another area a public row blew up over attempts by a member of the housing committee's attempt to gain access to a fostering file. A subsequent High Court judgement upheld the right of elected councillors to have such access (though the later successful appeal against this was due to go to the House of Lords in 1982 so the issue remained unresolved at the time of writing). One member of the team commented that if such a right were to be exercised he would have to consider what he wrote on files, since councillors were no respectors of confidentiality.

Following the publicity surrounding a court case in which another area of the social services department was criticized for condoning under-age cohabitation a memorandum was circulated from the committee to all areas and teams which laid down a reporting and case conference procedure for all such cases. For the team such a directive was clearly a threat and one inimical to their ideals of social work. One member summed up his reaction thus:

'You can have your private views but if you go against policy you will be sticking your neck out and they'll make mincemeat of you – it's a clear backward step – more and more social worker discretion is being eroded and supplanted by regulations and procedures you *will* follow. Social workers in the field of child care are being forced to become paranoid and forever looking over their shoulders . . . Public opinion is to blame. We're doing things in our interests rather than those of the clients.'

Management processes thus impinged on social workers' activities in various ways: direct and indirect, routinized procedures and policy statements, directives to employees and discussions with colleagues, the closure of cases and the closure of children's homes. In part these reflect the contradictory nature of managerial hierarchies and functions in social services departments, which may be endorsed by our comparative analysis. But there was also a simple absence of trust.

One social worker made unfavourable comparisons with a London borough where she had worked. A similar organizational structure had bred a very different set of managerial initiatives with an emphasis on innovation and flexibility in the deployment of resources. How far size, organizational structure, the recent history of industrial action, public opinion, or personnel and attitudes were to blame is not clear, but social workers did not feel positively supported by management, the less so the farther it was removed from them.

PART THREE

COMPARING THE TEAMS

6

Practice as a
Response to Local Needs

In this chapter we draw together the evidence of the three case studies to examine the degree to which one particular arm of the welfare state, the local authority social services department, adapts to the particular needs and circumstances of the people living in the area that it serves. We first consider the processes by which the demands of the community become the subject of intervention by the social services department and then analyse what implications this has for the nature of provision in the three areas. A final section pays particular attention to what this tells us about the general nature of social work practice within a local authority.

Chapter 7 considers more explicitly the influence of organizational structure on what we have found while Chapter 8 offers an overall summary and discusses some possible strategies for improving the adaptability of social services departments.

THREE CONTRASTING AREAS

Chapter Two provides a broad brush view of those area characteristics likely to be important in shaping the particular demands made on the three area offices. Hence in Selly Oak we expected to find a greater proportion of demands from families with young children, particularly those affected by the unemployment contingent on the decline of major centres of employment in the area. These were largely to be concentrated in the lower income areas of the large high-rise council estate and the core area of urban renewal and inadequate housing, from where we also anticipated many demands from elderly people.

We expected, however, that the proportion of demand arising from the elderly would be less than in Dereham and, more particularly, Aber, which has the highest proportion of elderly of all. The growing numbers of elderly, particularly the more dependent older group, represent a serious challenge to the ability of all three departments to adapt to local needs. All three authorities were pursuing policies of replacing institutional care by developing systems of care in the community. The extent to which this had resulted in coherent systems of care that are rooted in the community, particularly for elderly people, is something to which we will return.

The absence of meaningful measures of the incidence of mental handicap and illness prevented us anticipating the relative contribution of each to the work of the three study teams. We might have speculated about proportions of physically handicapped people living in the areas on the basis of the surveys conducted in response to the Chronically Sick and Disabled Persons Act. However, as has been pointed out elsewhere, the lack of uniformity in definition and method in the surveys would make an accurate comparison impossible (Bowl 1976).

Examination of these broad indicators serves only to highlight their relative inadequacy as indicators of social stress. Social conditions underpin, but do not determine, whether a request is made for the intervention of the social services department into the lives of particular individuals or groups of individuals. We know, for example, surprisingly little about the specific circumstances under which families, who have hitherto provided care and support for an elderly relative, are precipitated into calling in a social worker. Furthermore, we cannot be precise in taking into account the level of the support in the community that may thus delay or prevent demands on the social services department.

We can say something about the level of organized voluntary activity. In Selly Oak we found the range of voluntary organizations for the elderly that are typical of the urban setting and they made an important contribution to their care. They largely provide visiting services for the housebound and day clubs and centres for the fitter, ambulant elderly. Whilst some could take extra numbers, few could open more often and the overall view was that they could not meet the existing needs within the area. Provision was also uneven geographically and no facilities catered directly for the core area of Selly Oak, where many elderly people live alone. Formal voluntary provision for the other client groups was less prominent.

The pattern in the rural areas was rather different and more sketchy. In each, the voluntary sector provided community-based meals services, both mobile and in lunch clubs. Dereham also had a centre providing part-time day care and a number of social clubs for the elderly. In both areas too there were a number of play groups, and some support for the mentally ill and handicapped in Dereham, but beyond this little provision for other client groups. The formal voluntary sector is thus an important but limited contributor to levels of social care in the study areas and we must be sceptical about its ability to play an expanded role in the social services network under current conditions.

Some social workers placed more emphasis on regenerating the 'old community spirit' of informal care. Precise information on past levels of informal care in the localities was not available, though earlier writers on new communities have pointed to the implications of its absence (McKenzie 1955; Martin, Brotherston, and Chave 1957; Nicholson 1961). We are prepared to accept the argument that there is now less informal care in the localities (Abrams 1980) but are unable to offer systematic information on levels of support in our study areas because the task of 'measuring' such support would be a significant project in itself.

Other work has examined this issue and it is clear that informal support was, and continues to be, largely a function of women members of the extended family (Moroney 1976; Wilkin 1979). Such support has been eroded by the changing requirement of the economic structure for a labour force which is both geographically mobile and able to expand through the increasing employment of married women. Furthermore, there have been changes in social expectations. We cannot deny that women are less prepared to adopt the role of unpaid helper nor that working-class families expect to receive a degree of support from the welfare state. Nor would we claim these to be anything but legitimate expectations.

Informal care remains an important source of care in the community (Bayley 1973; Moroney 1976; Sainsbury 1974) but it is not a cheap panacea for the problems of social care just waiting for the community-oriented social worker to come along. Indeed if existing levels of informal care are to be sustained we may have to improve our support to the informal carers, many of whom carry unreasonably heavy burdens (Nissel and Bonnerjea 1982).

In our own study areas we saw how family and neighbours were important sources of support for many elderly clients but we also saw how relatives were sometimes stretched to the limit by the exclusive responsibility for care. We cannot precisely gauge the preventive value of this support. The evidence of elderly clients (and the voluntary workers we interviewed in Selly Oak) suggested that forms of care in the community provided by family and friends would benefit from the recognition and support of the statutory services. One measure of the adaptability of social services departments is the extent to which they are able to recognize, maintain, and develop such networks of informal care.

REQUESTS PRESENTED TO THE DEPARTMENTS

Information collected about demands made upon the three area teams does show congruence with the broad indications of need we established.

Selly Oak had the highest referral bombardment rate and a higher level of long-term cases per 1000 population than Dereham, though the tendency in Aber to retain cases as administratively open distorts their long-term figure. As we anticipated, elderly referrals predominated in Aber and Dereham, with family and child care referrals accounting for less than a quarter of all demands (in Aber constituting only a marginally greater proportion than the younger physically handicapped). In contrast, over a third of all referrals in Selly Oak concerned families and children and examination of the long-term cases shows them to be of even greater significance. Families and children were also the subjects of the largest proportion of long-term cases in Dereham, which, despite the greater significance of long-term mental health work, showed a pattern similar to that in Selly Oak.

The pattern in Aber was significantly different. The elderly were the most prominent group even in long-term work; the younger physically handicapped figured more significantly than elsewhere; the mentally handicapped were an important subject of long-term work and families and children a much less significant group. Another way to look at these figures is to compare percentages of long-term work in our study subject to a statutory order – 14 per cent in Aber, 22 per cent in Dereham, and 32 per cent in Selly Oak.

We have a clear spectrum of demands from the heavily family and child care influenced urban pattern with its higher overall level of bombardment, through Dereham's intermediate position to the extreme rural pattern dominated by referrals of the elderly. These differences in the levels and nature of demand may substantially

Table 6(1)   *Referrals and cases in the study areas*

	Aber	Dereham	Selly Oak
referrals in study period	269	481	418[1]
per 1000 population	8.8	10.4	11.1
% families and children	17	23	35
elderly	60	58	45
mentally handicapped	2	5	2
mentally ill	7	7	9
younger physically handicapped	14	10	9
long-term cases open throughout study period	515[2]	255	269[1]
per 1000 population	16.8	5.5	7.1
% families and children	20	40	46
elderly	33	26	38
mentally handicapped	18	12	6
mentally ill	9	17	10
younger physically handicapped	20	6	15

[1] These totals include cases excluded from other tables because of lack of information.
[2] This figure is adjusted to exclude 'cases' from the blind and partially sighted register.

explain the different structures of long-term work. Before we examine the other influences determining what does make up long-term work it is important to examine how far the pattern of demand represented real differences in the needs of the three areas.

ENGAGING THE SOCIAL SERVICES DEPARTMENT

Once an individual has decided to seek external help for themselves or for someone else, the likelihood of contacting social services is dependent on their appreciation of what the department can provide and their ability to make direct contact. For formal agencies with defined responsibilities, such as those of the police and courts for statutory child care, when and how to refer cases to the social services department is clearly laid down. For the ordinary citizen and indeed workers in other social agencies, this is rarely a clear-cut procedure.

In this respect, we found considerable similarities between the three study areas: all the offices suffered from poor physical amenities; even in the urban area the office was physically remote for most potential clients; there were few outward signs of the existence of the departments in their areas, and few examples of advice desks and other extra public points of referral. We did not find uniform attitudes to adopting strategies oriented towards positively seeking out those in need. In Aber considerable misgivings were felt about the department's invisibility. The most obvious way of remedying this deficiency would have been through extending formal liaison with members of the health services but they were seen as resistant to such a move. Yet social workers felt other forms of out-reach to be the province of community work, a specialist role from which they sought to divorce themselves. In Selly Oak there was more keenness expressed about out-reach work amongst some, though the insistence of the department on accountability for individual cases was a considerable deterrent. Nonetheless not everyone rued the lack of direct contact with the community and when the opportunity for an advice desk in a health centre did arise, suspicions over the expectations of the health service threatened the project.

The Dereham team's concern about their own accessibility had led to widespread recognition of the need for at least a sub-office at Swaffham. This came to naught, however, and as with the other teams there were few positive attempts to reach out into the community – they dealt with what came to them. The adoption of this passive position was likely to distort the picture of need that referral patterns provide, and clearly all three areas were affected. All had low percentages of referral by office visit and this was particularly true amongst the elderly, a point reinforced in the client interviews by the sparse numbers who would visit the office, or indeed ask a friend or relative to do so, if they needed to contact their social worker.

Of course, not all referrals are made by potential clients or their families. Many come by way of other agencies and clearly if these have their ears to the ground they could compensate for the distortions created by problems of direct access. The picture given by social services staff was an uneven one. Echoing other work on the subject, Dereham social workers felt other agencies lacked a clear picture of what was appropriate to social services and, in consequence, sometimes appeared to be simply passing on those cases they did not know what to do with (Bowl 1978).

Staff in Selly Oak and Aber were similarly aware of being used at times as the department of last resort and were critical of the perceptions which many other agencies had of their role. In both areas many formal agencies made insignificant contributions to the pattern of referrals. In Selly Oak most referrals came from informal sources, though more often relatives than friends or neighbours.

In all three areas it was significant that the development of personal relationships was seen as the means through which organizational interrelationships could be improved. Only members of the Dereham team articulated a more general educative role about what social services departments are about as 'part and parcel' of the social worker's job.

Table 6(2) *Informal and formal referral sources in the study areas*

	Aber		Dereham		Selly Oak	
	referrals	*long-term cases*	*referrals*	*long-term cases*	*referrals*	*long-term cases*
% referred by						
self	16	9	16	11	36	15
all informal sources	45	25	33	23	54	28
health services	31	32	38	33	13	23
other SSD personnel	12	20	13	18	14	27
all formal sources	55	75	67	77	46	72

We have only examined two of the factors determining how far referral patterns reflect the needs of the communities which the departments serve. We can only speculate, for example, on how far low expectations of service response depress the referrals of mentally handicapped people to the Selly Oak team. What is clear is that the congruence between our expectations of referral patterns and those we found cannot be taken as an indication that the three departments had a comprehensive awareness of the needs of the localities they serve. The differential problems of access and the dependence of links with individuals within other agencies introduced such random elements into the generation of requests that this could not have been so.

A SET OF FILTERS

Given that the respective referral patterns may be an inadequate representation of community need, how did the departments respond to these? If we accept the pattern of long-term work illustrated by the categories of *Table 6(1)* as one crude indication, clear differences emerge. Only in the archetypically rural area of Aber did the pattern of long-term work broadly reflect the pattern of referrals. Even here the proportion of elderly people tailed off as one-off service requests were met and the number of mentally handicapped was swollen by an administrative anomaly which meant that dormant cases were not closed. In Selly Oak we found that families and children dominated the long-term work while mental health work was under-represented. Surprisingly, Dereham more closely resembled the 'urban' area, though without the squeezing of long-term mental health work. These patterns can partly be explained by examining how the processing of requests influenced who became the subject of longer term intervention by the department.

An earlier study of 'The Point of Entry' emphasized the potential importance of the receptionist as a filter of initial requests to a department and in particular the unintended consequences that could arise if this is not appreciated (Hall 1974).

Some social work teams have responded by adopting systems which entail the duty social workers performing the reception work themselves. In Dereham and Selly Oak there was a receptionist and a combination of the complexities of their duties and the poor physical environment in which reception took place led us to question how seriously the influence of reception as a filter was taken. In Selly Oak a second filter was operative in the decision as to whether the caller could be dealt with on the spot by the duty worker or should be referred on to the Selly Oak team. Many requests for specific services and many financial and housing problems were dealt with on the spot, in most cases by the provision of information and without direct reference to other agencies that might be involved. A clear majority of self-referrals and referrals by office visit thus failed to reach the more considered assessment contingent on allocation to the Selly Oak team, though there was considerable confidence expressed in the duty officer's ability to make appropriate decisions.

The situation in Aber contrasted sharply. There was no

receptionist and the duty officer both met the infrequent office callers and answered the telephone. There were problems inherent in the need to leave the reception area to deal with these calls but the low level of bombardment and infrequency of genuine crises meant that duty was generally regarded as unproblematic. The vast majority of enquiries became referrals which were passed through to the specialist teams and became the subject of a home visit within a week. The Dereham system was similar to that in Selly Oak, though a major concern was that perhaps too much was passed through for allocation, often with inadequate information on exactly why. One reason for this was the physical environment which contributed to making duty a chore. Further discretion took place in Dereham and Selly Oak through the medium of the team leaders who sometimes decided not to allocate cases put through from the duty system or retained them as open but unallocated cases.

The influence of these filters is uncertain. In Aber most referrals were allocated for investigation. In Selly Oak the distribution of cases for allocation into client groups matched the referral patterns closely and there was considerable satisfaction that the differing skills and levels of experience of the personnel involved produced no undue distortion in the operation of these filters. We remain less certain. What is clear is that these filters contributed to a process by which certain client groups were less likely to become the subject of long-term cases in Selly Oak and Dereham as *Table 6(1)* illustrated. *Table 6(2)* demonstrates that a similar fate befell self-referrals, and referrals from informal sources generally. Although social workers in all three areas claimed equal respect for a wide variety of referral sources, particular sources appeared to serve as legitimators of need and more often led to long-term cases. Clearly the presentation of requests in a particular way that fits the social workers' view of their own function was critical to negotiating the filters of reception, duty, and allocation. The different systems we have seen could in themselves be seen as forms of adaptations to local circumstances, though not to needs but to pressure. In Aber, bombardment rates were low enough to create the possibility of a full-scale assessment allowed by allocation of all referrals, whilst in other areas systems were adopted that filtered out potentially important areas of work. In Selly Oak some of this was the result of definite policy decisions – for example on DIISS and housing problems – but apart from this there was little evidence that

considered judgement of needs and priorities guided the operation
of these filters.

FURTHER INFLUENCES ON LONG-TERM SERVICE RESPONSE

Not only the number of cases surviving, but also the type and
depth of work undertaken with each client group, were affected by
two further discretionary influences, those of allocation and
supervision.

In Dereham allocation took place at weekly team meetings.
Social workers and assistants made bids for particular cases and the
team leader attempted to keep an overall balance of work-loads.
No formal specialisms existed but the matching of social worker
preferences to cases did lead to the development of informal
specialisms. Although one qualified worker specialized in work
with the elderly, there was a clear division of labour between
qualified social workers' focus on cases involving the mentally ill or
families and children and the unqualified social workers' almost
exclusive concern with the elderly and the mentally or physically
handicapped. A similar pattern was found in Selly Oak, with an
otherwise stricter division of labour between qualified and unqualified staff slightly confused by the presence of the mental health
specialist. Here allocation meetings had been replaced by
individual negotiation between team and worker, which workers
felt lost them the opportunity to gain an overview of the work the
area generated.

The two problems of lacking an overview of demand and the
relegation of certain categories of work to secondary status implicit
in the systems adopted in these two areas could be avoided in Aber.
There allocation within the specialist teams took place on a geographical basis. Hence there was the opportunity for workers to gain
an overview of need, at least within their specialisms, within the
geographical area they served and the existence of specialist teams
formally recognized the significance of work with the less glamorous client groups.

In Selly Oak there was little perception of supervision intruding
into the area of the workers' own professional judgement on individual cases. Supervision was largely appreciated both as a sounding
board and in order to establish the legitimacy of their interventions
in the eyes of the department. There was closer supervision and
more frequent consultation with the less experienced workers. The

social work assistants in particular became concerned when this level of support was temporarily unavailable due to the team leader's absence through illness. Less problematic still was the decision to close, often largely statutorily determined, though the mental health and blind specialists felt that their open-ended approach to case-work was at odds with administrative pressure to close 'welfare' cases.

In Dereham a similar situation pertained though the team leaders adopted a slightly more interventionist mode of supervision and expressed the hope that they knew at least the broad outline of what was happening in every case. The main reservation expressed was that in cases where the provision of practical services was central, there was the danger of a tendency to close the case once the services were available without adequately exploring other, often less tangible, areas of need.

A much more active role in individual case management was signalled by the formal case review system operated in Aber. Seniors also used the opportunities that arose for becoming more involved in individual cases on a day-to-day basis. This direct influence on the service provided to clients, greater where less experienced workers were involved, was largely taken for granted by members of the social work teams and there was no articulation of this as influencing the nature of provision in any particular direction.

We have seen how the different demand patterns of the three areas, themselves not clearly representative of needs, became subject to further differential filters within the departments that regulated the pressures on the social work teams. The effect in two areas to different degrees is to allocate client groups to qualified and unqualified staff differentially and to restrict certain categories from long-term work. Other writers have noted similar, though not always identical, hierarchies amongst client groups (Howe 1980; Rees 1978; Stevenson and Parsloe 1978). Almost invariably it is the elderly who are at the bottom of the pile.

PROVISION FOR ELDERLY PEOPLE

In our study, social work with elderly people was also effectively given low priority in response to high levels of bombardment and was often allocated to unqualified staff. Even in Aber however, where these two processes did not particularly disadvantage this client group, provision for the elderly took on a different form from that for other client groups. It was often characterized in all three areas as 'routine', 'unglamorous', or even 'casual'. Visiting frequencies were lower and the characterization by one social worker of elderly clients as 'the recipients of services not individuals' has considerable force.

Social work with the elderly indeed had a remarkable similarity in the three areas. It was dominated by the tackling of practical problems of self-care, finance, and housing, and by activity characterized largely as assessment, advice, and the provision of practical services. The reason why many long-term cases were still open was because the clients were still waiting for practical services, which, with the exception of aids in the rural areas and home helps in Aber and Selly Oak, were not often made available immediately.

The involvement of social work staff was thus typically to organize a package of services at points of crisis and then withdraw. There were other problems recognized. Loneliness was seen as important in a third of long-term cases, a little less so in Aber. In the rural areas family problems were present in many long-term cases, reflecting the greater proportion living with their families amongst the elderly people referred to the two rural departments. As a result there was some long-term supportive activity, particularly in Aber and Dereham.

It was rare however for cases to be seen as being significantly complicated by interpersonal and emotional factors. While social work commentators have pointed to the potential of case-work with old people, in terms of adjustment to bereavement, loss, and adaptation to change (e.g. Mortimer 1982; Rowlings 1981) there was little evidence to suggest that these needs were met by workers. Other research has suggested that meals on wheels clients often derive more from the acceptance of a meal as a symbolic gesture of caring from the community than they do from the nutrition or company they provide (Johnson, Di Gregorio, and Harrison 1982). There may be a parallel in the large degree of satisfaction with the services they received expressed by clients in our study.

Certainly examination of the detailed responses of the clients made it clear that many did not get the help *they* felt they needed. These clients and their families were hesitant to turn to the social services department or were unaware that social workers were equipped to deal with stress and life crises at an emotional or interpersonal level.

Why does this neglect of the less tangible needs of elderly people continue in the light of the growing concern expressed in the social work texts and the increased prominence given to work with the elderly on social work training courses? The interest of social workers, many of whom expressed a preference for working with children and families, must be an influence. Only one qualified worker in our study chose to specialize with the elderly and, even within Aber's specialist team, the younger physically handicapped were worked with more intensively and visited more frequently than the elderly. It would however be unfair to single out social workers for blame, particularly those who do commit themselves to elderly people. Organizational processes and career structures are just two other factors that constrain the full development of this aspect of social work.

Furthermore, the roots of this neglect lie in wider societal attitudes, examined from different perspectives with telling clarity elsewhere (Faulkner 1980; Puner 1978; Walker 1981), that create a generation praised by our words whilst damned by our deeds. These attitudes also go a long way to explaining why, despite comparatively high levels of expenditure, workers in all three study areas still identified inadequacies in both the range and capacity of practical resources available for this client group.

It is thus difficult to accept the existence of systems of community care for the elderly in the three areas; rather there were sets of discrete unco-ordinated practical services (Plank 1978). Provision was not considered as a whole but referred to in terms of the adequacy of individual services or even specific facilities – this home is good, that club is unstimulating, etc. The development of care that was adapted to local needs hence inevitably became difficult and was not aided in Birmingham by occasional arbitrary policy decisions that changed the conditions governing the provision of important resources like home helps and telephones.

This was matched at the level of the individual case by a lack of continuity and co-ordination in the provision of services. Social workers in Selly Oak, for example, were conscious of the rather administrative nature of assessment for Part III accommodation, and the absence of follow-up to see that the placement had been successful. In this area, too, some of the most vulnerable elderly clients were being monitored by the organizationally discrete home help service without social work support. Yet links between the two services were tenuous, something avoided in Dereham by the inclusion of home help organizers in the same team as the social workers. Despite such a formal link, there was also still concern in Aber about the clarity of the division of labour and lines of communication. Social workers might have considered the home help organizers to be monitoring vulnerable clients but doubts were expressed as to whether a clear understanding of this existed and whether they could expect a clear referral back for their intervention.

The picture was of a lack of flexibility or adaptability to the needs of elderly clients at both the level of the individual case and the area as a whole. It was exemplified by the low level of service provided in Aber to elderly people living with their families, despite the evidently higher levels of dependency of this group and stresses on family relationships exhibited in the rural areas. To a degree we have attributed this lack of adaptability to factors specific to the elderly client group and we must now examine the extent to which it is a characteristic of general social work practice in the three areas.

MORE SECOND-CLASS CLIENTS

The composite picture of social work with the younger physically handicapped in Selly Oak and Dereham, where they form a significant proportion of social work assistant case-loads, was of a secondary component of 'unqualified' social work. Like work with the elderly, it was dominated by practical problems and the provision of advice and practical services. In Selly Oak only the particular problems of transport differentiated the client groups significantly and in both these areas the level of social work involvement was reflected in the lowest visiting frequency of all client groups.

There was however an urban–rural difference here in that in the rural areas long-term work was different. A wider range of problems was tackled including working with problems of interpersonal relationships arising from the disability of a member of a family. There was in consequence a higher level of positive intervention with these clients and those caring for them, exemplified by emphasis on supporting, sustaining, information-giving, and, especially in Aber, work directed toward specific problem-solving.

Only in Aber, however, did the younger physically handicapped appear to receive a significantly different service from that for the

elderly. Here visiting frequencies with long-term cases were considerably higher than with the elderly cases and the more intensive
social work input was matched by a wider range of service provision. Considerably higher proportions of clients received financial
or material support, or holidays, or were found places in day care
or 'clubs'. Complacency about the adequacy of provision would
not however be justified. Transport was identified as a serious
problem. The team had no access to an occupational therapist and
geography made it extremely difficult to bring clients with specialist
needs together for group activities. There were no easy adaptive
responses available to the team to overcome these problems.

The influence of lower levels of demand pressure and the specialist team structure in Aber did appear to facilitate a more varied
and considered service to younger physically handicapped people.
Increased awareness does not, however, solve the problems of
severe shortages of specialist facilities for the physically handicapped, particularly the hard of hearing or visually handicapped,
nor those additional problems created by the broad geographical
dispersal of those with the specialist needs.

In all the study areas social work with the mentally handicapped
was characterized by the diversity and intensity of problems being
tackled. Personal and emotional problems and the more tangible
material problems intertwined and there was a concomitant diversity of social work activity and contacts with other agencies.

Although there was a wide range of services to match the
problems identified, the level of provision was not always satisfactory. For example, day care facilities to provide occupation or
rehabilitation (and relief for hard-pressed carers) were in short
supply. In Dereham the absence of a local adult training centre
meant long journeys. Social work activity here was also rationed,
with over 40 per cent of long-term cases receiving a visit less than
quarterly. A developing lobby amongst the families of mentally
handicapped people was beginning to voice criticism of the department's efforts.

In Selly Oak many of those mentally handicapped people on the
long-term case-load received frequent visits but, as was demonstrated earlier, they were not very likely to achieve that status.
Here, too, there were still pressures on resources such as accommodation and despite the existence of a specialist worker they were
not a group that featured prominently in departmental priorities.

The position of the mentally handicapped in the social work

pecking order can be partially explained by the lack of a statutory framework for intervention in these cases, compounded by the limited range of resources experienced in working with most groups. Even in Aber, where different administrative practices meant that nearly all cases were long-term, intervention was limited and here too 40 per cent of all cases were visited less often than three-monthly, hardly the frequency needed to provide real support, for example, to the hard-pressed mothers of mentally handicapped children (Wilkin 1979). Problems of geography and transport hampered the development of day care and group-work but the role of the social worker was constrained to that of a co-ordinator or gatekeeper by other factors. There was an absence of a co-ordinated multi-disciplinary approach that might, for example, see them working – together with health visitors and other professionals – in partnership with parents providing home-based education and skill development for mentally handicapped children (Revill and Blunden 1977). Similarly, even given the paucity of employment rehabilitation facilities outside of the adult training centre, social workers experienced confusion over their possible role in the whole area of mobilizing training and employment opportunities for the mentally handicapped.

The mentally ill, to an extent, also formed part of this intermediate grade of social work that fell between the elderly and families and children in the hierarchy we have identified. The pattern was not uniform over the three study areas and was dependent on a diverse range of social workers' activities rather than practical services.

This reflects the breadth of problems tackled. Family relationship problems, finance and accommodation, and loneliness were important complications to the central health and self-care problems of the client.

For Aber's mental health specialist team these were the more favoured client group, and this was reflected in a high level of client contact, as well as interaction with psychiatric services, GPs, the DHSS, and to a lesser extent, housing authorities. Individual casework predominated, though some development of group activity in the face of low levels of day care provision had been started. Despite this high level of activity, the team were concerned about problems of communication with the geographically remote psychiatric hospital and the division of labour between themselves and the rapidly developing community psychiatric nursing service.

Without the protection of a specialist team, social work with this group was inevitably less intense in Dereham. Group-work was less prevalent, though day care was not in such short supply, and levels of social work support generally less intensive. Nonetheless provision, largely by qualified workers, more closely equated with that for families and children than the other groups.

It was in Selly Oak that this group attracted a Cinderella status. Levels of social work support were lower and assessment of the priority of the case often excluded it from allocation without client contact. The specialist along with other social workers felt the low levels of activity identified simply reflected the low priority accorded to mental health work generally within the department. Not everything was negative. The specialist had developed group-work and a divisional day care resource was well used but she felt that needs were not adequately monitored. Even information on compulsory admissions was not considered comprehensive. In recognition of these problems a district mental health liaison officer had been appointed with a view to developing work in this area, and a mental health lobby in the department had grown more vociferous, but there was a considerable legacy of low levels of provision to overcome.

CORE SOCIAL WORK

For the qualified social workers in Selly Oak and Dereham intervention with families and children was the core of social work. In all the study teams it was in talking about this group that the interdependence of emotional and material problems was made most explicit, and particularly the influence of the employment problems of the three areas. The major problems tackled with new cases in the Selly Oak areas were child abuse and financial problems, with housing an important subsidiary problem. In the two rural areas child abuse was less often identified and problems of family relationships and child behaviour more frequently so. Whether this represents real differences in the prevalence of abuse in the three environments or greater organizational emphasis on the issue in Birmingham is difficult to assess. Nonetheless, given public concern about this area, it did contribute to pressures creating priority for child care work in relation to that with other client groups.

The long-term pattern was more uniform, with child abuse less clearly identified than family relationships and child behaviour as problems to be tackled, with problems of finance and housing still prominent in all three areas. Social work activity reflected the limited range of available practical services relevant to this client group. Assessment and information-giving were key activities with new cases. In the rural areas, there was more active intervention in providing support, and in Dereham, advocacy in dealing with resource distribution agencies. This latter difference was reflected in the visiting frequencies in the rural areas, which largely matched the intensive input given to long-term cases. This was rarely true in Selly Oak where much assessment work was of necessity restricted and levels of client contact low. Long-term work was again more uniform, characterized often as supervision, review, supporting, and sustaining. Personal problem-solving also appeared more frequently than with other client groups.

Our categories mask considerable variety in the work actually carried out which was largely individual case-work and as such, invisible. Though this group received the highest level of social work input, it was not easily measured. We can identify some further differences. Group-work was a limited activity in Dereham and Selly Oak, where a voluntary sector unit did provide some alternative, but it was totally absent in Aber. Practical services that were regularly used were mainly financial help in cash or kind and alternative placements for children. In the latter respect, the rural areas made less use of residential care and more of fostering placements.

Work with children and families involved a wide range of external contacts. In over half of long-term cases liaison with schools and the education department was identified. GPs were particularly important in Dereham: indeed few agencies were not a regular feature of the work. This reflected the social workers' identification of unfulfilled basic needs that lay in the domain of other agencies as fundamental to the social work problems presented, especially in the areas of employment, education, and income. Yet relationships with these agencies were highly individualized and 'social action' aimed, for example, at clarifying or even changing the policies of those agencies was not considered to be a legitimate social work activity. Similarly, work in the community itself was limited to service mobilization, a view with important implications for the role of social workers extending beyond work with children and families. Indeed it is to a broader view of practice that our analysis now turns.

There are many ways in which we have identified differences in the patterns of social work with the different client groups both within our study areas and between them. Pressure of demand, particularly in the urban area, worked to the disadvantage of particular client groups. The process of disadvantage was furthered by a division of labour which operated against the 'less glamorous' groups. Even in the low pressure area of Aber aspects of this process were evident in work with the elderly and mentally handicapped. It was exemplified by the neglect of the more tangible needs of the elderly and younger physically handicapped, particularly where practical services could readily be made available. This reflected a more general demand/response pattern of social work with all clients that operated within clearly defined boundaries. These were set by legislative demands, the existing structure of resources, and the methods of work with which workers felt comfortable. Consequently, much social services provision had an almost automatic quality. It reflected a lack of awareness of the structure of overall needs and circumstances of an area, let alone adaptability to them. It is within this pattern that the significant urban and rural differences were attributable to demand pressure or the impediments created by large geographical distances. In other senses urban and rural provision seemed remarkably similar. At the root of this is a remarkably consistent view of social work itself.

THE DOMINANCE OF CONVENTIONAL MODELS

The first point of congruence that we noted was the absence of explicit theoretical models in the way social workers described their practice. Rather they were guided not by intuition but by a common-sense framework based largely on their own individual experience of training and subsequent work with clients. Work was client-centred and focused on the interpreted needs of individuals, though heavily constrained by legal requirements and available resources.

Nonetheless the divide between theory and practice could be seen as more apparent than real. The absence of opportunities to develop group-work and community work meant most interventions were family based. Even the family was more often the locus than the focus of intervention and hence intervention became largely 'individual case-work'. It was clear too that although not articulating case-work principles as underpinning their work, concepts such as 'individualization', 'acceptance', and 'self-determination' were central to the approach of social workers. Several of them also expressed the view that they felt more secure working in this way. It was the form of intervention for which training best prepared them, in which they were most experienced and towards which the procedures of the organization were geared.

Given the growth of support for 'unitary' or 'integrated' models of social work practice (Goldstein 1973; Pincus and Minahan 1973; Specht and Vickery 1977) a first reaction might be surprise at the degree to which practice was dominated by case-work. There was little group-work, few examples of team working, no systematic monitoring of the needs or resources of particular areas, and a circumspect attitude to the stimulation and support of informal caring networks. Yet at an abstract level, workers in all three teams did recognize the influence of wider social forces on the problems with which they had to deal and how they affected different communities differentially. There are a number of levels of explanation for this discrepancy.

All three teams recognized differences in the characters of the area they served. For example, in Dereham particular reference was made to the different demands created in communities dominated by recent in-migrants often without local sources of informal support. Similarly the definite differences in the distribution of client groups between the sub-areas of Selly Oak were noticed by the Selly Oak team. Yet there was little evidence of the use of skills of data collection and analysis other than at the individual level and hence no identification of the strengths and resources of particular locations in a systematic way. In Aber, where work was allocated geographically, there was not even monitoring of referrals on a geographical basis.

One approach to developing this level of intimacy with the locality has been the development of 'patch' working, where areas of 5,000–10,000 population are served by a specific patch worker or groups of workers (Hadley and McGrath 1980a, 1980b). This would, however, clash with the informal specialization favoured by Dereham's social workers; it was considered apprehensively by social work assistants in Selly Oak who saw it as a threat to their autonomy; and the evidence of the geographical allocation of work in Aber is that it is not a panacea if unaccompanied by changes in other attitudes to practice. In particular it implies the development of advocacy and social action roles in working with local people in influencing the area policies often operated by other welfare state agencies that shape their needs. Not all social workers saw this as legitimately part of their role, particularly in Aber, but nearly all considered it impossible given the current pressures from casework.

True patch work would also imply a different relationship to informal networks. This would imply providing 'replacement', 'reinforcement', and 'relief' to existing informal networks (Wolfenden 1978) and working to link those in need with potential resources. This sort of networking might be particularly useful in developing the sort of mutual support already identified as desirable amongst, for example, the elderly and parents of mentally handicapped children. To work in comprehensive partnership with the community however implies something further. It calls for a change in the nature of a team's relationship to its locality so that both clients and the wider community have more direct influence over what needs are to be met and how to meet them. It is evidence of one of the major contradictions in social work that, despite articulating a desire for the truer picture of community need that this would allow, social work staff were very wary of developing their work in this way.

Whilst patch work was considered a 'good thing', Dereham staff tended to think in terms of 'using volunteers'. Aber workers too, in seeing their role very much in terms of bringing people to services or vice versa, did not see stimulating and developing informal networks as part of their role. There was a fear of 'tampering' with something outside of their sphere of control. In Selly Oak lack of both authority and time were cited as deterrents.

We have seen how the division of labour between qualified and unqualified workers, which went largely unchallenged by the workers themselves, did disadvantage certain client groups. Yet within an 'integrated' approach or 'patch' system, there could be advantages to an alternative division of labour based on task, allowing different workers to develop specialist skills. This would require a team approach. That many workers prefer individual allocation and individualized practice is compounded by the absence of regular opportunities not only to share work but to discuss together the development of particular expertise. There was also little communication, except in Dereham, between social workers and the home helps working on their areas.

A final point of similarity to note was the extent to which workers assented to the pecking order that exists between client groups. This was not helped by the uncertainty expressed by generically trained workers over their role with mentally ill and handicapped clients. Yet the forms of specialization favoured in our study areas did little to redress the balance in favour of mental health work and in Aber the elderly and mentally handicapped were disadvantaged even within specialist teams.

We have now described a picture of social services departments being only minimally adaptive to the needs or characteristics of the areas they serve. Central to this has been a style of social work that is rarely conducive to the development of adaptive and imaginative responses. We have in part attributed this to the experience, training, and preferences of the individual social workers. It would be negligent of us to allow this to be interpreted as necessarily a criticism of their effectiveness at the work they actually do, which we have not set out to gauge, or their will to adopt different, more creative approaches. We tackle the problems of how it might be possible for social work teams to develop such approaches in our concluding chapter. First we consider more explicitly the influence of organizational structures on the nature of social services provision and social work itself.

7

Practice and the organizational context

FRAMEWORK FOR ANALYSIS

Introduction

In describing the processes that govern social work activity and service delivery, previous chapters have provided glimpses of the many influences on that practice. We now consider how far organizational factors shaped the ways in which workers operated. Comparative analysis is not made easy by the absence of clearly defined and empirically tested classifications of organizational structures in social services departments. Neither the general organization theory literature nor the more immediately relevant theoretical models (Billis et al. 1981; Rowbottom, Hey, and Billis 1974) provide such a template.

The most appropriate source of an organizational framework for this analysis remains the Seebohm Report (1968). Though some doubts remain about whether the spirit of Seebohm's thinking was actually implemented it has been the nearest to a blueprint we have for the organization of social services departments. In this chapter we first attempt to identify the organizational pre-requisites for the effective provision of personal social services that Seebohm defined. We then test the findings of our case studies against these and discuss the extent to which they proved influential, over a decade after Seebohm's publication, in shaping the service that was provided.

Organizational cornerstones of Seebohm

Clear patterns of communication and the operation of delegated authority through area teams were seen as essential to the discharge of responsibilities in the new departments:

'The social services department can only work effectively through area teams, drawing support from the communities they serve, with a substantial measure of delegated authority to take decisions, and able to call on the more specialized resources, advice and support of the departmental headquarters when the need arises. The effective exercise of delegated authority necessarily implies that the headquarters should produce statements of guidance on general policy.'

(para. 594)

The position of area teams is therefore pivotal, but do they have enough autonomy and what degree or type of administrative and managerial centralization is required to enable them successfully to discharge their duties? Hence we are concerned with workers' vertical relationships with professional, administrative, and management colleagues and the extent to which these power relations shape activities with clients and community.

Seebohm also stressed the importance of making services accessible to the public, so reducing ambiguity about where responsibility for providing assistance lies. Given that social services have limited resources this inevitably raises questions about how far they can be involved with early identification of need and to what extent services can be distributed equitably between geographical areas and different social groups. This, as we shall see, is very much tied up with wider matters concerning the planning of services. The effects of these factors on field-work practice therefore require careful consideration.

Opportunities for the development of new specialisms were perceived by Seebohm in the emergence of integrated departments, yet the need for greater citizen and community participation was also recognized. Views of practice which take on board enhanced participation hardly fit well with the decision-making discretion synonymous with specialist models where workers are assumed to be privy to bodies of knowledge, skill, and expertise not possessed by others. Many ideas about specialization have parallels in professions such as medicine and law where more rigid distinctions and status differences between clients and professionals have been traditionally recognized or accepted. Seebohm's participative model is not only about local democracy but also the exposure of defects in services, mobilization of new resources, early identification of need, and development of preventive work. It was also seen as a means to reduce rigid distinctions between givers and takers of services and the stigma which being a client has often involved in the past (cf. paras 491–92).

Whether the inevitable tensions between community participation and professional or bureaucratic authority compromises effective action may be a moot point. We were concerned therefore to examine how the different patterns of labour division and specialist orientation in the study teams reflected a commitment by their employing agencies to either or both of the models identified by Seebohm and to assess what impact this had on practice.

On the question of functional responsibility and comprehensive service delivery the report laid great stress on co-ordination:

'The staff of the social services department will need to see themselves not as a self-contained unit but as part of a network of services in the community. Thus effective co-ordination with other services and individuals and the mobilization of community resources, especially volunteers, to meet need are as important aspects of the administration of the social services department – and demand as much skill – as its internal management.'

(para. 478)

Co-ordination is about relationships between staff within and outside the agency. We have seen how many other professional groups and statutory bodies filter and receive referrals and provide complementary services. There are many aspects of the relationships between these groups and social services departments, such as perceptions of status differentials and professional responsibilities, that may be important in determining social workers' tasks. Similarly, the post-1974 departments are organizations of considerable scale with most employing thousands rather than hundreds of persons. The machinery for co-ordinating the activities of field-workers and other service delivery arms of departments may therefore be important in shaping what those field-workers can do. Even within teams there are workers of different types and with different skills so there exists scope for joint and complementary action. Hence, whether teams operate as teams or as collections of individuals may simply reflect the presence or absence of formal co-ordinating machinery or of effective informal liaison. All these facets of internal co-ordination clearly have implications for the delimiting of social work tasks and roles.

To recapitulate we can conceptualize social services organization under four overlapping headings:

1 administrative centralization;
2 distribution of services;
3 professional role;
4 intra- and inter-agency co-ordination.

The first and last of these concern the interface between the teams, their employing organizations, and other agencies. For example, teams may be subject to varied policy and practice directives from the administrative centre or equally to the vagaries of policy change in other agencies. It is probable that the character of power relations between teams and these surrounding bodies tells us a great deal about what residual influence teams themselves can exert on practice. The other two factors might be considered as more controlled by the teams themselves and thus more closely resemble their own internal goals.

Parallels to this framework can be seen in the work of Gilbert and Specht (1974) in the USA. They note that each of these elements has the potential to strain against the others. For example it may be possible to reduce inaccessibility by developing widespread community 'out-reach' strategies but only at some risk of increasing problems of co-ordination and accountability. Thus in our discussion it is important to remember the same interaction between the elements of analysis.

THE TEAMS COMPARED

Administrative centralization

Though popularly conceived as types of bureaucratic organization where formal authority, backed by well-defined rules and procedures, is vested higher up the managerial hierarchy, social services departments appear to have more in common with matrix organizations (Knight 1976). In these organizations the normal vertical hierarchy is overlayed by lateral authority, in this case professional discretion, which gives workers necessary decision-making authority. Whilst the literature suggests matrix organization is appropriate in managing situations of uncertainty or rapid change, typical in the personal social services, Smith

(1965) reminds us that where executive decision-making is decentralized to workers in front-line units uncertainties and conflicts may arise from imbalances between professional and bureaucratic authority. Moreover, whilst social workers have a considerable measure of professional autonomy, they are at the very periphery of their employing organizations and distant from the source of bureaucratic power. How does this influence workers' visions of practice?

Overall policy and budgetary control were determined by headquarters rather than at area team level. Even the internal organizational structure of the teams was very largely determined by headquarters. In Aber this reflected senior management's desire to impose county-wide uniformity following the 1974 amalgamation of three former authorities and this in itself was seen as an example of management's unwillingness to let teams adapt their pattern of work, and underlying organization, to local conditions.

Nevertheless mechanisms had been developed to encourage participation in policy creation and decision-making in all the teams. In Aber this hinged around the pivotal role of the area officer who took advice and opinion from his own team meetings whilst acting as spokesman for the team at management group meetings. In Dereham a monthly dialogue took place between a representative of the senior management group and the area officer both to explicate and clarify policy intentions and to give headquarters an idea of the temperature of feeling in the area. Finally in Selly Oak, where representation and team involvement was perhaps less obvious, the team leader acted as team spokesman at area management meetings which were seen as the real locus of power. Workers in Selly Oak seemed the most openly critical of the vertical command structure and they had been in open conflict with central management over the vetoing of the idea of having team observers attend area management meetings.

Each team talked about the infrequent and spasmodic nature of their contacts with headquarters staff. Physical distance between the area teams and headquarters appeared to make little difference either to the quantity or quality of these contacts. While in Aber some 45 miles separated headquarters from the team, in Dereham divisional staff shared the same building as the area team but even this proximity made little impact on the smoothing of liaison between management and teams. In essence our study highlighted the existence of a psychological gulf between area teams and headquarters, identified before as a widespread phenomenon in UK social services departments (Parsloe 1981). However we can provide some elaboration about the nature of this gulf.

Practitioners considered they had a more intimate knowledge of the areas served, and their needs and resources, than did management, yet felt uninvolved in forward plans and policies. Furthermore forms of innovation which went beyond the individual case level generally had to be sanctioned by headquarters. This left the teams feeling that management lacked confidence in them and they accepted with some reluctance and scepticism that innovation was in reality someone else's job.

Occasionally they received directives appearing to threaten professional freedom out of the blue from headquarters. Sometimes this could be attributed to poor communication about the reasons behind policy changes, but workers also felt themselves to be increasingly rule-bound. For example the fact that it is the local authority rather than the professional worker who assumes parental rights when a child comes into care justifies a level of clear accountability. Nonetheless, emphasis by management on close adherence to social policing duties with the attendant red tape resulted in social workers undertaking various tasks to cover themselves as much as their clients.

We also sometimes saw the 'involvement' of senior management personnel in case-work decisions. Although hierarchical intervention in Aber was often validated on the basis that 'county' resources were implicated such tampering tended to be viewed as a breach of a social worker's professional discretion. In Dereham we saw that the imposition of a new system of stand-by duty caused some consternation although the team responded by developing their own system. To sum up, there were aspects of the delegation of responsibility to the areas from their respective managements which were not as clear cut as first appeared.

The perceived threat to local discretion was compounded for the two rural teams who had already lost power and control, even identity, since the 1974 amalgamation into the geographically larger county councils. They had particularly strong feelings about the need to assume control over their own budgets. In Dereham it was mentioned that the allocation of fixed sums to particular budget heads cramped flexibility and diluted the desire for responsive and innovative action. Similar sentiments prevailed in

Aber. Perceived inconsistencies in the way financial authority and responsibility were delegated also aroused intense feelings in all teams. We saw how on the one hand home help organizers were at least able to deploy their budgets with a high degree of autonomy but social work use of section 1 monies was generally tied up with considerable red tape. Thus the very design of management systems fuelled avoidable petty jealousies between different sections of the agency. The formal regulation of financial discretion was then as much an issue as that concerning the degree to which decision-making was centralized.

Symbolic of the absence of more complete systems of delegated authority was the prescribed role of the area officer, or in Selly Oak, the team leader. Each sat uncomfortably at the interface between their own teams and central management. It was possible to detect in them a dissonance about the exercise of authority. An outward indicator that their control over the organization and deployment of teams was far less than complete was seen in the appellations of area 'officer' rather than area 'director'. Their supervisory position presented them with the classic dilemma of having to rationalize loyalties to departmental management as well as to their own teams. More serious for practice was the fact that the attendant uncertainties sometimes left workers pondering whether these immediate bosses were agents of management or full members of their team.

Such alienating consequences have been noted time and again in the literature on organizations. In one comparative study of social work in the USA it was found that an ability of leadership to provide support and structure was the chief factor discriminating workers with high and low job satisfaction (Armstrong 1977). Other commentators have suggested how vertical command and control may affect worker–client relationships, either through reinforcing authority and directiveness or in producing split values and frustration (Brenton 1978; Glastonbury, Cooper, and Hawkins 1980). Workers in all the study teams quite frequently pointed the finger at respective managements as the source of much frustration in what was already a taxing job but we suspect that there was an element of scapegoating in this. For example we were to witness some 'legitimate' misuse of power in the teams to keep unwarranted changes, instigated by managements, at bay.

Mechanic (1968) has argued that the exercise of power in organizations can be threatened or diluted by controlling access to

204 Social work in context

information, even by those who operate at the base or periphery of the structure. During the course of our case review exercise we became aware that the state of case records and files was highly variable between the teams. The client information system in Dereham made routine internal monitoring the norm and it was generally accepted as a legitimate channel to keep management informed. By contrast lack of a routinized procedure in Aber was a contributory factor forcing management to devise a case-load management system to systematize review procedures and tighten control from the administrative centre. Paradoxically this was the reverse of what workers wanted for it was read as yet another attempt to erode professional autonomy. Before long we were to witness cynical comments from workers about their intentions to undermine the new system. It had after all been invented elsewhere and was not seen as a gesture aimed at helping front-line workers to be more self-managing.

Clearly much centre–periphery communication rests on front-line supervision and this took place within the areas and was not controlled from outside. Discussions with seniors suggested that ensuing implementation of headquarters policy was only one small part of their role. Also, except at the crudest level, senior social workers and area officers had no aggregate overview of case profiles, area needs, or resource shortfalls. Hence the actual tools or technology required for effective monitoring by the agency were not available, so in a circular way the teams were contributing to the inability of their employing agencies to monitor policy implementation and, paradoxically, to perpetuation of inequities in resource deployment.

Our analysis suggests that agencies have not yet come to grips with balancing professional and bureaucratic authority in ways that will be liberating and satisfying for front-line workers yet effective in terms of administrative performance.

Deployment of services

What factors determining resource distribution limit and shape the work of practitioners? First we must remember that many of the resources which are a social worker's stock in trade – day centres, residential care facilities, hostels, community centres, and so forth – are inherited from historical planning decisions. Hence community resources were not always in the right place or necessarily of the right mix. Also capital programmes were frequently tied to broader local authority plans, often structure plans, of which social workers were virtually unaware. Hence teams were generally not tuned in to ways in which their employers had chosen to tackle economic and social problems on a broader front. This planning was carried out by senior management or in other local authority departments. The separation of resource-planning from practice had several consequences.

First, social workers felt powerless to do much about the siting of their team bases or other facilities since there were other parties with vested interests. For example, decisions about siting of services required interventions from planning, legal services, treasurers, and possibly highways departments so service redeployment was regarded as a major undertaking largely beyond area team control. Second, this separation of function led to a conceptualization of planning which was often of the bricks and mortar type. The teams tended to measure unmet needs in terms of shortfalls in the volume of formal services so the idea of 'comprehensive' family services mooted by Seebohm became reinterpreted as 'comprehensive' statutory services. Measuring deprivation by statutory service shortfalls is misleading and conceptually narrow since it tends to overlook the culture context in which informal care takes place whilst also de-emphasizing the possibilities for collaborative action with informal carers. Indeed there is a growing body of research pointing to the burdens and obligations on family and other informal care-givers which often go unrecognized by statutory bodies (Equal Opportunities Commission 1980; Nissel and Bonnerjea 1982), yet there are indications that this informal care is a vital means by which groups like the elderly are able to adapt to the challenges of daily living (Wenger 1982). Third, we are not convinced that managements were using to best advantage all the intelligence information which teams potentially had at their fingertips about needs and resources. Extracting this data is itself a vexed technical question but the prevailing separation of planning from operational activity did nothing to make it easier. It all but obliterated possibilities for 'bottom-up' designed planning systems.

The whole of the preceding chapter could be considered a catalogue of how teams had failed to adapt fully to 'local' conditions and we saw how this partly explained the prevailing uniformity of social work practice. To this we must add that management's understandable concern for conformity in targeting for minimum standards of provision, equitable distribution of resources, and forms of manpower deployment all exerted powerful influences here. Chapter 2 reported how the teams and their agencies had at their disposal varying mixes and levels of formal resources. Given the readiness of the teams to conceptualize interventions in terms of available services it was therefore to be expected that resources mobilized on behalf of clients largely reflected the prevailing patterns of social services expenditure. This, for example, could be clearly seen in terms of the low levels of community provision for the mentally ill in all the study areas. Ultimately, expenditure levels are tied up with questions to do with the complexion of local political control and the priorities that councils place on social services as against other services. Though we did not attempt to make any study of relationships between the teams and council members our impressions were that contacts were informal, *ad hoc*, and, for the most part, spasmodic. Workers were not therefore in a good position to lobby for more resources. Councillors who effectively made the decisions about resourcing were in this sense remote from the teams.

Nevertheless, the 1970s saw a high priority placed on raising levels of social services provision in response to exhortations from successive governments. Hence the whole system was engaged in building up a minimum stock of statutory service provision, thus laying the foundations for a hoped-for accessible service. This thrust seems to have permeated the very heart of social work for practice ideology in the teams seemed rarely to take account of wider conceptions of welfare pluralism (Webb 1981) which sought to draw balances between contributions from the statutory, voluntary, and informal care sectors. This matter is strongly connected to conceptions of professional role which is the next subject for consideration.

Professional role

We can confirm the challenge and job satisfaction which workers derived from the discretion allowed in their activities with clients. This has been noted before (Stevenson and Parsloe 1978). This activity was highly privatized, extending only rarely beyond the individual client or family, and in this limited sense all workers could be considered specialists. How far, however, was the absence of, for example, group or community work endemic in social workers' predispositions when considered against the pervading organizational determinism described so far?

Team members felt ambivalence, if not misgiving about viewing community work or 'social action' as an integrated part of team social work. Furthermore only one of those who had undergone professional training felt equipped to assume such a role. Nonetheless there existed other factors affecting the scope for community work.

In the two rural teams there was uncertainty about the philosophical basis for rural community work since theoretical underpinnings had traditionally been associated with notions about urban deprivation. In short there was ambiguity about whether 'rural' as opposed to 'urban' community work actually existed, never mind what its place in the priority of things should be.

In Aber there was a community worker, financed through urban aid, working in a northern town. Management however viewed this as an experiment which was not to be tampered with by the social work team. Writers have suggested that community workers fear their roles may be colonized by social workers (Thomas and Warburton 1977), especially with the growth of interest in integrated social work methods (Specht and Vickery 1977), but thoughts of colonization were furthest from the minds of Aber workers.

Williams (1979) has suggested that voluntary service or rural community councils have a vital part to play in the launching of community initiatives but their relationships with the study teams were very tenuous. In Aber the rural council was perceived largely as a white elephant given its perceived preoccupation with conservation issues and environmental improvement rather than with social or community need. Consequently there was little motivation for collaborative action. The Dereham team had no rural community council with which to collaborate and in Selly Oak the voluntary services council in the city was viewed as so physically and psychologically remote that the idea of joint action rarely entered people's consciousness.

Thus, besides feelings in workers about the dubious nature of the community work model and their own lack of competence or skill there were barriers presented both by management and by the absence of collaborating agencies. The case studies bore testimony to the ability of workers to recognize distinctive structural problems in their areas as well as to their own powerlessness to deal directly with them. This disjunction remains a pressing problem for all who are concerned about community need.

Social workers did not only reject as legitimate a community work role and fail to collaborate with voluntary agencies but they were also disinclined to build working partnerships with either volunteers or informal carers. Yet Seebohm's concept of a community-based agency was one founded on informal networks: 'The notion of a community implies the existence of a network of reciprocal relationships which, among other things, ensure mutual aid and give those who experience it a sense of well-being' (para. 476).

The risks and balances in social work deployment of volunteers have been reported elsewhere (Holme and Maizels 1978) but this reluctance to engage the community raised complex questions about the permeable boundaries of social work. Lying very much at the heart of this was the issue of accountability to the agency. All three teams were constantly reminded about their overriding responsibility to the agency. The associated paper-work, review procedures, and supervisory checks re-emphasized this whilst occasional memoranda from management underlined the need for workers to be discrete in their dealings and at all costs preserve client confidentiality. Against this background it is easier to understand the prevailing conservatism in social work and a reluctance to integrate non-professionals or even third parties acquainted with clients into case-work relationships. However, it was not just as simple as that.

Like successive governments, the respective managements exhorted the social work teams to develop links with the community, but there were few indicators about how this end should be achieved without turning accountability, traditionally defined, on its head. Agency policies on this subject were therefore regarded as incomplete or confused.

A growing body of writers have proposed acceptance of Seebohm's second practice model which puts a higher value on client and community participation in case management and service delivery, arguing that this would give greater prominence to consumer rather than agency sovereignty (Froland *et al.* 1981; Gottlieb 1981; Hadley and Hatch 1981; Molnar and Purdhit 1977). With statutory work or activity with a high risk element, workers felt secure with a traditional system of accountability and it is difficult and probably undesirable to see the concept of agency accountability being removed. Indeed state legislation played a strong hand in defining social needs for social workers and prescribed that certain tasks and functions were carried out as we saw in the last chapter. This was a significant element legitimating the idea of a worker's primary accountability to the agency. On the other hand none of the agencies made it clear how far workers could go in experimenting with alternative accountability frameworks in an endeavour to engage untapped community resources or to give clients more self-determination or greater choice over needed support packages. Hesitancy can be understood if such alternatives are seen as no more than an easy way of shifting problems to the community or volunteers. Concepts of accountability to consumers or more directly to the community still require further definition and it is hoped that this will emerge from continuing experimentation in the field. This matter is taken up in the final chapter. In the meantime our results lend support to the work of Froland and others who found that agencies giving greater emphasis to bureaucratic procedures, professional norms, and formal authority in service delivery are less likely to develop participatory roles with the community that emphasize mutual decision-making and shared responsibility.

Experimental initiatives which play around with differing concepts of accountability are only just beginning to produce their substantive findings. In one model where social workers are learning to apply opportunity cost principles to their decision-making frameworks, coupled with substantial delegated authority to maintain self-managing budgets, cost-effective and customized support packages are beginning to emerge (Challis and Davies 1980). In the patch experiments it is claimed that greater emphasis on client involvement in decision-making is a key factor facilitating flexible community-oriented social work (Hadley and McGrath 1981). It seems from these preliminary findings that it may be possible to reconcile accountability to both the community and the agency.

We reported earlier that workers in all the teams had sympathy with the idea of being more self-managing in terms of their budgets and resource deployment. They were less sure about 'going local' to the extent of both living and working on the patch, which raised problems associated with the visibility of professional roles and with the management of workers' personal and professional lives. Some American practitioners appear already to have discussed the pros and cons of rationalizing these conflicting elements and management of the problem does not appear to be completely hopeless (Fenby 1978). This underlying reluctance amongst workers to develop more intimate links with the patch seemed linked to their acceptance of a service delivery model dictated by referral demand. With one or two exceptions they were not predisposed to a more active case-finding approach. Their central bases in any case militated against this. Hence the idea that the teams could engage in preventive work, arising from early identification of need, was a non-starter. The entire service delivery system did not operate that way and as if to illustrate the point one team was occasionally reminded not to generate undue demand for fear that agency resources would be overwhelmed. The notion that earlier identification of need and preventive work might make agency responses easier or less costly appeared not to have been taken on board, either by the teams or by their managements.

Within this framework it is easier to understand how the formal and more informal approaches to professional specialization by client group espoused by the teams were inextricably linked to a selectivist, resource-rationing, and reactive paradigm favoured by their agencies. At the beginning of this discussion we mentioned that workers derived job satisfaction from professional autonomy as mirrored in their privatized work. This enabled workers to escape the undoubted stresses associated with the formal rules and regulations of their centralized administrations as others have already surmised (Satyamurti 1979). It militated against the development of what might be termed resource creation activity in relation to informal carers, volunteers, and voluntary bodies and it also severely affected the flexibility and diversity of response to presenting client needs. The variants of genericism and specialism reflected by the teams seemed minor adaptations aimed at securing some minimum level of job satisfaction for workers rather than as attempts to deal more directly with these wider issues.

Co-ordination

The ability of social workers to meet client need depends on effective co-ordination at an intra-and inter-agency level. Co-ordination should not be viewed however as an end in itself and here we try to examine those aspects that lead to a better quality service to clients and community.

Intra-agency co-ordination has connotations of teamwork but how was this expressed and what impact did it have on practice?

Co-ordination within teams was typified by interactions between supervising senior social workers and social workers. What brought them together most frequently was case allocation and case review. These activities were unquestioned and considered a vital part of social work. Though frequently a private affair between senior social workers and field-workers group allocation meetings were also evident as we saw in Dereham.

Webb and Hobdell (1980) have suggested that the language of teams is often used prescriptively but without regard for what it is that teamwork is supposed to achieve. They argue that two related purposes can be identified: to overcome the disadvantages of specialization by increasing co-ordination, and to exploit the advantages of a division of labour by facilitating specialization. Despite contrasts between the forms of specialization and division of labour in the Aber, Dereham, and Selly Oak teams we noted no obvious differences in emphasis given to promotion of co-ordinated activity. Case allocation and review aside, we seemed to be dealing with three separate teams of individualists rather than mutually interdependent specialists. Webb and Hobdell use a sporting analogy in differentiating these models, the co-equal individualists resembling a tennis team and the division of labour team that of a football or cricket team. The study teams conformed to neither of these types for each member was mostly using his or her own set of common-sense rules. The overriding degree of privatization in activity coupled with an emphasis on one-to-one working relationships with clients has already been the subject of comment but it escapes description by means of a sporting analogy!

Cases involving more than one social worker were rare. In Aber and Dereham senior social workers were able to invest much of their time supervising and counselling workers. Occasionally this resulted in visits to clients to offer second opinions and this may have obviated the need for other workers to be involved. In Selly Oak the team leader took on a substantial case-load of his own to relieve pressure on his colleagues but individual case-work was the *sine qua non* of activity, apparently the result of an active selection of priorities. Shared working was only exceptionally pursued. To what extent the absence of teamwork hindered development of group and community methodologies we cannot be entirely sure but our observations suggest it to be a contributory factor.

Others have advanced the opinion that training does not equip social workers particularly well to work in teams (Parsloe 1981). In trying to pin down obstacles to team approaches Briggs (1980) has suggested that 'an atmosphere of openness, adventure, trust, support, and a tolerance for ambiguity, must be present to enable persons to risk new behaviour'. In our earlier discussion about administrative centralization it was evident that workers in all the teams had reservations about these conditions being present.

Briggs (1980) offers another perspective on this issue by suggesting that status comes to those practitioners who could work independently. The social work profession's arguments about promoting levels of working are certainly couched in these terms and in the teams there were evident signs that most practitioners guarded their own roles and functions with a hint of jealousy. For example, status divisions between qualified and unqualified workers, or formal divisions of labour by client group tended to make workers anxious to protect and conserve their position. Any proposals for teamwork could be seen as eroding autonomy. In short each agency was as if engaged in rewarding certain kinds of behaviour and independent practice, thereby providing role models to be emulated. At the same time much social work, especially that with the elderly and handicapped, appeared to have been routinized to the extent that it was possible for workers to function without having to rely on each other. Home helps and their organizers, occupational therapists, voluntary visitors, and social workers rarely consulted with each other over particular cases.

This did not necessarily result in the most flexible and best-tailored responses to presenting needs. In the management of non-routine situations of uncertainty senior social workers were always available for consultation and advice but formal collaborative action between field-workers was still rare. Informal, interpersonal relations between peers in all the teams were generally positive and there is no doubt that this provided individuals with a source of expressive support necessary to sustain them in their privatized roles. The senior social worker's role was often a vital 'ingredient' in keeping such interpersonal relations buoyant and free from unnecessary rivalry and dispute. However the seniors too were rarely directive in creating opportunities for joint methods of work between practitioners.

If intra-agency teamwork was not viewed as a priority then inter-agency co-ordination was seen as highly desirable but annoyingly elusive. Activity in this field raised the inevitable question of status differentials between different professionals, especially those in the health and social services. Though, individually, social workers had been working hard to establish forms of liaison with primary health teams the occasional blunt rejecting response was often sufficient either to undermine confidence in teamwork or to invoke sceptical attitudes.

Sometimes too the seemingly all-powerful medical consultants and those independent contractors, general practitioners, manipulated the service delivery system on behalf of 'their' patients, often without due consultation or proper negotiation with the social work teams. On a corporate level workers reckoned that there was little they could do on their own to promote organizational flexibility on the part of other agencies or a softening of attitudes towards social services from other professionals. This was seen as part of management's job but confusion about which party should be taking the initiative deflected energetic corporate action.

Returning to the sporting analogy Dingwall (1980) reminds us that with their strong sense of individual responsibility doctors belong to the football team where they occupy the positions of captain, manager, and coach. Our own data suggest that social workers occasionally get a touch of the football when it is kicked to them, but for most of the time they are playing a different game on the touch-line. Such incompatabilities and imbalances reflected the reality of practice as we perceived it. As Dingwall suggests, these factors constitute significant barriers to organizational change which might promote inter-professional teamwork.

Most inter-agency contact was referral activity rather than collaborative action. On the other hand redirection of clients to resource distribution agencies like housing departments or the DHSS was often all that was required so it would be wrong to stretch the notion of collaboration too far. Nevertheless, real barriers still existed. As Sainsbury (1981) has tellingly commented in this connection, 'it is easier to refer a situation than to share it'. To share can mean to make complex, to lose control of responsibility, or to take risks. This applies to social workers' dealings with voluntary bodies or informal carers as well as with other formal agencies. From our less than systematic contacts with voluntary bodies in the areas we gained the impression that independence and self-determination were greatly valued so the idea that many are just ready and waiting to engage in partnership experiments may have to be questioned.

There were success stories in partnerships with voluntary agencies. The Selly Oak team was working with voluntary bodies in the child care field and this was accepted as greatly expanding the range of work possible. The WRVS and other agencies also frequently figured in discussions about inter-agency work. Sometimes, however, voluntary bodies were conspicuous by their absence. In Aber, for example, workers were very much aware of their monopoly position in the provision of social services and the team was not under the magnifying glass of pressure groups or competing voluntary social work agencies. We can only conjecture from our data whether purposive duplication, coined by Webb (1981), in service provision between the statutory and voluntary sector would result in a greater conciliation aimed at promoting partnerships or merely open conflict and retrenchment. Nevertheless, there was some confusion about what precise model of welfare pluralism should exist. Questions about whether services from the statutory and voluntary sector should supplement, complement, or substitute one another were germane to this in our discussions with all the teams.

We should remind ourselves of exactly what expectations are implicit in all this for social work teams. Can we realistically expect the social worker to scale the heights of medical dominance, transcend bureaucratic intrusions, and find flexible ways of working in partnership with ordinary persons as care-givers, volunteers, or para-professionals? These requirements pull in different directions and beg questions about not only tasks and roles but also alternative models of professional and bureaucratic organization. This has been a central feature throughout the present discussion and one to which we return in the final chapter.

DISCUSSION

Irrespective of their territorial base the teams were all deeply concerned about their position within larger bureaucratic structures. Professional autonomy was seen as being cramped by centralized systems of administration and resource deployment but also by co-ordination with other agencies and problems of status rivalry with fellow professionals. These powerful forces not only narrowed the focus of practice but also seriously undermined the possibilities of collaborative multi-disciplinary action in the community. Social workers were not masters of their own destiny and the resulting feelings of powerlessness caused some frustration and resentment. These feelings had more to do with the working environment in which practice was carried out than the nature of the social work task itself. There are clear parallels with job satisfaction theories which demonstrate the pervasive effects of organization policy, working conditions, and hierarchical relations, work climate in short, on worker dissatisfaction (Herzberg 1966).

Faced with having to adapt to pressures from their employing agencies, the social work profession, clients, and the community at large, the teams in this study tended to accede primarily to agency and professional forces. To do otherwise would emphasize competition and rivalry with peers and appear as if to threaten agency control. In this sense our findings parallel those of American studies which demonstrate how social workers tend to accommodate conflicting loyalties by falling in with bureaucratic and professional norms (Billingsley 1964; Green 1966). What remains unclear is how far this pattern of accommodation is or should be compatible with resolution of pressing client and community needs, for our data suggest that an effective service would be one dependent upon certain forms of adaptation by agencies towards clients and community. This scenario is elaborated in the next chapter.

Organizational variations in social services departments appeared not to have provided an adequate solution to this overriding dilemma. The generic and specialist team approaches made little difference in the management of these stresses or to the form that practice took, so we were left wondering why this question about labour division has been so much debated when there remain important contextual organizational problems to sort out. The teams saw themselves as denuded of decision-making responsibility by the separation between bureaucratic power and professional discretion. When these two power sources came together however it was usually interpreted as interference rather than as enabling. Forward planning and development, budgetary control, and innovation beyond the case level were the job of middle and senior management and this contributed in its own way to an overriding privatization and conservatism in social work practice.

We are mindful that our account is based almost entirely on the views, orientations, and practices of teams and that there may have been some misinterpretation of managerial intent. The picture we paint is one of considerable organizational determinism but it is important not to overstress this. Workers did not dislike routine and their privatized working methods provided a way of coping with the day-to-day stresses of a taxing job. The idea of community-oriented social work or any multi-professional activity generated subtle threats to autonomy or implied risks and uncertainties. Hence there was an inevitable in-built inertia, resulting in an unwillingness to change established methods existing in the teams, and this should not be overlooked. There were also indications of a dissonance between workers' beliefs, aspirations, and their actual practice. They wanted to be involved in the community but did not see it as their job to do community work. To varying degrees they recognized the existence of informal care networks but did not work with them. They perceived structural problems but felt powerless to deal with them direct or manipulate the organization to better effect in serving the community. They were, after all, accountable to the agency, not the community.

In microcosm the study teams reflected many of the unresolved debates in the literature about the scope, direction, and organization of social work and social services which have raged since the publication of the Seebohm Report. That there appears to be no easy answer is indicative of the complexities involved. It was as if the teams and their managements were colluding together to minimize avoidable risks, to keep practice within measurable dimensions, and to distance themselves from public glare, so mutual scapegoating was to be expected. The central challenges presented by change were therefore met by tactics aimed at avoiding them; hence the rather inflexible but understandable concern with preserving the *status quo*. Although the effectiveness of social work is inevitably tied up with the nature of professional tasks and roles, our description of the three study teams suggests it is inextricably linked with organizational structure and inter-organizational relations in the personal social services. Any attempt to divorce practice from the administrative determinants of effective service delivery would be like taking a scalpel away from a surgeon. Front-line workers cannot work in a vacuum as if independent contractors, nor is it right for them to do so. The organizational cornerstones proposed by Seebohm appear only to have been partially adopted but our analysis has at least identified some explanation of this. The final chapter attempts to synthesize the main findings before moving to a prescriptive account of how personal social services might be organized and tailored to meet community needs in a more adaptive and flexible way.

8

Conclusion:
Social Work in Context

SOCIAL WORK IN THE NATIONAL CONTEXT

This book has been written at a time when the post-war consensus about welfare policy has broken down. On both right and left there is a fundamental disagreement about the ends and means of welfare policy. Not the least consequence has been a felt sense of crisis in social work. Since our study might be misconstrued as yet another attack on social work we need to relate our analysis to this crisis as it provides the context for our study.

We see the crisis as having three dimensions: economic, ideological, and scientific. Each has different sources, motives, and methods of criticism, yet together they have contributed to a questioning of the traditional premises of social work and its role as part of state welfare.

Economically, social workers in particular have a serious crisis in their role in rationing the rapidly decreasing resources available to local authority departments. It has become hard to escape the recognition that social services have been and are being treated as luxuries in times of economic recession.

The difference between the major political parties on this issue has only been one of degree. However, the Conservative Party has distinguished itself by conducting a moral crusade against the very idea of welfare. Under the banner of individual self-reliance there has been a concerted campaign to detach the idea of welfare from any implication it may have for universal rights or models of citizenship. Instead, welfare has been redefined as a safety net available only to those too inadequate to provide for themselves through the market system. In this version social work is symptomatic of society's moral degeneration. It is seen as having no role outside the discharge of narrowly defined statutory obligations. In consequence, government has called for a return to the virtues of self-reliance and voluntary effort and a reduction in state intervention (Jenkin 1980; Thatcher 1981).

Strikingly, there has been no effective counter campaign against this revival of Poor Law philosophy. On the one hand, this reflects the questioning of Fabian solutions encompassing social planning from the centre (Cockburn 1977; Hadley and Hatch 1981) and on the other the ambivalence of radical groups towards the welfare state. Significantly, this radical critique can be seen in social work itself. The community action movement of the late 1960s and 1970s typified social workers as concentrating on individual pathology, neglecting inequality and discrimination. In fact the emergence, and very existence, of community work in its more radical form was an implicit criticism of the perceived irrelevance of social work practice and case-work in particular (Henderson, Jones, and Thomas 1980).

If, for very different reasons, both right and left attacked the welfare state and the role of social work, the effectiveness and demonstrable outcomes of social work, as tested by social work research, have been seriously questioned (Fisher 1976; Reid and Hanrahan 1981). Even in the provision of practical services there was criticism that delivery systems were over-bureaucratized, governed less by individual need than routinized procedures and not subject to control by service users (Illife 1980; Leonard 1979).

Faced with these criticisms, social work is on the defensive. From the right, it is seen as morally degenerate and inordinately expensive, from the left at best ameliorating, at worst reinforcing inequality and the suffering it purports to relieve; from the perspective of technical evaluation too vague and unsystematic to realize the most modest of goals. A succession of widely publicized cases of child abuse have simply endorsed these criticisms publicly.

No one should write critically about the personal social services heedless of this crisis about the legitimacy of social work. Our own position must be made clear. If we have made criticisms of social work, they are not intended to call into question the integrity of social workers nor to suggest that social work has no moral or political justification.

In this last chapter we shall argue that social workers should make better use of what limited discretion they have but we are aware that they have little control over the organizational context of their work. While social workers, their clients, and the general public may see social work as the embodiment of the social services, social workers are crucially dependent on public sponsorship, public financing, public control, and public administration for their occupational mandate. This is the primary context of social work. Those who believe, from whatever perspective, that social work is in need of reform should be mindful of these factors.

Were this a different kind of book we would be tempted to pursue these questions further. However, we have been concerned with a much more limited analysis. If only to help those readers who start a book by reading its conclusion, we start by reviewing our major findings.

SOCIAL WORK IN THE LOCAL CONTEXT: SUMMARY OF FINDINGS

As the introduction explained, we set out to analyse two related yet distinct problems. The first was about the extent to which each social work team had adapted its practice and organization to the particular characteristics of the area it served. The second was a rather different concern, but in a sense to do with adaptation: it was about how social workers met the problems presented by elderly clients. The previous two chapters have compared the three teams in detail. Here of necessity we must be cruder in our argument. We first summarize the main findings and offer our interpretation of them. The last part of the chapter discusses the implications of our analysis for social work teams.

Our answer to the first question has to be that there was little evidence of any team significantly adapting its organization and practice to the local context. We arrived at this conclusion by using a number of criteria. None of these were designed to examine the relationship between team response and sophisticated, direct measures of need. The conceptual and methodological problems involved were sufficiently daunting to dissuade us from such an enterprise (Bradshaw 1972). Nevertheless, we posed a number of questions which set out to test this relationship, albeit more indirectly. In this summary we consider five potential adaptations that the teams could have made in their work: (1) to the local social and economic infrastructure; (2) to the problems of groups of clients; (3) to informal care and voluntary services; (4) to the work of other statutory agencies; (5) to the problems presented by individual clients.

Beginning with the local social and economic infrastructure, we saw that social workers knew well enough what the problems were, but felt helpless to do anything about them. Unemployment and poverty, inadequate housing, and the absence of community facilities were identified as the most serious problems of communities. Further, these structural factors were seen to lie at the root of many clients' problems. While beyond workers' perceived remit, such problems could not be ignored in day-to-day work. However, adapting to them was less a question of having a team strategy; rather individual workers attempted to deal with them as they appeared within each case.

The second test was the extent to which teams had adapted their activity so as to recognize and act on the collective problems of groups of clients. We found little evidence of this. The rarity of group-work cannot be explained simply by logistical problems. Rather it reflected the working assumptions of social workers – that clients were perceived and treated as discrete individuals or occasionally as families. Nor did team members develop joint strategies for helping particular groups of clients. A less tangible indicator was the extent to which the teams adapted their work to meeting and managing referral demands. This was not an adaptive process of planning to local needs and conditions and was not led by explicit local policies.

The third measure of adaptability involved the ability of teams to dovetail their activities into such frameworks of caring as existed outside statutory agencies. Social workers were often unsure about the existence or effectiveness of informal networks. Even where recognized, they were thought to be damaged or undermined by social work intervention. Similarly, workers were sceptical about volunteers and voluntary organizations as being any more than peripheral sources of support.

The development of co-ordinated approaches with other statutory agencies represented in the locality to the problems of communities provided a fourth possible indication of adaptability. Here we found evidence of considerable liaison over individual cases, but little evidence of joint working or planning between services in their approach to specific client groups or localities.

The fifth and final test of adaptability was whether team activity actually constituted an appropriate response to the needs of those individuals who sought help. From the evidence we have available, our conclusion must be that needs were adapted to the remit of social work and the social services department. For instance, for families, help with financial problems was not generally available unless they were presented as part of emotional or behavioural difficulties. For elderly people, problems were redefined to fit the available solutions of existing practical services. This is not to suggest a consistent mismatch between the problem presented and social work intervention. Frequently there was congruence, but there was a tendency to define some problems as not the concern of social work and to redefine others so that they appeared to be met.

On these particular criteria the social work teams studied did not appear to adapt their work to local needs and conditions. What explanation can be offered for the similarity and rigidity of this response? The answer, as far as we can see, is that social work, as practised by these teams, was adapted to a different set of influences stemming from the political and organizational context.

First, social services departments are public agencies and social workers as employees have defined duties. Local authorities have mandatory statutory obligations to discharge and such discretionary powers as they are prepared or able to pursue. Additionally, senior officers of the department are responsible to a committee of elected councillors who may dictate local policy through their ability to allocate resources. The political context serves to define legitimate needs and their resolution. Thus, the reluctance of social workers to depart from a relatively narrow interpretation of their role simply reflects the occupational mandate they have been given and their accountability to their employer. Hence, workers and their departments were guided by a client's eligibility to social services and this framework underpinned the whole basis of practice.

Second, social services departments as complex organizations have other goals which do not always appear on the agendas of social services committees. Our own focus on the bottom of the organization has served to reinforce the notion of organization as process within which individuals and sub-units have a vested interest in pursuing their own self-interest. In this respect, it seemed that some of the features of social work practice we observed could be described as survival strategies. Field social workers coveted the freedom they had as individuals in their work with clients. Through working their own case-load, practitioners sought to maximize their own job satisfaction while at the same time remaining within their mandate.

If the significance of case-work as it is generally taught on social work training courses is added to the political and organizational context, it is not surprising that 'the one-to-one relationship' between client and social worker epitomized team members' work. To move outside this model would not only provoke insecurity in an organizational sense but also give rise to feelings of uncertainty in terms of basic skills or method. Furthermore, moves towards change might be seen as endangering the limited freedom given to workers in their case-work activity. Thus, it was safer to operate along existing guidelines. Faced with the pressing problems of their own clients, the individual workers who comprised the three 'teams' we studied neither had the time nor were given the encouragement to innovate or challenge policy or practice.

Understanding the appropriateness of social work's response to elderly people took forms very similar to those for the more general question about adaptability. First, problems of the social and economic structure tended to affect more those of working age than the elderly. Yet it would be possible to see the elderly as having a quite distinctive cluster of financial and material problems to do with housing, and income maintenance. However, that the elderly may be underprivileged in a material sense did not seem to be an idea which informed social work practice.

Social workers were considerably more conscious of shortfalls in departmental services available to the elderly. Since these gaps were often the result of a local authority declining to allocate the necessary resources, it was to be expected that social workers were not campaigning for new facilities or even lobbying informally within the department.

Socio-economic problems and service deficiencies experienced by elderly clients were often acknowledged by social workers. They provided the fixed boundaries within which the teams operated but did not constitute the focus of their professional activity. Social workers did not see their role as improving the general lot of the elderly, but rather as providing what services and support they could within the existing system.

That system took little account of informal care networks. What we have already said on this topic applied most of all to the elderly as a client group. There was some involvement of neighbours, individual volunteers, and voluntary groups. Yet as a generality, it was difficult to identify anything which could be accurately described as community care outside the provision of practical services and supervisory visits.

The level of co-ordination with other services supporting the elderly was considerable in relation to individual clients, but we found no instances of joint monitoring of actual or potential elderly clients in their locality. What we have termed 'reactive' social work was especially evident here. Monitoring the needs of the elderly was not at the centre of social work.

The presentation of such cases was frequently by third parties, often lay rather than professional people. The role of social work assessment was thus crucial in delving beneath the surface to underlying problems. There is no doubt that in general elderly people were grateful for the services they received and felt they were appropriate to their needs. But our client interviews suggested that amongst elderly clients there were signs of considerable psychological distress felt by clients and their carers which went unnoticed by social work assessment. It is too easy to pass critical judgement. Those who need help may be resentful or fearful of asking for it and may not see that anything can be done. Indeed it is not easy for us to see what remedies social work can offer to ease the problems of isolation and loneliness which appear to accompany the ageing process in our society. However, these problems seem to require more active acknowledgement than they appear to receive from current social work intervention.

Our understanding lies again in the formal and informal priorities set by the organization. Whatever the relative importance of legislation covering different client groups, in practice they are graded in terms of status and priority. Family and child work is held to be of major importance; that with physically and mentally handicapped and mentally ill people of intermediate status; that with the elderly of least priority. Because of the restricted scope of our study, we have little evidence of whether or how such priorities appeared at committee and senior management levels. This pecking order certainly filtered through to the teams and was endorsed by them as a set of working priorities.

Evidence for the relatively low status of work with the elderly was not hard to find in any of the teams, whether the formal structure was generic or specialist. Case allocation consistently defined elderly clients in the category of 'welfare work' dealt with largely by unqualified workers. This reflected organizational priorities and their endorsement by trained social workers. The skills they wished to exercise and the satisfactions they sought were more obviously and readily realized in cases involving children and families.

Work with the elderly was routine and routinized, apparently offering little challenge to the social workers involved. The typical response was initially and often exclusively based on a list of services: aids and adaptations, home help, meals on wheels, lunch clubs, visiting services, day care, assessment for residential accommodation. Once the appropriate and available services had been supplied, the brief of the social worker had been met. Often the client neither wanted or needed any more. The problem is whether this strategy, appropriate for some clients, had become a generalized routine.

It was significant that many of the most vulnerable elderly had ceased to receive social work support but were being monitored by ancillary services, especially the home help service, which had certainly not been designed with these functions in mind. This was well understood by social workers and endorsed by them. But, if long-term social work with the elderly is often being undertaken by home helps, some organizational recognition of this may be overdue. Certainly the tangential status of the home help service to social work teams would require some remedying and some more systematic review and co-ordination adopted.

Adaptability, whether to local communities, or to the elderly as a client group, was not a prime feature of the teams we studied. Their priorities as defined by statute, departmental policy, and casework tradition lay elsewhere in reactive individual case-work, bounded by available service provision. We do not seek to blame individuals for this state of affairs. Nor is it just a question of management or of social work attitudes. Rather the organization of social work implicitly and explicitly endorses some kinds of social work activity and not others. Ultimately this is a question of the legal and administrative structures operated by the central and local state. Reform, if it is to come, would have to change this context. The prospects for that seems minimal. Since those struggling with these problems in their daily work may feel the need for more immediate possibilities of reform, we focus our final argument at the level of the team. That they might use differently what autonomy they have, and make viable claims for more autonomy, seems to us to offer some hope in the otherwise bleak prospects for social work.

THE CASE FOR AN ADAPTIVE SERVICE

What then are the prerequisites of an adaptive service; a service which would be more responsive and accountable to a particular locality and its people? What effects would these changes have for team organization and teamwork? Within the limits of this book we can only sketch the direction of these changes and their implications.

Any suggested changes in the way services are organized must take into account not only the advantages that would accrue for clients and social workers but also the implications for departmental administration. To argue for a more responsive approach to local conditions implies more than merely developing a service which will be more visible and open to community members. As we have seen, local authorities are essentially concerned with the rationing of resources so as to balance demand against supply. It seems sensible to assume that rationing will remain at the heart of any model of service response. What is at issue is the way in which demand may be more effectively managed and met by available resources. To accomplish these tasks, it is our conviction that the responsibility should lie with the decentralized social service team. It is the team which is clearly in the best position to balance this equation within the general policy set by their department.

In Chapter 6 we have shown that factors in the intake process reduced demand to a manageable level. Our concern was not that these filters existed, but rather that they were not based on explicit statements of team priorities. Added to this were social workers' own stereotypes – whether clients were perceived as having high or low status; and the almost automatic responses within limited options that team members typically pursued in their privatized work. It seemed therefore that the relationship between competing needs and team response became buried in the routines of the area teams. Certain clients became relatively disadvantaged by default rather than design. Workers prized their freedom to pursue their own predilections and the potential for teamwork, and team planning was lost.

It seems necessary for *teams* consciously to attempt to control these processes; recognize and accept their accountability to their locality; and develop patterns of working which are seen to be based on an assessment of local needs and conditions. If these aims are accepted the decentralized team would become of necessity the focal point for planning both operational activity and resource deployment.

Hence a necessary precondition would be for social work teams to be identified with a specific locality and arrangements made whereby the team is readily available and visible to the area it serves. While it may be difficult to arrive at an acceptable definition of 'neighbourhood' or 'community' at an abstract level, defining a locality is arguably less problematic in practice. From this study, workers in the three teams had few difficulties agreeing the physical and cultural boundaries of the areas and sub-areas they served. Hence, the workers themselves could have defined localities within which decentralized teams could have operated if they had so wished. As Hadley and McGrath (1981) have demonstrated, attempts at providing 'local' or 'patch-based' services have reasserted the relevance of a community-oriented approach to social services which we have seen was embodied in the Seebohm Report. No clear model emerges from these accounts as to the ideal focus, form, or operation of teams which claim a patch orientation. We must await the outcome of evaluative research of experimental initiatives such as in Normanton (Hadley and McGrath 1981) and Dinnington (Bayley *et al.* 1981) which may provide some answers to these questions. Nevertheless, there can be discerned a move towards a more decentralized form of service organization running counter to the model of centralized control which has characterized the work of many social services departments (Kakabadse and Worrall 1978).

Being locally based would not only raise the visibility of the service but also expose the team and its operational policies and activities to the general public. As Currie and Parrott (1981) found in the operation of a patch team in Nottinghamshire this had the effect of increasing referrals. As teams move towards a more adaptive model of delivery, the discovery of previously unmet needs would inevitably lead to greater referral bombardment. If they are to respond to local conditions, it seems vital for them to develop explicit policies and priorities which seek to balance the equation between demand and the resources they have available. Without such attempts at local planning, the filtering systems employed to manage demand would inevitably remain unrelated to the local context. By concentrating planning at this level, it would enable teams more easily to identify the potential contribution of voluntary and informal systems of care, which taken together with departmental services would form the resource context of work. This approach would imply that the discretion given to teams and team leaders over the use and allocation of resources would be much greater than it is at present.

All this would imply a shift away from the conventional model
of service response we observed, which raises three immediate sets
of questions. First, is it possible for social work teams to gather the
necessary information to formulate local plans? Second, what
would be the effect of delegating planning functions to front-line
units and what consequences would these changes have for line
management relationships and local government administration?
Third, in arguing for teams to be locally based, what implications
are there for team and worker accountability?

The freedom we would envisage for decentralized teams to
realize their own priorities would necessarily be bounded by the
parameters set by the statutory duties and obligations of social
services departments. Nevertheless, if teams are to be adaptive and
oriented towards local needs and conditions, then collectively
acknowledged need, embodied in central government legislation
and general policy statements of departments, must be related to
the local context. However, decentralized teams will never be in the
position of acting as a clearing house through which all those in
need will be identified or through which social care will be
provided in a particular locality. Health services, housing departments, and the DHSS are equally engaged in state provision.
Further, voluntary organizations, volunteers, mutual aid groups,
and the whole system of informal care provided by families,
friends, and neighbours constitute alternative or complementary
ways in which social need is met.

If we are to arrive at a position where teams can begin to assess
need and set local priorities new ways of addressing their responsibilities will have to be worked out. In order to achieve planning at
the local level teams themselves would have to analyse the relationship between expressed and hidden needs and the ways in which
these can be met. Hence the opinions of suppliers – the team, other
statutory agencies, and the voluntary organizations operating
locally – and users – represented by local interest groups of clients
and their carers – would have to be taken into account.

As a first step teams could consider using the information which
already exists as raw data within team and departmental records.
None of the teams we studied monitored demand locally. Given the
amount of information collected at the point of referral and during
case episodes, the potential for monitoring and evaluating team
activity is obvious. A number of models already exist at various
levels of complexity which could draw on this data base. For

example, the case review form employed in this study was derived from an experimental case review system which has been evaluated elsewhere (Goldberg and Warburton 1979). Algie (1974) and Vickery (1977) provide other alternatives. If these or other models were used it is possible to envisage a much more effective use of departmental intelligence through which work could be planned and monitored. Such a system has the potential to provide a core of data about expressed needs, case management, team activity, resource utilization and shortfalls and it would enhance the ability of teams to co-ordinate their activity and set priorities.

Second, it seems feasible to consider the development of locally co-ordinated service delivery strategies, as for example between the team and a group practice, a local housing office, or voluntary groups so that they might pool their information and arrive at a better understanding of both the needs and resources of the area served or a particular group of clients. While there may be deep-seated problems in the relationships between all of these groups, the development of a more responsive service would require their mutual co-operation and partnership in developing care in and by the community.

Third, there is the more difficult problem of obtaining users' and potential users' opinions. While local pressure groups may be available to represent groups of clients, any attempt at local planning would have to take into account those needs which may be left unrepresented. There are needs expressed in problems such as poverty, inadequate housing, and unemployment which emanate from structurally determined deprivation and inequality. Social workers have traditionally been concerned with the most dis-advantaged groups in society and many recipients of services are faced with these problems. However, their role in this arena is riddled with contradictions (Parry, Rustin, and Satyamurti 1979; Pritchard and Taylor 1978). Nevertheless, it seems necessary for workers to consider these individual examples of personal or family distress as representative of collective disadvantage of significant sectors of society. We have reported that workers were aware of these inequalities. However organized it seems unlikely that workers have the mandate to intervene directly at this level. Nevertheless the consequences of these structurally determined needs would have to be evaluated in team planning. Inevitably, by arguing for teams to locate themselves within neighbourhoods and to orientate themselves to the individual and collective needs of people within them these contradictions would be more rather than less apparent.

We now turn to the implications this delegation of authority might have for local authority administration. Undoubtedly it would affect the relationship between senior management and the decentralized team. As we saw in Chapter 7 there are inherent tensions in social services departments since the organization is dependent on the front-line worker to identify its clientele and to pursue its primary goals. These tensions have been described as a problem of managerial control (Smith 1965), as a conflict between administrators and social workers (Blau and Scott 1963) or from the workers' point of view as a problem of survival in a hostile environment (Glastonbury, Cooper, and Hawkins 1980; Stevenson and Parsloe 1978). Arguing for more delegated authority for front-line units and a loosening of central control would in all probability add to these tensions. Social workers would remain employees of the local authority and the system of administration would continue to provide the links between the field social worker, senior management, the director of social services, and the social services committee. Central government would continue to provide legislative definitions of need. As Johnson (1972) points out local government provides the means through which state provision is controlled, its clientele identified, and services guaranteed and this position would not change.

However, we would contend that a shift towards greater *team* autonomy within these constraints is possible. In discussing the use of authority in social service departments, Warham (1977) suggests that for effective role performance three conditions are necessary. First, that authority is reasonably clearly defined and its limits understood; second, that it is real and that front-line workers are trusted to 'get on with it'; and third, that it is commensurate with the job to be done. We would suggest that if *teams* were given the mandate to operate within these limits some of the flexibility necessary for local adaptation of service response could take place. This would imply both greater freedom and in consequence greater responsibility to be situated at the team level. It would result in more complex relationships between departmental staff at all levels. Taken with the need for local planning it would require decision-making discretion over the deployment of a wide range of resources to be vested with the team. Obviously such changes would beg the question of the leadership qualities necessary of team leaders and more fundamentally the willingness of councillors and senior management to operate in a looser system, in which both political control and the management of resources would be more open to scrutiny by users and the general public. Further, they would affect the relationships between the centre and the periphery of the organization. While general statements of policy would remain the province of senior officers and committee, the role of the former would be primarily geared to enabling and monitoring front-line units in the pursuit of the tasks we have outlined.

ACCOUNTABILITY AND LOCAL CONTROL

So far our concern has been to suggest some practical ways in which the work of social work teams could become more adapted to local needs and conditions and their implications. However, if teams are to be responsible as well as responsive to the area they serve, it is necessary to consider their accountability to local people. So far we have stressed the occupational mandate given to workers by virtue of their employment by the social services department and the importance of this aspect of accountability. However, social workers represented by their professional organization (BASW 1977), consider themselves as equally responsible and accountable, as individuals, to their clientele. While social work ethics are largely covered in the rules of the departments in which they work, professionalism, epitomized by individually focused case-work and its principles and methods, remains at the heart of social work practice. We would contend that the balance struck between these two notions of accountability, between state and bureaucratic hegemony, on the one hand, and professional hegemony on the other, should also take into account the responsibility of the social work team to the people of a particular locality.

By arguing for decentralization, local planning, and a delegation of authority, we also hope for greater participation by users and the general public in the ways in which services are planned, run, and developed. Earlier we suggested the means through which various groups might be represented in the process of setting team priorities. By raising the visibility of teamwork in this way, the needs and requirements of local people would be more readily recognized. However, greater emphasis on public participation, accountability to the area served and on the development of mechanisms of local control, would bring a number of consequences.

First, these changes most obviously would threaten the present structure of political control over the work of social services departments. Hence, ways would have to be found to incorporate elected members into the development of greater user and public participation. Second, the recognition that teams should be subject to local control would expose workers and departments more openly to public scrutiny and to possible criticism. Third, such changes could produce their own brand of hegemony by failing to take into account the most vulnerable and least articulate citizens' needs. There are probably other reasons why 'community participation' as envisaged by the Seebohm Report has rarely been attempted. Without changes to the political structure, we cannot be surprised that such attempts fail. Nevertheless, we feel that for social work teams to adapt to local needs and conditions, they should recognize the three aspects of accountability which we have outlined:

1 accountability to their employing authority and the central state;
2 accountability in terms of personal responsibility to individual clients;
3 accountability to local people and interests.

Each can be seen as a competing requirement which needs to be taken into account and through which team responses to local needs should be legitimated. The third aspect is crucial if local adaptation is to be attempted.

TEAMWORK AND THE SOCIAL WORKER

In discussing how social workers might better address local needs we have placed the onus on *the team* to develop its own priorities and stressed the importance of the delegation of authority over the use of departmental resources as a crucial element in that process. In the social work literature, the internal organization and functioning of teamwork has been given considerable attention (cf. Parsloe 1981; Payne 1982; Rowbottom, Hey, and Billis 1974; Stevenson 1981)

We feel that much of the debate about how teams should be organized has failed to take into account the primary factor which should govern team organization and teamwork at the local level, namely that teamwork implies a group of people coming together to co-ordinate their work to prescribed goals. Hence, it is our view that there is a need to relate team structure and teamwork to a set of priorities which are subject to local conditions. By doing so, social work teams would be forced to consider not only the most appropriate internal division of labour for their own locality but also the ways in which team responsibilities interweave with other agencies, voluntary organizations, and informal care in developing an adaptive response. Such an approach would imply that departments would be willing to accept much more local variation in team organization for front-line units.

Arguing for *the team* to take on the responsibilities we have outlined would have the effect of enhancing its freedom as a corporate body but it would inevitably result in restricting the freedom of social workers in their own work within their privatized case-loads. We have seen that this freedom was prized by the workers we interviewed. While our argument has led us to this conclusion we are less certain how far social workers would be prepared to accept our view that the pursuit of individual job satisfaction should take second place to a team consensus, which might for instance place greater priority on work with low status clients, and lead to a more considered service for elderly people for which we have argued.

In this regard, it was clear that the low status position ascribed to elderly people was as much to do with social workers' own preferences for work with children and families as to how priorities were set by departments. Hence to redress the balance it would be necessary for both social work – its educators and practitioners – and policy-makers in both central and local government to acknowledge explicitly the needs of elderly citizens and their carers.

Again, too, we must remind ourselves of the limits of a social work team's autonomy. Here, we are less than clear whether the freedom we envisage for teams, set in the context of local accountability and local control provides social workers with the structure they might prefer. Public participation and moves to involve the community would bring workers face to face with the social and economic issues of which they were aware but for which they had no remedies within the repertoire of case-work. Given the limited control that team members have over the political and organizational context of practice, it may be unfair to expect them to expose themselves in this way. As the blunt end of state welfare provision their options and their role are predefined. Inevitably, arguing for teams to acknowledge their responsibility to local people would place workers within a political arena within which their primary concerns with meeting the needs of individuals rather than collectives might be called into question.

Thus in outlining our own views as to how teams might be more adaptive to local needs, we are left with some nagging doubts. It was clear that social workers were united in their view that the balance between central control and front-line autonomy should be redressed in their favour. However, the logic of our argument has left us questioning whether social work or social workers as employees of the local authority would prefer the system we have outlined. We are convinced that, given the necessary autonomy, social work teams could better address the problems with which they are faced. But what are the incentives for social workers and departments to move towards a more adaptive and proactive approach to local welfare provision? At the beginning of this conclusion we pointed to a crisis in welfare policy and its consequence, namely that social work is on the defensive. In this climate, any change is potentially threatening. We feel the risks implied by the changes we have suggested are worth taking. But, in the last analysis, are the choices open to social workers their own?

Postscript:
The Barclay Report

During the time that we were undertaking our research a working party, headed by Peter Barclay, was established by the then Secretary of State to examine the role and tasks of social workers. Whilst we were aware of this committee, its membership, and terms of reference, its recommendations were kept a closely guarded secret until shortly before their publication in May 1982. As a result we were unable to weave our reactions to the report into our conclusions and decided instead to add this postscript.

As it turned out the working party produced not only a majority report but also two minority reports which stand in sharp contrast to each other. Commenting on the Barclay Report thus becomes problematic since minority reports have a way of becoming majority recommendations. It is clear, however, that a majority of members of the working party favoured a move towards what they call 'community social work'.

In our own research we have been aware, in reaching our conclusions, of the dangers of providing prescriptions for either social work in general or for the three teams we studied. The objectives of social work will be decided largely outside the research community and professionals, politicans, clients, and the wider community will all, in varying degrees, be involved in deciding its future role.

The Barclay Report has provided a prescription so we felt it appropriate to stand our findings against those of the working party in an attempt to assess the extent of congruence. More especially, just how relevant is the strategy the Barclay Report recommends to the area teams we studied?

We have looked at a number of possibilities that might be considered in efforts to make social work more adaptive to the localities it serves. Generally, our analysis has pointed towards a more community-based approach. The majority of social workers we talked to felt this to be a more responsive, flexible, and potentially effective way of doing social work. Nonetheless, in spite of this *geist* alighting on most social workers, we saw, like the working party, precious little evidence of much being done to promote it. Like them, we saw a social work task essentially dominated by a one-to-one client relationship responding to demand pressures and subject to various kinds of bureaucratic constraints. In addition, we saw a lack of variety of response between the different area teams, an absence of teamwork and locally based policies, and, perhaps more clearly than the working party, the different status ascribed to separate groups of clients.

Thus we were led to wonder, as did Barclay, why the community approach, advocated by the Seebohm Report over a decade ago, had not taken root. Or, as the Barclay Report asked in more prescriptive style, why might it now?

LEGISLATIVE REFORM OF THE PERSONAL SOCIAL SERVICES

The Barclay Report represents the first major government-inspired review of social work since the Seebohm Report and there are many similarities of content and inspiration. The Barclay Working Party was clearly disappointed by the limited ability of social services departments to follow the Seebohm Report's direction in developing a closer involvement with the community. In essence the Local Authority Act that followed Seebohm represented an administrative reorganization of service function rather than any fundamental restructuring of the relationship between social worker, client, and community. This may have been inevitable but the lack of political will to achieve anything more than administrative changes now seems painfully obvious. Richard Crossman's *Diaries of a Cabinet Minister* shows the lack of interest that he, as a senior Cabinet Minister responsible for social services, had in the Seebohm Report: 'My first job was to see Seebohm of the Seebohm Committee . . . he told me in great secrecy what was to be the central recommendation of the report. I didn't particularly want to know, but he told me it was going to be a demand for a reorganization of social services.'

In fact, five months after this meeting Crossman's interest had increased. The burning issue of the day was parliamentary devolution and Crossman was responsible for this issue in Cabinet. He saw the need to wrest the responsibility for children from the Home Office into one central government department (the DHSS) and proposed a trade-off. Devolution, 'as a swop for the Children's Department?' asked James Callaghan the then Home Secretary.

From exchanges such as these it is not hard to see why the Local Authority Act was more administrative than it was fundamental in its structuring of the tasks and role of social workers. In contrast, the Barclay Report makes no such recommendation for organizational change and concentrates instead on encouraging changes of attitude and a commitment to community social work. We accept that an approach based on administrative reform alone does not seem to have been effective. However, structural alterations to the format of local government are not the only factors explaining why community social work has not developed. Overwhelmingly the legislation which empowers local authorities to act and social workers to undertake social work, points directly to the needs of individual clients rather than communities. Thus the whole system of accountability and legitimacy in social work is oriented in clear contradiction to a central element in the philosophy of community care. Only legislative change would remove this impediment altogether – a point we feel is undervalued by the working party.

Based on the findings of our research, our contention would be that the working party are underestimating the power of legitimacy and accountability and overestimating the will of social workers and managers to change their patterns of work to meet this new challenge.

RESISTANCE TO CHANGE

The influence of the 'culture' of social work in maintaining existing structures should also not be underestimated. As we saw in Chapter 6, a lack of any underpinning theory of intervention and the reassurance felt in the one-to-one client relationship seemed to be a strong factor in maintaining its existence. There are relevant and powerful reasons which help to explain the lack of a more community-based approach. In spite of the existence of some radical workers in Selly Oak, the majority of workers we surveyed displayed what can best be described as a 'Common-Sense, Band-Aid' approach to social work. The possibilities for change were sometimes raised but these were generally directed at removing existing work pressures. Anticipated changes tended to be piecemeal and administrative modifications to the duty system or to referral, allocation, and standby procedures, rather than fundamental changes to social work's tasks and roles.

A community-based approach poses threats not only to senior managers within a department, as the Barclay Report seems to suggest, but also to the security that social workers themselves have established. Increasing accountability and responsiveness to client need, social care planning, and the stimulation and maintenance of informal care networks suggested by the report all add major dimensions of responsibility to a group of workers who have, we might suggest, spent the time since Seebohm defining their role downwards rather than outwards; rather in a way that Professor Pinker advocates they should continue to do.

The potential bifurcation of role for senior managers that is envisaged by the Barclay Report is even more impressive. The contention that increased social work autonomy will mean that 'it will be impossible for senior management to continue to hold all the reins of departmental resource allocation', would be welcomed by most of our social workers. But the report's acceptance that such 'delegation may be found to give rise to differences in standards of practice and levels of provision' and thus 'it is necessary for senior managers to retain clear and unequivocal responsibilities for co-ordination of policies and priorities and maintaining standards of provision' will we feel be met with an ambiguous response by practitioners and managers alike. In thinking about their relationship to the community and to other organizations our practitioner respondents foresaw problems emanating from planning processes. Lack of involvement in planning and development activity was irksome to them considering their day-to-day understanding of the areas served. Even though the Barclay Report suggests that senior managers will be the primary co-ordinators and monitors, our findings indicate the need for greater involvement of front-line workers on a collegiate basis. The implications for a participative management style are clear and failure to latch on to this may yet prove a deterrent to the emergence of 'community social work'.

Finally, it must be said that social workers were ambiguous about *their* own belief in the strength and reliability of informal care networks in the community. Some of this ambiguity came from the political manoeuvres of both national and local government whose efforts to encourage development of informal care were seen as thinly disguised attempts to save money. The Barclay

Report recognized this and suggested that their desired approach would require resources initially which would yield 'value for money' in the long term. Rightly, social workers have been suspicious of such optimistic prospects for resources. Whilst identifying some under-use of community resources, practitioners we interviewed saw the funding of the statutory services as a major priority. This was not in opposition to the encouragement of informal caring but based on the conviction that whilst the majority of care is carried out informally within the community, statutory resources are and will continue to be called upon when these networks break down. Although investment in prevention may reduce this dependence it would not solve the problems of an acute deficiency in many statutory services.

TEAMWORK

The Barclay Working Party lays great emphasis on the concept of teamwork but does not seem to have understood its frailties or the autonomy of workers within it. Stressing the need for supervision and support of all but the most experienced worker to safeguard both the public and social workers themselves, the report stresses the 'check and scrutiny provided by the team organization within which social workers operate and the opportunities of consultation which are afforded to them' (9.15).

In discussing teams and teamwork in more detail the report recognizes the potential of teamwork, arguing that 'a well organized team . . . is far better placed than any individual social worker could be to assess the levels of social need, reach decisions on priorities and provide an appropriate service'. We would agree, but the report is clearly talking about teams and teamwork outside the experience of our research findings. 'Work must be distributed', the report argues, 'among team members, for example, in such a way that the *collective resources of the group* are available, when needed, to all clients' (our italics). This, the report admits is a considerably more dificult operation than simply allocating 'one worker to one client' (9.23). We would agree again, but would ask once more why has this fundamental change not taken place in the past ten years?

The concept of teamwork, especially between social workers and their residential, day, and domiciliary colleagues is most underdeveloped. This, in an Annex to the report (page 224) is argued to flow from the development of 'service delivery' structures which divide rather than integrate the functions of social work. Our respondents also saw the potential of integrating work within the team, working with other agencies, and supporting local communities but quite simply the task was too daunting. The width of tasks envisaged for the community social work team is elaborated in the Barclay Report (10.28/29) but responding to such a task specification in times of public expenditure reduction would seem foolhardy rather than responsible. Not without reason have formal and informal client specialisms, noted in our research, developed in post-Seebohm departments. While some social workers may feel uneasy about this development, it *is* a highly adaptive response to the dominant demands of their employers.

Our impressions are that the majority of social workers may wish to develop a wider community remit but find security and job satisfaction within the model championed by Professor Pinker which argues for specialist social work within adequately staffed generic teams.

Our research supports the conviction of the working party that referrals to social workers are sometimes made 'with only the haziest notion of what they [social workers] can or should be able to do to help resolve the problem in hand' (8.4). If a move towards a more community-based orientation is attractive to social workers, its acceptability to the medical profession (with whom we found the vast majority of liaison took place) is far from certain. Research on the relationship between medical practitioners and social workers emphasizes time and again the differences in perception of professional role and accountability. Greater autonomy for social workers would go some way to providing, in GPs eyes, a more equal partnership but there is no evidence to suggest that this in itself would lead GPs to adopt either a more community-centred approach or, for that matter, a more appropriate style of referral. Rather the expectations placed on social workers would be likely to increase.

WELFARE STATE: SERVING OR SERVICING?

There is much within the Barclay Report which breathes soundness and sense over the troubled state of social work, but then so did the Seebohm Report, and as we have noted, the necessary radical changes of philosophy in that report have not taken root. We have tried to show why the Barclay Report is likely to encounter similar problems in finding its own rooting hormone and in so doing we have pointed to some oversights, contradictions, and shortfalls.

The working party argues that a slavish attitude towards public accountability and an overbearing interest in getting the structure right has given us our present state of social work and a half-hearted commitment to community social work. A refocusing away from these concerns will provide an opportunity for change. Of course, our findings have shown clearly the attitude of social workers to the oppressive effects of structure and accountability and often this has been accepted as the reason for things being as they are. However, can these issues really explain the findings of our study which showed a willingness to ignore the community and even in many cases dismiss the relevance of volunteers; to adopt a client specialist approach by design or by stealth and to work in a privatized and *ad hoc* manner in relation to individual cases and other agencies? Most of all, is it a sufficient explanation of the low status given to elderly clients? Our answer would have to be NO.

If we were to indulge in speculation we would argue that the Barclay Report will not induce the changes it desires; not because many of these are not highly laudable but because their strategy for change fails to remove the major impediment to this change. As we have argued in our conclusion this lies in a deeply held notion concerning the nature of the social work client and the individual client's relationship to the provider of services: the state. The Barclay Report will not achieve a fundamental change in this relationship because it does not recommend any changes that might allow social workers to adapt from a servicing to a serving role (Cockburn 1977). Equally we believe this to be the reason that Seebohm failed.

Our suggestions for the teams we studied and social work in general relate to an increase in visibility at a local level and hence public debate; only in this way will social work become more responsive to community needs. The issue is not, as Barclay suggests, one for the profession to resolve. The profession is one participant in the debate; the debate if it is to be resolved will be resolved outside social work and beyond the Barclay Report.

*Appendix: Research Instruments**

A. CASE REVIEW FORM

Please read the guide notes before completing the questionnaire.

1. Your initials
2. Case status: type 1   type 2
   - new referral   ☐   ☐
   - re-referral   ☐   ☐
3. Case identity no. _____
4. Source of referral code   ☐☐
5. Method of referral code   ☐
6. Date present case opened _____
7. Date of first ever referral to area _____
8. Principal client's age or 'family' _____
9. Sex. M or F or 'family'
10. Status
    - single ☐
    - married ☐
    - widowed ☐
    - divorced/sep. ☐
    - or 'family' ☐
11. Has ability to converse
    - in English only ☐
    - in Welsh only ☐
    - bilingually ☐
    - other (specify below) ☐

    _____

12. Residence: client lives
    - alone ☐
    - with family ☐
    - with others (specify) ☐

    _____

13. Accommodation:
    - owner-occupied ☐
    - council rented ☐
    - private rented ☐
    - other (specify below) ☐
14. Client category
    (tick *all* applicable categories)
    - physically handicapped ☐
    - elderly (persons aged over 65) ☐
    - 'mentally ill' ☐
    - mentally handicapped ☐
    - family problem ☐
    - child care ☐
    - other ☐
15. If child in LA care ☐
16. If child under statutory supervision ☐
17. Registered:
    - chronically sick/PH ☐
    - blind ☐
    - deaf ☐

Case Allocation

18. If the case has been transferred to you on what date did you receive it? _____

    Not transferred ☐
19. How many workers *other* than yourself have been involved previously? _____

---

* Full details of the research instruments and copies of the interview schedules can be obtained from Dr Gordon Grant, Department of Social Theory and Institutions, University College of North Wales, Bangor, Gwynedd, Wales.

Duration of case:		21. Approx. visiting frequency was/is	
up to 3 months	☐	weekly or more	☐
up to 6 months	☐	monthly or more	☐
up to 1 year	☐	less than once a month	☐
up to 3 years	☐	less than once every 3 months	☐
over 3 years &	☐	less than once every 6 months	☐
indefinite		22. Date of last visit	_____

	1	2
23. Tick those problems occurring in current case episode or in last episode if case is closed.	Tackled to date	Still to be tackled, i.e. problems additional to present ones or present problems requiring work additional to present service

Code		
1 None	☐	☐
2 Health/self-care	☐	☐
3 Loneliness	☐	☐
4 Family relationships	☐	☐
5 Child behaviour	☐	☐
6 Child abuse/deprivation	☐	☐
7 Education	☐	☐
8 Employment	☐	☐
9 Financial	☐	☐
10 Housing	☐	☐
11 Transport	☐	☐
12 Other, specify	_____	_____
24. Using appropriate code nos code major problems at each period	☐	☐

	1	2
25. Which social work staff	have been involved to date?	would you consider necessary for future work?
1 Qualified social worker	☐	☐
2 Unqualified social worker	☐	☐
3 Social work assistant	☐	☐
4 Occupational therapist	☐	☐
5 Craft instructress	☐	☐
6 Home help	☐	☐
7 Volunteer	☐	☐
8 Other (specify)	_____	_____

	1	2
26. Which practical services	have been provided to date?	would you consider necessary for future work?
1 Aids	☐	☐
2 Adaptations	☐	☐
3 Home help	☐	☐
4 Meals on wheels	☐	☐
5 Clubs	☐	☐

		6 Day care	☐	☐
		7 Adult training centre	☐	☐
		8 Hostel/temporary accommodation	☐	☐
		9 Sheltered housing	☐	☐
		10 Residential care, long term	☐	☐
		11 Residential care, short term	☐	☐
		12 Foster care	☐	☐
		13 Adoption	☐	☐
		14 Formal supervision (statutory)	☐	☐
		15 Informal supervision	☐	☐
		16 Holidays/outings	☐	☐
		17 Financial/material	☐	☐
		18 Craftwork supplies	☐	☐
		19 Other (specify)		

		1	2
27.	Contact/liaison With which other agencies	have you had contact to date?	would you consider it necessary to have contact in future?
	1 None	☐	☐
	2 GP	☐	☐
	3 HV/DN	☐	☐
	4 Psychiatric services	☐	☐
	5 Other health services	☐	☐
	6 Child guidance	☐	☐
	7 Marriage guidance	☐	☐
	8 Education/school	☐	☐
	9 Housing department	☐	☐
	10 Employment agencies	☐	☐
	11 DHSS	☐	☐
	12 Probation	☐	☐
	13 Voluntary agencies	☐	☐
	14 Other (specify)		

		to date?	in the future?
28.	How would you characterize your work with this client Tick social work activities/tasks (more than one may be involved)		
	1 Investigating/assessing	☐	☐
	2 Giving information/advice	☐	☐
	3 Mobilizing resources	☐	☐
	4 Acting as an advocate	☐	☐
	5 Educating/developing skills	☐	☐
	6 Helping to solve personal problems	☐	☐
	7 Supervising/reviewing	☐	☐
	8 Supporting/sustaining	☐	☐
	9 Providing group activity	☐	☐
29.	(If appropriate) 1 Closure	☐	
	2 NFA	☐	
	Reason for closure or NFA		
30.	Other comments:		

31. Location:
  1 Parish code   ☐
  2 Proximity of nearest neighbour
    next door attached   ☐
    next door detached   ☐
    across road   ☐
    500–100 yards   ☐
    100 yards–¼ mile   ☐
    more isolated   ☐
    (comment if necessary)

(NB. Question 11 was only used in Aber, questions 13, 25, 29, and 31 were varied according to local circumstances. These were also covered by the written instructions for completing the form, which also provided detailed notes on each question, especially definitions of referrals and long-term cases, lists of thirty-one possible referral sources and six referral methods, indications of permitted multiple classifications, clarification of ambiguous terms, instructions about missing information.)

B. MAIN HEADINGS FOR SOCIAL WORKER INTERVIEWS

Personal background

Time spent on area, changes since been here.
Job before, attraction job, area, expectations.

Perceptions of community

Distinctive features of area and changes seen.
Most serious social problems, most widespread, root of problems, town and country differences.
In and out-migration.

Informal care

Conceptualization, distribution, factors promoting informal care in communities, groups not supported by informal care, promotion by social workers, attitude to development.

Intake and allocation

Where referrals came from.
Who refers/how enlightened?

How handled – duty, standby, management, mechanics, team
structure, supervision, allocation, policy, referrals – to cases – to
closure.
Seniors' role.

Voluntary agencies/volunteers

Voluntary agencies: how used, sources, problems.
Volunteers: recruitment, tasks undertaken, which clients, roles.

Professional image

Clients' expectations, images of social work.
Statutory agencies, fellow professionals – understanding SSD,
integrated working, expectations.
Personal orientation – practice, methods of work.
(Importance of Welsh – Aber only.)

Resources and needs – unmet

Unmet needs – which client groups, service shortfalls, town/
country differences.

Untapped resources in community

Resources untapped in communities.
Alternative ways of delivering services.

Organization of field-work

Patch/district, specialist/generic. Linkages – residential, day care,
domiciliary. Ideal versus reality.

Headquarters and area linkage

Area freedom to develop local priorities and policy. Budgetary
control, delegation of decisions versus central control.
HQ involvement in day-to-day decisions – bureaucracy, monitoring, advisory functions, boundaries and constraints on
workers and team.

Seniors/teams leaders only

Management of team's overall case-load.
Supervision: frequency, nature, objectives.
Autonomy granted to individual social workers.
Accountability to higher management.
Senior/team leader role.
Freedom to manage: set priorities and modify policies.

C. SPECIMEN LETTERS TO CLIENTS

From the social services department

Dear

I am enclosing a letter explaining some research which asks for your agreement to be interviewed privately in your own home by a representative of the University of East Anglia. As you will see the research team is working with the Social Services Department to find out the views of people living in rural areas who have been in touch with us in the past. This project has the full backing of our Department.

Already many people in this area have been visited and interviewed and I understand they enjoyed being able to help with this piece of research. I wonder therefore if you will feel happy to assist the research in this matter. Any information you give will be treated in the strictest confidence and known only to the researcher.

If for any reason you do not wish to take part then please complete the attached reply slip and return it here in the enclosed pre-paid envelope. If you do decide to take part then just keep the letter and do *not* bother to return the slip. One of the interviewers, who will have proof of identity, will then call round in the next few weeks to find out when it may be possible to see you.

The research team will only attempt to contact you after two weeks have passed to give you some time to decide whether or not you wish to take part. The decision is entirely yours and you should not feel obliged to agree unless you wish to assist in this research.

Yours sincerely,

Tear off here

IMPORTANT. ONLY COMPLETE THIS IF YOU DO NOT WISH TO HAVE AN INTERVIEW

I would prefer not to be interviewed, thank you.

Name (in capitals) ....

Address ....

....

....

Signed ....

From the research team

Dear Sir/Madam,

Delivery of Social Services in Rural Areas

I am writing to you from the University of East Anglia about a major piece of research concerning the delivery of social services in rural areas. As part of a larger exercise my colleagues and I are seeking to interview a large number of people who have been in touch with the Social Services Department. We would like to talk to you about your experiences of social services and to learn more about what, as a consumer, you think about social services and about living in a predominantly rural district. This is the first time that the views of rural consumers have been sought in this country and Norfolk County Council has given us its full backing in the matter.

We hope that you will agree to allow one of our interviewers to come and see you but if you feel you would prefer not to take part then of course we will naturally respect your wishes. The accompanying reply slip should be completed and returned in the pre-paid envelope if you DO NOT WISH to be interviewed. Otherwise an interviewer will call round during the next few weeks to arrange a convenient time to see you.

I would like to stress that information collected will be treated in the strictest confidence and personal details will not be divulged to anyone other than the interviewer.

You may be interested to know that we are collaborating with teams in the Midlands and North Wales in gathering information and that great interest is being taken by the Department of Health and Social Security and the Welsh Office. We hope that you will feel able to help us to make this a worthwhile and successful exercise. May I thank you in advance for giving this matter your consideration.

Yours sincerely,

D. MAIN TOPIC OF CLIENT QUESTIONNAIRE

(1–7)   *Residence and migration*
  – birthplace of
    self/spouse
  – when and why moved
    to community

(8–16) *Accommodation*
  – type and tenure
  – amenities
  – problems and
    satisfactions

(17–19) *Household composition*
  – number in household
  – relationships

(20–3) *Social services**
  – referral: means and
    reaction to
  – previous sources of
    informal care
  – services provided and
    perceived benefit
  – general satisfaction with
    SSD
  – current means of
    contacting SSD

(36–7) *Community services*
  – type of other services
    received
  – frequency of contact

(38)   *Morale scale**
  – modified Philadelphia
    version (17 questions re
    emotional state with
    positive/negative/don't
    know responses,
    numerically scored)

(39–52) *Family, friends and
    neighbours*
  – if living alone
  – relatives alive
  – contact with neighbours
  – degree of and
    satisfaction re contact
    with immediate

    relatives (siblings,
    children,
    grandchildren.)

(53–67) *Loneliness and isolation**
  – access to telephone, car,
    buses
  – feelings of loneliness: if,
    when
  – times spent alone
  – existence of friendships

(68–70) *Mobility/dependency**
  – Harris/Hunt
    Dependency Inventory
    (ability to perform 13
    items of self-care and
    mobility with or
    without help)
  – if bed-fast and when
    last up
  – if housebound and
    when last out

(71–2) *Health*
  – specific ailments and
    disabilities
  – subjective assessment of
    health

(73–7) *Help with common
    problems**
  – sources of help with
    personal problems
    (finance, illness,
    depression, etc.)
  – sources of help with
    practical tasks
    (shopping, cooking,
    laundry, etc.)
  – access to and
    satisfaction with
    specified goods and
    services (shops,
    chemist, post office,
    GP, etc.)

(78–81) *Ethnicity* (Aber only)

- identification of Welsh
  speakers
(82–5) *Employment*
  - previous job of
    self/spouse
  - age of and reasons for
    retirement
(86–90) *Income*
  - sources

- amount
- adequacy
- budgeting problems

(   ) question numbers on
      interview schedule
*   data most often used in
      case studies

References

Abrams, M. (1978) *Beyond Three Score and Ten: A First Report on a Survey of the Elderly*. London: Age Concern.

Abrams, P. (1980) Social Change, Social Networks and Neighbourhood Care. *Social Work Service* **22**: 12–23.

Algie, J. (1974) *Social Values, Objectives and Action*. London: Kogan Page.

Armstrong, K.L. (1977) *An Exploratory Study of the Interrelationships between Worker Characteristics, Organizational Structure, Management Process and Worker Alienation from Clients (How to Avoid Burnout)*. Berkeley, University of California: unpublished PhD thesis.

Association of County Councils (1978) *Rural Deprivation: An Association of County Councils Study*. London.

Barclay Report (1982) *Social Workers, Their Role and Tasks*. London: Bedford Square Press.

BASW (1977) A Code of Ethics for Social Work. In BASW *The Social Work Task*. Birmingham: British Association of Social Workers.

Bayley, M.J. (1973) *Mental Handicap and Community Care*. London: Routledge and Kegan Paul.

Bayley, M., Parker, P., Seyd, R., and Tennant, A. (1981) *Neighbourhood Services Project Dinnington. Paper No. 1. Origins, Strategy and Proposed Evaluation*. Sheffield: Department of Sociological Studies, University of Sheffield.

Bebbington, A.C. (1979) Changes in the Provision of Social Services to the Elderly in the Community over Fourteen Years. *Social Policy and Administration* **13** (2): 111–23.

Bell, C. and Newby, H. (eds) (1977) *Doing Sociological Research*. London: Allen and Unwin.

Billingsley, A. (1964) Bureaucratic and Professional Orientation

Patterns in Social Casework. *Social Service Review* 38: 400–07.

Billis, D., Bromley, G., Hey, A., and Rowbottom, R. (1981) *Organizing Social Services Departments.* London: Heinemann Educational.

Blau, P. and Scott, W.R. (1963) *Formal Organizations: A Comparative Approach.* London: Routledge and Kegan Paul.

Bowl, R.E.E. (1976) A Survey of Surveys. *New Society* 38 (734): 195.

—— (1978) *The Role of the Social Services Department and Its Relationship with Other Welfare Agencies.* Birmingham: Hereford and Worcester CC/Social Services Unit, University of Birmingham.

Bradshaw, J. (1972) The Concept of Social Need. *New Society,* 30 March: 640–43.

Brenton, M. (1978) Worker Participation and the Social Service Agency. *British Journal of Social Work* 8 (3): 289–300.

Briggs, T.L. (1980) Obstacles to Implementing the Team Approach in Social Services Agencies. In S. Lonsdale, A. Webb, and T.L. Briggs (eds) *Teamwork in the Personal Social Services and Health Care.* London: Croom Helm.

Bultena, G.L. (1969) Rural-Urban Differences in the Familial Interaction of the Aged. *Rural Sociology* 34: 5–15.

Challis, D. and Davies, B. (1980) A New Approach to Community Care of the Elderly. *British Journal of Social Work* 10: 1–18.

Chartered Institute of Public Finance Accountants (1978/1979) Personal Social Services Statistics (Actuals).

Child Poverty Action Group (1978) *Rural Poverty: Poverty, Deprivation and Planning in Rural Areas.* London.

Cockburn, Cynthia (1977) *The Local State.* London: Pluto Press.

Crousaz, D. (1981) *Social Work: A Research Review.* London: HMSO.

Currie, R. and Parrott, B. (1981) *A Unitary Approach to Social Work – Application in Practice.* Birmingham: British Association of Social Workers.

Davies, E. and Rees, A. (eds) (1960) *Welsh Rural Communities.* Cardiff: University of Wales Press.

Denzin, N.K. (ed.) (1970) *Sociological Methods: A Sourcebook.* London: Butterworth.

Department of Health and Social Security (1980) Mental Handicap: Progress, Problems and Priorities. A Review of Mental Handicap Services in England since the 1971 White Paper 'Better Services for the Mentally Handicapped'. London: HMSO.

Dingwall, R. (1980) Problems of Teamwork in Primary Care. In S. Lonsdale, A. Webb, and T.L. Briggs (eds) *Teamwork in the Personal Social Services and Health Care.* London: Croom Helm.

Emmett, I. (1964) *A North Wales Village: A Social Anthropological Study.* London: Routledge and Kegan Paul.

Equal Opportunities Commission (1980) *The Experience of Caring for Elderly and Handicapped Dependants: Survey Report.* Manchester.

Faulkner, A. (1980) Ageing and Old Age: The Last Sexist Rip-off. In E. Norman and A. Mancuso (eds) *Women's Issues and Social Work Practice.* Itasca, Illinois: Peacock Publications.

Fenby, M.L. (1978) Social Work in a Rural Setting. *Social Work* **23** (2): 162–63.

Fisher, J. (1976) *The Effectiveness of Social Casework.* London: Charles C. Thomas.

Fisk, M. (1980) Poverty and Housing in Wales: An Account of Current Problems. In G. Rees and T.L. Rees (eds) *Poverty and Social Inequality in Wales.* London: Croom Helm.

Frankenberg, R. (1966) *Communities in Britain: Social Life in Town and Country.* London: Penguin Books.

Froland, C., Pancoast, D.L., Chapman, N.J., and Kimboko, P.J. (1981) *Helping Networks and Human Services.* Beverly Hills: Sage.

Gilbert, N. and Specht, H. (1974) *Dimensions of Social Welfare Policy.* Englewood Cliffs: Prentice-Hall.

Ginsberg, L.H. (1976) *Social Work in Rural Communities.* New York: Council for Social Work Education.

Glampson, A. and Goldberg, E.M. (1976) Post Seebohm Social Services: The Consumers' Viewpoint. *Social Work Today* **8** (6): 7–12.

Glastonbury, B., Cooper, D., and Hawkins, P. (1980) *Social Work in Conflict: the Practitioner and the Bureaucrat.* London: Croom Helm.

Goldberg, E.M. and Connelly, N. (eds) (1981) *Evaluative Research in Social Care.* London: Heinemann Educational.

Goldberg, E.M. and Fruin, D. (1976) Towards Accountability in Social Work: A Case Review System for Social Workers. *British Journal of Social Work* **6** (1): 3–18.

Goldberg, E.M. and Warburton, W.M. (1979) *Ends and Means in*

Social Work: The Development and Outcome of a Case Review System. London: Allen and Unwin.

Goldstein, H. (1973) *Social Work Practice: A Unitary Approach.* Columbia: University of South California Press.

Gottlieb, B.H. (1981) *Social Networks and Social Support.* Beverly Hills: Sage.

Green, A.D. (1966) The Professional Social Worker in the Bureaucracy. *Social Service Review* 40: 71–83.

Green, R.K. and Webster, S.A. (eds) (1976) *Social Work in Rural Areas: Preparation and Practice.* Knoxville: School of Social Work, University of Tennessee.

Hadley, R. and Hatch, S. (1981) *Social Welfare and the Failure of the State: Centralized Social Services and Participatory Alternatives.* London: Allen and Unwin.

Hadley, R. and McGrath, M. (eds) (1980a) *Patch Based Social Services Teams, Bulletin No. 1.* Lancaster: University of Lancaster.

—— (eds) (1980b) *Patch Based Social Services Teams, Bulletin No. 2.* Lancaster: University of Lancaster.

—— (1981) *Going Local: Neighbourhood Social Services.* London: National Council for Voluntary Associations.

Hall, A.S. (1974) *The Point of Entry.* London: Allen and Unwin.

Harris, A.I. (1971) *Handicapped and Impaired in Great Britain.* London: HMSO.

Henderson, P., Jones D., and Thomas, D.N. (1980) *The Boundaries of Change in Community Work.* London: Allen and Unwin.

Herzberg, F. (1966) *Work and the Nature of Man.* London: Staples Press.

Holme, A. and Maizels, J. (1978) *Social Workers and Volunteers.* London: Allen and Unwin.

Howe, D. (1980) Divisions of Labour in the Area Teams of Social Services Departments. *Social Policy and Administration* 14 (2): 133–50.

Hunt, A. (1978) *The Elderly at Home: A Study of People Aged 65 and Over Living in the Community in England in 1976.* London: Social Survey Division, OPCS.

Illife, S. (1980) Dismantling the Health Service. *Marxism Today* 24(7): 14–19.

Isaacs, B., Livingstone, M., and Neville, J. (1972) *Survival of the Unfittest: A Study of Geriatric Patients in Glasgow.* London:

Routledge and Kegan Paul.

Jackson, B. (1968) *Working Class Communities.* London: Routledge and Kegan Paul.

Jenkin, P. (1980) Speech to the 1980 Conservative Party Conference.

Johnson, M.L., di Gregorio, S., and Harrison, B. (1982) *Ageing, Needs and Nutrition.* London: Policy Studies Institute.

Johnson, R.L. and Knop, E. (1970) Rural–Urban Differentials in Community Satisfaction. *Rural Sociology* 35: 544–48.

Johnson, T.J. (1972) *Professions and Power.* London: Macmillan Press.

Kakabadse, A. and Worrall, R. (1978) Job Satisfaction and Organizational Structure: A Comparative Study of Nine Social Services Departments. *British Journal of Social Work* 8 (1): 51–70.

Knight, K. (1976) Matrix Organization: A Review. *Journal of Management Studies* XIII: 111–30.

Lawton, M.P. (1975) The Philadelphia Geriatric Centre Morale Scale: A Revision. *Journal of Gerontology* 30: 85–9.

Leonard, P. (1979) Restructuring the Welfare State. *Marxism Today* 23 (12): 7–13.

McGrath, M. and Hadley, R. (1981) Evaluating Patch Based Teams. In E.M. Goldberg and N. Connelly. *Evaluative Research in Social Care.* London: Heinemann Educational.

McKenzie, N. (1955) The New Towns: The Success of Social Planning. *Fabian Research Series No. 172.* London: Fabian Society.

Martin, F.M., Brotherston, J.A.F., and Chave, S.P.W. (1957) Incidence of Neurosis in a New Housing Estate. *British Journal of Preventive and Social Medicine* 11(4): 196–202.

Martinez-Brawley, E.E. (1982) *Rural Social and Community Work in the United States and Great Britain: A Cross-Cultural Perspective.* New York: Praeger.

Mechanic, D. (1968) *Medical Sociology: A Selective View.* Appendix 1: Sources of Power of Lower Participants in Complex Organizations. New York: The Free Press.

Michaux, M.H., Pruim, R.J., Foster, S.A., and Chelst, M.R. (1973) Relatives' Perceptions of Rural and Urban Day Center Patients. *Psychiatry* 36: 203–12.

Molnar, J.J. and Purdhit, S.R. (1977) Citizen Participation in Rural Community Development: Community Group Perspectives. *Journal of Voluntary Action Research,* January: 48–58.

256   *Social work in context*

Moroney, R.M. (1976) *The Family and the State.* New York: Longman.

Mortimer, E. (1982) *Working with the Elderly.* London: Heinemann.

Moseley, M.J., Harman, R.G., Coles, O.D., and Spencer, M.B. (1977) *Rural Transport and Accessibility,* vols. I and II. Norwich: Centre of East Anglian Studies, University of East Anglia.

Nicholson, J.H. (1961) *New Communities in Britain: Achievements and Problems.* London: National Council of Social Service.

Nissel, M. and Bonnerjea, L. (1982) *Family Care of the Handicapped Elderly: Who Pays?* Report No. 602. London: Policy Studies Institute.

Nissel, M., Maynard, A., Young, K., and Ibsen, M. (1980) *The Welfare State: Diversity and Decentralization.* Discussion Paper No. 2. London: Policy Studies Institute.

Parry, N., Rustin, M., and Satyamurti, C. (1979) *Social Work, Welfare and the State.* London: Edward Arnold.

Parsloe, P. (1981) *Social Services Area Teams.* London: Allen and Unwin.

Payne, G., Dingwall, R., Payne, J., and Carter, M. (1981) *Sociology and Social Research.* London: Routledge and Kegan Paul.

Payne, M. (1982) *Working in Teams.* London: MacMillan Press and British Association of Social Workers.

Pincus, A. and Minahan, A. (1973) *Social Work Practice: Model and Method.* Itasca, Illinois: Peacock Publications.

Plank, D. (1977) *Caring for the Elderly: Report of a Study of Various Means of Caring for Dependent Elderly People in Eight London Boroughs.* London: Greater London Council.

—— (1978) Old Peoples Homes Are Not the Last Refuge. *Community Care,* No. 202, 1 March.

Pritchard, C. and Taylor, R. (1978) *Social Work: Reform or Revolution?* London: Routledge and Kegan Paul.

Puner, M. (1978) *To the Good Long Life.* London: MacMillan.

Rees, S. (1978) *Social Work Face to Face.* London: Edward Arnold.

Reid, W. and Hanrahan, P. (1981) The Effectiveness of Social Work: Recent Evidence. In E.M. Goldberg and N. Connelly (eds) *Evaluative Research in Social Care.* London: Heinemann.

Revill, S. and Blunden, R. (1977) *Home Training of Pre-School Children with Developmental Delay.* Cardiff: Mental Handicap in Wales Applied Research Unit.

Rojek, D.G., Clemente, F., and Summers, G.F. (1975) Community Satisfaction: A Study of Contentment with Local Services. *Rural Sociology* **40** (2): 177–92.

Rowbottom, R., Hey, A., and Billis, D. (1974) *Social Services Departments: Developing Patterns of Work and Organization.* London: Heinemann.

Rowlings, C. (1981) *Social Work with Elderly People.* London: Allen and Unwin.

Sainsbury, E. (1981) Sharing in Welfare: Community Resources and the Work of Area Teams. *Social Work Service* **27**: 11–17.

Sainsbury, S. (1974) *Measuring Disability.* London: Bell.

Satyamurti, C. (1979) Care and Control in Local Authority Social Work. In N. Parry, M. Rustin, and C. Satyamurti *Social Work, Welfare and the State.* London: Edward Arnold.

Sauer, W.J., Shehan, C., and Boymel, C. (1976) Rural–Urban Differences in Satisfaction amongst the Elderly: A Reanalysis. *Rural Sociology* **41** (2): 269–75.

Seebohm Report (1968) *Report of the Committee on Local Authority and Allied Personal Social Services.* London: HMSO.

Shaw, J.M. (ed.) (1979) *Rural Deprivation and Planning.* Norwich: Geo Abstracts.

Smith, D. (1965) Front Line Organization of the State Mental Hospital. *Administrative Science Quarterly* **10**: 381–99.

Smith, H.W. (1975) *Strategies of Social Research: The Methodological Imagination.* London: Prentice Hall International.

Specht, H. and Vickery, A. (1977) *Integrating Social Work Methods.* London: Allen and Unwin.

Stevenson, O. (1981) *Specialization in Social Services Teams.* London: Allen and Unwin.

Stevenson, O. and Parsloe, P. (1978) *Social Services Teams: The Practitioner's View.* London: HMSO.

Thatcher, M. (1981) Speech to the Annual Conference of the Women's Royal Voluntary Service.

Thomas, D. and Warburton, W. (1977) *Community Workers in a Social Services Department: A Case Study.* London: NISW/ PSSC.

Vickery, A. (1977) *Caseload Management.* National Institute for Social Work Paper No. 5. London: National Institute for Social Work.

Walker, A. (1981) Towards a Political Economy of Old Age.

Ageing and Society 1(1): 73–94.

Warham, J. (1977) *An Open Case. The Organizational Context of Social Work*. London: Routledge and Kegan Paul.

Webb, A. (1981) *Collective Action and Welfare Pluralism*. ARVAC Occasional Paper No. 3. Wivenhoe, Essex.

Webb, A. and Hobdell, M. (1980) Coordination and Teamwork in the Health and Personal Social Services. In S. Lonsdale, A. Webb, and T.L. Briggs, (eds) *Teamwork in the Personal Social Services and Health Care*. London: Croom Helm.

Wenger, G.C. (1980) Mid-Wales: Deprivation or Development. A Study of Patterns of Employment in Selected Areas. *Social Science Monographs No. 5*. Cardiff: Board of Celtic Studies, University of Wales.

—— (1982) Ageing in Rural Communities: Family Contacts and Community Integration. *Ageing and Society* 2 (2): 211–29.

Wilkin, D. (1979) *Caring for the Mentally Handicapped Child*. London: Croom Helm.

Williams, G. (1979) Community Development in Rural Britain: The Organization of Local Initiative. *Community Development Journal* 14 (2): 107–14.

Williams, W.M. (1963) *A West Country Village. Ashworthy, Family, Kinship and Land*. London: Routledge and Kegan Paul.

Wolfenden, J. (1978) *The Future of Voluntary Organizations*. London: Croom Helm.

Young, M. and Willmott, P. (1962) *Family and Kinship in East London*. London: Penguin Books.

Name index

Subject index